Relationships
and
How to Survive Them

CPA Seminar Series

Relationships
and
How to Survive Them

Liz Greene

CPA

Centre for Psychological Astrology Press
London

First published 1999 by The Centre for Psychological Astrology Press, BCM Box 1815, London WC1 3XX, GB, Tel/Fax 0181-749-2330.

First paperback edition published 2004.

RELATIONSHIPS AND HOW TO SURVIVE THEM

ISBN 1 900869 26 8

British Library Cataloguing-in-Publication Data. A catalogue record for this book is available from the British Library.

Printed in Great Britain by Antony Rowe Ltd, Chippenham, Wiltshire, SN14 6LH.

Table of Contents

Part One: The Composite Chart

Part Two: The Eternal Triangle

Part One: The Composite Chart

This seminar was given on 27 April 1997 at Regents College, London as part of the Summer Term of the seminar programme of the Centre for Psychological Astrology.

The meaning of the composite chart

Technical matters

I am assuming all of you here today know what a composite chart is. But it might be helpful to mention some basics, just in case someone is lurking behind a chair who isn't familiar with this astrological approach to exploring relationships.[1] A composite chart is based on the midpoints between two birth charts. Although each individual in a relationship has his or her own independent identity, when we look at the composite chart we are viewing a third entity, different from either of the two individuals, which needs to be considered along with the more traditional synastry between the two charts. This third entity has its own psychological dynamics and its own mode of expression. The composite chart may not look a lot like either of the charts of the two individuals, and may contain configurations which do not appear in the natal charts. The composite chart has a distinct nature of its own.

Before we explore what the composite chart might tell us about a relationship, I should point out that working with composites may involve a number of different techniques. For example, it is useful to look at the progressed composite during a critical time in a relationship, so we should know how to calculate this. It is also useful to compare the composite with the charts of the two individuals, using basic synastry techniques, and also to look at how the progressed composite affects the two people and how the progressed charts of the two people affect the

---

[1]Available astrological literature on composite charts is not extensive, but the reader should see Robert Hand, *Planets in Composite,* Para Research, Gloucester, Massachusetts, 1975. This remains the best introduction to the subject.

composite. Most computer programmes will calculate a composite chart, but we should still understand how to work one out "by hand", as it were, so that we have a real sense of what we are dealing with.

If we are going to set up a composite chart without a computer, we must work out the midpoints or half-sums between each pair of identical planets in the two birth charts. We take the degree and minute of the Sun of one person and the degree and minute of the Sun of the other, and we find the midpoint between them; that gives us the composite Sun. We take the degree and minute of the Moon of one person and the degree and minute of the Moon of the other; the midpoint between them gives us the composite Moon. And so on. That is simple enough.

There are always two midpoints for any pair of planets – a "near" one and a "far" one, depending on whether we measure the distance between the planets in the direction of the order of the zodiacal signs, or in the opposite direction. The two midpoints between any pair of planets are always exactly opposite each other. If one person's Sun is in 5° Cancer, and the other's Sun is in 5° Virgo, the "near" midpoint will be 5° Leo, the half-sum of the distance of 60° between the two Suns measured by moving in the natural order of the signs. The "far" midpoint will be 5° Aquarius, the half-sum of the distance of 300° between the two Suns measured by moving in the opposite direction around the zodiac circle. The midpoint usually used in the composite chart is the "near" one, although there may be times when this has to be adjusted. We will deal with this issue later.

With the house cusps and the Ascendant, there seems to be some argument amongst astrologers. I don't really understand why this should be. If we are going to do a midpoint chart, then we do the whole thing as a midpoint chart, and this includes the midpoint between the two Ascendants, the midpoint between the two MCs, and the midpoints between every other pair of house cusps. For reasons which I can only attribute to the creative fertility of the human mind, the idea has arisen in some quarters that we should find the composite MC by taking the midpoint between the two natal MCs, and then look in a Table of Houses to find the Ascendant for the latitude and longitude where the two people are living.

Now, that sounds very interesting. But what is the logic behind it? People in relationship do not always live together. Also, it is possible to do a composite between oneself and someone who has been dead for six hundred years. What longitude and latitude do we use then? The location of the remains? More importantly, in practise, when I have looked at the repercussions of important transits moving across the composite Ascendant, it is the midpoint Ascendant that seems to be operative, not the one based on the longitude and latitude of the couple's domicile – if there is a domicile to begin with.

Having drawn up a composite chart with either a computer or our own mathematical skills, we may occasionally find some astronomical anomalies. Using the "near" midpoint, we may find Mercury or the Sun opposite Venus. Some astrologers correct these so that they make astronomical sense. But I feel we should leave such anomalies alone if possible, because this is not the birth chart of a human being. It is a mathematical abstraction. The Sun opposite Venus in a composite chart will tell us something important about the relationship. It may be impossible astronomically, but a composite is not a map of the heavens. It has nothing to do with where the planets are actually placed.

Occasionally we will get other anomalies. If two people have the Sun in exactly the same degree and minute of opposite signs, there is no "near" midpoint. This is obviously not a common occurrence. But if one person has the Sun in 3° 24′ Aries, and the other person has the Sun in 3° 24′ Libra, the composite Sun could be placed in either 3° 24′ Cancer or 3° 24′ Capricorn; and which midpoint do we then use? When this happens with any composite planet, it is helpful to look at the houses in which the planet is placed in the two birth charts, and try to place it in the quadrant of the composite chart which seems to reflect this most accurately.

One plus one equals three

The concept behind the composite chart – or, as Erin Sullivan sometimes calls it, the compost chart – is that it represents the relationship itself as a third factor. Two people create a third thing between them. The composite chart is like an energy field, which affects both people and draws certain things out of each individual as well as imposing its own dynamics on both. The composite doesn't seem to describe what either person feels about the other. In this way it is very different from synastry, which describes the chemistry between two people in terms of how they affect each other. When we are exploring the synastry in a relationship, we say, "Your Venus is on my Mars. You are activating my Mars and bringing a Mars response out of me, and I am activating your Venus and invoking a Venus response in you. Consequently we feel a certain way about each other." When we are looking at a composite chart, we are not exploring what two people activate in each other or feel about each other. We are interpreting the energy field they generate between them. The composite chart is like a child, a third entity which carries the genetic imprints of both parents but combines these imprints in an entirely new way and exists independently of either of them.

Because the composite has all the same features as a birth chart, we need to approach its interpretation in more or less the same way. The composite chart has a core identity which signifies its "purpose" (the Sun) and a characteristic set of emotional responses and needs (the Moon). It has a mode of communication (Mercury) and a distinctive set of values and ideals (Venus). It has a mode of expressing energy and will (Mars). It has its own way of growing and expanding (Jupiter) and it has innate limitations and defence mechanisms (Saturn). It has a specific vulnerability to the collective due to patterns from the collective background of the relationship (Chiron). It reflects certain collective ideals which strive for change and progress (Uranus). It has innate aspirations which reflect certain collective fantasies (Neptune). It has a bottom-line survival instinct which can prove supportive to the relationship's continuity but can also be destructive if the relationship is under threat (Pluto). It has an image or role to play in the eyes of society (MC), and it has a "personality" which will express itself in certain characteristic ways to the world outside (Ascendant). The signs in a composite chart describe the basic stuff or "temperament" of which the relationship is made; the planets describe the motivating energies; and the houses describe the spheres of life through which the planets express themselves. All this is basic astrology, and it is no less applicable to the composite than it is to the individual birth chart.

Relationship as an entity

We do not usually think of our relationships as independent entities. More often, we think in terms of our own feelings and attitudes, or the feelings and attitudes of the other person. Yet every relationship creates its own ambience. None of us behaves in the same way when we are half of a couple as we do when we are operating solo. We might have characteristic behaviour patterns when we are alone, but the moment we are with our partner, a certain kind of energy dynamic is set in motion and we behave in particular ways which are sometimes very noticeable in the company of other people.

Two people in relationship create an atmosphere around them, not by conscious choice, but because that is simply what happens. Other people will often reflect this back to us. "The two of you seem such a lively, attractive couple," a friend might say, or, "What an exciting life the two of you must have!" Meanwhile, one is thinking to oneself, "What on earth are they talking about? That isn't how I feel." We might see something like composite Jupiter rising in Sagittarius and Libra at the composite MC, and other people perceive the relationship as an exciting and glamorous Jupiter-Venus entity. But one's partner's Saturn might be conjunct one's Moon and opposition one's Sun, and the synastry between the birth charts might make one feel more like Sisyphus and his rock than Mick Jagger and Jerri Hall. The opposite can also occur. The composite may have Saturn rising and Chiron culminating, and the world sees something quite heavy when one is with one's partner. But the synastry may involve lots of Venus-Jupiter-Uranus contacts, reflecting an excitement within the relationship which both people personally feel but which does not express itself to others.

We can learn a lot about the angles of the composite chart for an important relationship by asking other people how they see the relationship. Often we might be in for quite a shock, because the answer may not reflect how we actually feel about the other person. The composite, like a natal chart, presents itself to the world according to its Ascendant and MC. It has a ruling planet which will focus the expression of the relationship in a certain house or sphere of life. The houses of the composite work in the same way they do in a birth chart, reflecting spheres of emphasis through which the dynamics of the relationship are manifested. When composite planets highlight a composite house, that area of life will be extremely important to the relationship, and both people will be impelled to focus on it, even if the same house is empty in both birth charts. A relationship can push us into having to confront certain areas of life, even if natally we are neither predisposed nor well equipped to cope in that area.

Composites have their own laws and energies, and these have nothing to do with whether we are "well matched" with someone. A composite in itself will not tell us about compatibility. That is what synastry is for. The composite won't reveal whether the relationship is "good" or "bad" in terms of the chemistry between two people. The composite says to us, "If you choose to enter this relationship, here is its meaning and pattern of destiny. This is what it is made of and what it is for." If we want to get a sense of whether or not that meaning and destiny are going to make us feel good, we have to compare the composite with our own chart.

If we examine the synastry between the composite and the chart of each individual in the relationship, we can learn a lot about how the relationship makes each person feel. We can also take a third party and compare that person's chart to the composite. This is a fascinating exercise. Let's say that I am in a long-term relationship, but also have a lover. I can take that third party's chart and look at how it affects the composite chart between me and my partner, and I can get a very clear picture of how my lover affects the relationship. We can also look at the chart of a child in relation to the composite between the parents. This is very useful in terms of understanding family dynamics. Some children have a way of really disrupting the parental relationship, while others help to glue it together. We can see this by looking at the child's chart in relation to the parents' composite. We might not see this dynamic by merely exploring the synastry between the child and each individual parent.

Freedom and fate within relationship

Working with composites makes us think in terms of something larger than ourselves as individuals. Wherever we go, we create interfaces with other people, and we may not have the same amount of choice in dealing with those interfaces as we might when we deal with our own personal issues. If one has a Sun-Saturn square in the birth chart, one can actively do something with it. One doesn't have to be its victim, or live solely from the darker side of it. It may be a difficult aspect in early life, and it may reflect deep feelings of insecurity or inadequacy. But one can say, "I know that a lot of my self-doubt is connected with my father and my childhood. I sabotage myself because I am sometimes afraid to aim high. I am often too hard on myself, and expect too much. But I'm going to try to work on these issues. I'll make an effort to understand what they are about. I may need some psychotherapy to help me to learn to trust myself more. And I'll try to develop my Saturn sign so that I have more confidence." Gradually one can shape that Sun-Saturn square into something very strong and creative, if one is willing to put the necessary effort into it.

But when a Sun-Saturn square appears in the composite chart, the relationship cannot go into psychotherapy. The relationship cannot say, of its own volition, "I'm going to work on these feelings of limitation and self-doubt." The relationship does not "feel" self-doubt. Both individuals can work on their own Saturns. But neither may have a Sun-Saturn square, and neither may really understand why, when they are together, something in the relationship thwarts and frustrates their joint goals. The external limitations which often accompany a composite Sun-Saturn may seem strangely impersonal and beyond one's control.

The impersonal feeling of the composite may be very uncomfortable for us if we are psychologically inclined, because psychological astrology implies individual responsibility and a belief that we can change many things in our lives if we are prepared to do the inner work. Because we view the birth chart as an inner picture, we can take responsibility for how we express it, and consciousness can make a huge difference. A psychological approach to astrology allows us to transform many things if we make sufficient effort. But one can be deluded by the fantasy that one can change anything, and some things lie beyond the individual's scope of influence. I am not suggesting that composites are not psychological, or that we should abandon this approach when interpreting them. But "psychological" does not always mean free, and change may mean a change in the attitudes of both people toward the relationship, rather than a change in the endemic pattern of the relationship itself.

We can do nothing to change the fundamental patterns in the composite chart. Of course the same may be said of an individual chart. But we seem to have more room to affect the levels on which we express our natal patterns. This gives us the inner sense – valid or not – that we have the power to participate actively in, or even create, our own future. Maybe we do, at least in some areas of life. But a composite presents us with a different experience, if not a different reality at core. We can change how we react to the patterns in the composite, and we can make the effort to provide creative outlets for its energies. But even with the maximum cooperation with a partner, the patterns of a composite still *feel* "outside" our sphere of personal influence. A composite will not say, "This is a bad relationship – get out of it." But it may say, "This relationship has got an inherent restriction which neither person is going to be able to alter. If you want this relationship, accept this issue." If the composite chart has a Sun-Saturn square or a Sun-Chiron conjunction, it contains built-in limits, often of a very concrete kind. These limits may prove to be creative and positive for either or both individuals. But they feel as though they have been imposed on us. A Sun-Saturn square or a Sun-Chiron conjunction in the natal chart also contains built-in limits, but we *experience* them differently.

Audience: Could you give an example of how that sort of issue might work with one of the aspects you just mentioned?

Liz: Let's take composite Sun-Chiron aspects. I have seen these many times when a relationship involves the unavoidable inclusion of limits from the past. The past may be an ex-partner who wants big maintenance payments, or it may be children from a former marriage. These situations can cause a lot of pain, especially where children are involved, because no matter how mature and conscious the two people are, there will be conflicts, divided loyalties, hurt feelings, and perhaps also financial restrictions. It is not a question of altering attitudes; *a priori* families, for any couple, are a built-in fact which will always impose limits. If a couple do not experience limits in such circumstances, then we probably won't see Sun-Chiron in the composite chart.

We know that Chiron is connected with experiences of wounding, particularly those which seem unfair and unmerited, and which are a product of the state of the collective at the time rather than some particular person's fault or act of malice. Sun-Chiron contacts in a composite suggest that the relationship itself carries an unhealable wound, usually from the past of both parties, or from the nature of the world in which the two people are living. At the same time, the relationship may provide deep healing for both people, or for others who come in contact with the couple, because the inherent limits invoke suffering and consequent understanding and compassion.

I have sometimes seen Sun-Chiron in a composite when two people want very badly to have children but are unable to do so. This is a wound which can make people think much more deeply about who they are and what purpose their lives serve, because they do not have the collectively sanctioned "purpose" of a family to give them a direction in life. Another example might be a partnership where there is a great age difference, and the younger partner must watch the other grow old and frail. No amount of love and commitment can turn the clock back. Or there might be a physical handicap in one partner which may be genuinely and deeply accepted, but which limits the mobility of both people. Yet another example might be a racially mixed marriage, or a homosexual relationship, both of which may provoke animosity among neighbours who are xenophobic or too rigid in their definitions of normality. Xenophobia and rigid opinions are characteristic of many, many people, and no amount of agonising or raging will alter this unfortunate flaw in human nature. Both people may be hurt through the relationship, not because it is "bad", but because there is something about the way the relationship "sits" in the collective which limits its possibilities.

Audience: Are you saying that the composite chart is a static picture? Can't something like that be healed?

Liz: I am not saying that it is a static picture. As far as healing is concerned, it depends on what you mean by the word. Chiron's wounds do not heal in the sense of going away. Something has been permanently twisted out of shape, even if the poison has been released and cleansed. One cannot regain innocence once it has been destroyed by the kind of wounding this planet reflects. But one's attitude toward the wound can change, and greater tolerance, compassion, and wisdom can result. That is a kind of healing; but it cannot undo the past. One cannot, for example, make one's children by a former partner vanish in a puff of smoke. One can try to numb the wound by cutting off from the children emotionally, and never seeing them again; and then there is another sort of wound that must be dealt with. Or one can work very hard to face all the emotional complications, and eventually establish rewarding relationships with everyone concerned. But there will always be compromise and sadness and a sense of loss. Such aspects in the composite chart do not mean that the effects of the difficulty remain static and unchanging. Both people may be deeply and permanently transformed. But the past cannot be remade.

The composite chart progresses like a birth chart, and this reflects changes within the relationship just as it does within the individual. But the composite chart as an entity doesn't have the same capacity as an individual for deciding of its own volition to change or fight against something. It is not a conscious individual. Both people may work to become more conscious, and the ways in which they experience the relationship may change accordingly. But the basic patterns of the relationship unfold like a seed growing into a plant, with a natural inevitability that may feel alien to our ego-centred consciousness.

"Inside" and "outside" the relationship

Audience: Presumably the composite will be affected by transits.

Liz: Yes. I am going to talk about this in more detail later. The composite chart responds to transits. Each time a major transit moves over a point in the composite, things happen within the relationship. There is change. But the change often feels very impersonal. For example, we might see transiting Pluto about to arrive on the composite Sun. If we saw this transit approaching in a client's natal chart, we could say to the person, "In the next year or two, Pluto is going to spend a lot of time moving back and forth over your Sun. It might be wise for you to start doing something with this now. Prepare for it, because a chapter of your life is ending and a new one is beginning. Your sense of who you are and what you want, the role you seek to play in the world, your goals and values, are all in need of change. You may need to let go of certain things in order to make room for a new direction and a new sense of individual identity. Start thinking about it, because then you can give the transit creative channels instead of fighting against your own necessity."

The situation feels rather different when Pluto moves over the composite Sun. If we see this in the composite for two clients in a relationship, we can certainly say to both people, "A chapter in the relationship is coming to an end and a new one is beginning. It would be wise to prepare." But the changes which occur may not feel as though they are the product of either person's feelings and actions, although both people may have been contributing to the outcome over a long period of time. While they themselves can prepare, the relationship is following a course which is part of its fate. A couple may have an unplanned child, for example, and that may be the irrevocable change which the transit describes. The relationship itself may end through impersonal factors such as a war. The couple may have to uproot and move to another country to begin a new life. These things do involve a whole series of past choices, conscious or unconscious, on the part of both people. But the effects and repercussions of those choices are virtually impossible to foresee, and the relationship will take its own course.

Audience: Then is the composite chart more external than internal?

Liz: I don't think so. But it may *seem* as if something else has decided for us, which doesn't "think" or "feel" as humans do. Composites are made up of midpoints between two people, and reflect the pattern which arises when two people create a relationship. Transits and progressed aspects in a composite describe the way the world impinges on the relationship, and the pattern of its internal development. In that sense, because it is the product of two people, there is no "something else" outside those two people which decides for them. But the relationship as a separate entity is neither of the two people individually, and the expression of the composite can feel alien and "outside". Composites often seem to exteriorise transits in ways which are very literal. This isn't always the case, especially if the transit is hitting a composite planet placed in a subtler house such as the 12th. But most of the time, if there is a powerful transit over the composite Ascendant or composite Sun, something will happen to the relationship on an obvious, concrete level. The kinds of things that happen don't always appear to be directly linked to either individual, although such events faithfully reflect the astrological meaning of the planets involved.

For example, one's husband's mother has to move in and be looked after when transiting Saturn is on the composite Moon in the 4th. Or one's partner is required to go on a prolonged business trip when transiting Uranus is opposite composite Venus in the 9th. There is a strange simplicity about the way these transits are reflected. There are obviously choices involved. One's husband could put his mother into a nursing home, and one's partner could go and look for another job. But usually, by the time the transit arrives, there isn't really a choice at all, because the situation, rather than the couple, demands that things happen in that particular way. It is hard to work on such things psychologically, as we might if it were Saturn going over our natal Moon. We can choose to respond according to our own level of consciousness. The burden or responsibility reflected by transiting Saturn over the composite Moon, embodied in the arrival of one's sick mother-in-law, may provoke many different responses, depending on how we elect to deal with the situation. But composites often present us with a *fait accompli.*

Choices and consequences form an interlocking chain over time, rather than representing a series of independent, unconnected occurrences. There is a point where individual choice and capability end, and once our interface with other people begins to involve such a chain of mutual choices and consequences, the outcome is no longer in our hands. It is a product of who both people are, which is in turn reflected in the choices both people make – as well as those made before they become involved with each other, and those made by their families before their birth. I am not trying to make a case for composites being fated in a way which is different from individual fate. But as I said, they can *feel* strangely impersonal.

Heavy transits in the composite are not necessarily "bad". A Pluto transit over the composite Sun may reflect the birth of a relationship – when two people actually meet – as often as it can connote the end of a bond. We need to remember that a composite exists forever, as it were – there is no "beginning" or "end" because it is an abstract map which only becomes relevant if two people actually interact with each other. Transits and progressions in the composite usually signal quite clearly when this direct interaction begins. But we could do a composite chart between ourselves and a film idol or pop star whom we will never meet, and the composite, although a valid map, remains in the realm of unlived potential.

No astrological movement is inherently malevolent by nature. Often what we think of as "malefic" planets or aspects are reflected in very positive, constructive events in a relationship. And we also need to remember that, as individuals, we may "feel bad" when a hard transit is occurring in our own chart, but the relationship itself does not "feel bad" when a hard transit hits the composite. The transit simply describes how things are at the time within the relationship. It is the individuals who, for their own reasons, may experience a negative reaction to a transiting square or opposition in the composite. A challenge to the relationship may not carry the same sense of anxiety and distress that a challenge to the individual does. It is only when the same transit hits the individual chart that we may experience "bad" feelings, even if the ultimate meaning of the transit is very positive.

We can learn a great deal from this. Transiting Saturn on the composite Moon may coincide with one's mother-in-law arriving on the doorstep, but that does not imply the event is "painful" or "depressing". It is the individuals who may begrudge the additional responsibilities. "Bad feelings" are more typical of Saturn on the natal Moon. The composite does not describe an individual psyche, and changes within the relationship do not reflect emotional conflict as they might in a person. We are complex creatures and often react to change with fear and anger, even if we have chosen the change ourselves. A relationship as an entity changes in a natural way in accord with the transits and progressions in the composite. But when a powerful transit hits a person's natal chart, psychological defence mechanisms are mobilised. No matter how enlightened we are, we may fight the unknown, even if we know it is going to be good for us. Anxieties may rise to the surface, particularly if childhood issues are triggered. But a composite does not have a childhood.

Chiron, Pluto, or Saturn over an individual's natal Sun or Moon may coincide with painful emotional experiences, because inner conflicts are activated. We may recognise that these transits are actually working to our benefit, but we may fight them emotionally because we don't welcome the issues that are thrown up. Then we may struggle against the transit, and create additional problems for ourselves. But the entity described by the composite doesn't fight its pattern of unfoldment, because it is not a human psyche. Often what we expect to be horrible events, from our personal experience of a particular transit, in fact turn out to be very rewarding ones when a similar transit occurs in the composite. Change may be involved, but it is often a change which both people are really pleased about. This may take a bit of the sting out of the fact that we can't "work on" a composite chart in the same way we can "work on" ourselves.

Consciousness and orbs

Perhaps we need to think more deeply about the philosophical and psychological implications of composites. When we work with an individual chart, we have to consider the issue of orbs. We don't wake up on Thursday morning at 7.30 am with Saturn suddenly on the natal Sun. We can feel a transit coming when it is up to 10° away from its exact aspect, just as we can feel its aftermath when it is up to 10° past its exact aspect. Certain psychological processes are already at work beneath the surface during the buildup time, and we often get heralds in our dreams of the meaning of the transit, long before anything comes to the surface. Events relevant to the transit may occur long before and after the transit is exact. Inner processes are still completing themselves during the ebb of the transit. Transits of heavy planets take a very long time to unfold, and minor transits such as Mars or a new or full Moon may trigger the bigger transit several times during the course of its buildup and ebb.

Although we may often see events precisely synchronous with transits in the composite, orbs are relevant in a composite, too, and the heavy planets have a long buildup and ebb time. But we cannot speak of an individual psyche in which processes are taking place. This makes me ask the question: What is occurring within the relationship during the buildup and ebb of a transit in the composite? And can we, as individuals, affect it in any way? We all have a consciousness that senses something shifting, and we can work on this, ignore it, suppress it, or fight it as we choose. How we react may affect the way things manifest. This opens up the very complex issue of which events – if any – are "fated" in our lives, and which are of our own creation. Individual consciousness does seem to have an effect on the way transits manifest. In a composite, something is indeed building up, but neither individual can lay claim to it. I don't know whether, if two people are actively working with the energies in a composite, it makes any difference to the manifestation of a transit, except in terms of how those two individuals feel. This question will, I am sure, keep arising throughout the day.

Audience: Is this similar to working with national charts?

Liz: There is a similarity. A country, like a relationship, can't say to itself, "I think I need to work on my upcoming Saturn transit." A national chart is an entity which has a real birth moment, unlike a composite, but it is going to react in a very impersonal or natural way to transits. This may depend on the level of consciousness of the people. I don't know to what extent a composite may be affected by the consciousness of the two people involved. I am sure it is. But I am not clear about the limits involved.

Audience: So the composite really is more fated.

Liz: I only know that it *feels* more fated. But this terrain is too subjective and complex, and I don't know what "fated" means in terms of where our own – and the collective's – chain of choices and consequences begins and ends.

An example: Sun-Uranus in the composite

Let's think about a Sun-Uranus conjunction. If we see this aspect in a natal chart, there are many levels of meaning which we could discuss with a client. We could say, "You need a lot of space and freedom; you are probably not overly fond of authority; you enjoy being at the forefront of new ideas." We could use Uranian keywords like "eccentricity" or "inventiveness". We could be more psychological, and say, "You seem to have experienced some distancing in your early relationship with your father. Perhaps he was not available physically or emotionally, or you perceived him as embodying qualities of intellectual brilliance or exacting standards which you felt you couldn't live up to. But this father-figure is an inner image, a dimension of your own nature, and you may set unrealistically high standards for yourself which place you under a lot of inner pressure."

We could also see that individual as especially receptive to new collective ideas and visions. He or she would need to find a place in life which allowed for a contribution to the larger collective. Then we might say, "You would probably feel most fulfilled working in a field where you can contribute to human progress according to your ideals and talents. The Sun describes vocation and purpose, and Uranus is concerned with the evolution of the larger system." Now, let's say we have a relationship with Sun conjunct Uranus in the composite chart. What do you think this says about the relationship?

Audience: It's unstable.

Liz: Yes, fair enough. But in what sense? Sun-Uranus in a composite doesn't necessarily mean the relationship will break up. But it will always have an element of unpredictability because its essence is Uranian, which is to say, a vessel for new ideas and inspirations arising in the collective psyche. With this kind of nature, the relationship will resist being grounded in quite the same way as one with Sun conjunct Saturn; otherwise it cannot fulfill its purpose. The more rooted something is in the earth, the less receptive it is to the revelations of the airy, inspirational realm. We could say the same thing about an individual with Sun conjunct Uranus. We could advise that individual to make sure he or she has creative channels through which the progressive and anarchic qualities of Uranus can be expressed. With a composite, we can likewise advise a couple to make sure there is some room for a little unconventionality in the relationship. Conventional roles and overly rigid security structures might not be a good idea. Perhaps some shared political, social, or spiritual commitment would provide a constructive outlet for the Uranian core of the relationship. But despite this good advice, neither individual may be temperamentally equipped to act on it.

Audience: I think it would be a very creative relationship.

Liz: It would, at least potentially. The "purpose" of the relationship – its solar essence – is to act as a vessel for collective inspiration. A great deal depends on how this affects the two people, and whether either or both are able to relate to Uranus well. This is why we have to compare the composite with the individual charts. Let's say that the composite Sun is in 13° Capricorn, and composite Uranus is in opposition in 15° Cancer. The composite is making a definite statement about the relationship as an entity. There is no way that this couple, no matter how conservative and well-rooted and earthy and secure they try to make life, are going to keep this Uranian element out of the relationship.

    If one partner has Uranus at the MC, trine the Sun, and the other has a relatively low-key Uranus, then the Sun trine Uranus person may wind up acting out all the Uranian qualities in the relationship. That can prove very problematic, because acting out Uranus may mean just up and vanishing one morning. If neither is able to relate to Uranus, then Uranus may manifest as an external situation which forces instability or separation. If both people are able to relate to Uranus, or at least make the effort to try, then the prospects are more creative. An individual with Sun-Uranus will be pushed from within to recognise and develop the aspect, because it is his or her own. But in a relationship, if neither person feels able to relate to Uranus, what are they to do with a composite Sun-Uranus? As individuals, they cannot become other than what they are.

Let's look again at our hypothetical couple with the composite Sun in 13° Capricorn opposite composite Uranus in 15° Cancer. Let's call them Arthur and Brenda. Partner A (Arthur) has the Sun in 8° Scorpio, opposite Uranus in 13° Taurus. Partner B (Brenda) has the Sun in 18° Pisces, opposite Uranus in 17° Virgo. We would find the composite Sun opposite composite Uranus, because both natal charts have this configuration and so it would inevitably be reproduced in the midpoint pattern. So far, so good. Both people are Uranian, in the sense that the Sun is strongly aspected by Uranus. But Brenda also has a natal Moon-Saturn conjunction in 15° Cancer.

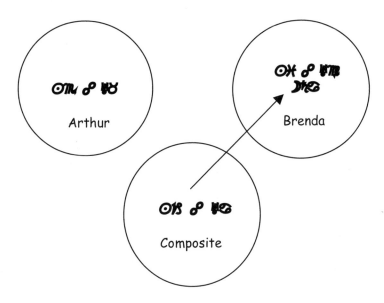

This Moon-Saturn conjunction in Brenda's chart complicates matters. Although the conjunction makes a benign trine-sextile configuration with her natal Sun-Uranus opposition, it is still Moon-Saturn in Cancer, and will reflect a deeply conservative, tenacious, and defensive quality within Brenda. Moreover, composite Uranus falls on Brenda's natal Moon-Saturn conjunction. Throughout the day we will be looking at the way the composite chart affects individual charts, but for the moment just keep that point in mind. When transiting Uranus comes into mid-Capricorn and triggers the composite Sun-Uranus opposition, it will also move into opposition with Brenda's Moon-Saturn conjunction. Meanwhile, transiting Uranus will trine Arthur's natal Uranus in Taurus and sextile his natal Sun in Scorpio.

The effect the relationship has on both individuals will be quite different, apart from any transits affecting the composite. The composite may generate anxiety in Brenda as a matter of course, because of the way her natal Moon-Saturn conjunction is being affected by composite Uranus. Brenda may feel threatened by the unconventional element in the relationship, or by the fact that Arthur must do a good deal of travelling for his work. But the relationship may have quite a different effect on Arthur. When the Uranus transit comes along, he may rise to the occasion with a sense of enthusiasm and excitement. We cannot tell what the changes are likely to be, but let's say there is an opportunity to emigrate because of a new work situation. That is a typical expression of transiting Uranus moving over the composite Sun. Or they have an unplanned-for child, or one of the in-laws dies and there is money inherited. Transiting Uranus over the composite Sun can describe any sudden, unpredictable change which frees energy and highlights the basic "purpose" of the relationship.

Arthur may say, "Great! I needed something new." But Brenda's response may be deeply ambivalent. Remember that composite Uranus is on her Moon-Saturn, so even before the Uranus transit comes along, there is something about this relationship that triggers a feeling of deep emotional unease in her. Composite Uranus stirs up her childhood experiences, constantly reminding her of the sense of restriction, responsibility, or emotional loneliness which belongs to the early part of her life. Issues with mother and feelings of being emotionally shut out and undernourished may be activated in her – not by Arthur, but by the mysterious "third" entity which the composite describes. This is not a bad thing, because the relationship also gives Brenda a chance to face and work with these issues from the past. Composite Uranus wakes her up to dimensions of her emotional life which may previously have been avoided, breaking apart old, entrenched patterns and allowing greater insight and emotional flexibility. Nevertheless, the relationship has a way of making her feel very anxious indeed, especially if she is not conscious of what is being constellated.

Now transiting Uranus activates this synastry between composite Uranus and Brenda's natal Moon-Saturn. The same transit also hits the composite Sun by conjunction, and composite Uranus by opposition. This transit describes some deep change which awakens or crystallises the essential purpose of the relationship. But the change, however positive, is going to be felt as very threatening to Brenda because transiting Uranus is opposing her Moon-Saturn conjunction. A great deal may depend on how she reacts. Change in the relationship is inevitable, but Brenda can react in a range of different ways to the transit which is triggering her natal chart as well as the composite. As astrologers, we might say, "Brenda experiences this transit in an uncomfortable way. The relationship is changing and she may react defensively to the change. Is she aware of the psychological dimension involved? Can she take it as an opportunity to ask some important inner questions?"

If Brenda remains unconscious of what is happening, then things may just roll along blindly, and perhaps also destructively. Arthur may be looking forward to emigrating to France, but Brenda may suddenly get sick because of the anxiety and tension. She may do everything possible to prevent change. Then one of those situations erupts which happens so dreadfully commonly – just as there is a big move planned, or a major step in a relationship, one of the two people suddenly says, "No, I can't go through with this." Then the relationship itself may be in danger, and the composite Sun-Uranus enacts itself literally. Does it have to? I don't know the answer. But individual psychology may be extremely important in relation to how transits are expressed in the composite, especially when there are strong natal-composite links.

Heimarmenê

The transit of Uranus will affect Arthur and Brenda very differently, but it will still be Uranus transiting over the composite Sun and opposing its own composite place, and there will be change within the relationship. Neither Arthur nor Brenda can stop this change, nor can they alter its fundamental nature, even though the reactions of both people may ultimately influence – or even create – certain external results. If we think in terms of cause and effect, we can view the expressions of such transits over the composite as the consolidation of a whole series of choices that have been made by both people over a long period of time. It is a bit like the Stoics' idea of the endless weaving process, the causal "chain" that we experience as fate. They called it *heimarmenê*. We all make an infinite number of choices that we are not even conscious of making, and these choices then produce consequences, which then require us to make other choices which produce further consequences.

By the time two people in a partnership have made a sufficient number of choices, some of which may have emerged out of consequences produced by choices made by family members or "outside parties" even before they were born, events begin to crystallise in the relationship which look as if they have come out of the blue. These events coincide with transits over the composite chart. Because of the peculiar fact that composites exist on an abstract level between everyone and everyone, always and forever, we may be looking at the astrological image of *heimarmenê*.

Many of the things that happen in a relationship are the result of one's own choices. One has many options with, say, a natal square between Saturn and Venus. One can choose to respond to the characteristic dynamic of this aspect in a variety of ways, ranging from cold criticism and rejection of the beloved to a compassionate understanding of one's own fears and a willingness to be vulnerable. A transit which triggers this natal square may be seen as an opportunity to bring the dynamic into consciousness and work on it. In doing so, one may affect the course of one's relationship. But the composite cannot work on its own transits. And as individuals, we cannot truly grasp that enormous cosmic chain of cause and effect that seems encapsulated in "what happens" when the composite chart is triggered. Our individual responses to these experiences may affect the future of the relationship – but I don't know to what extent, however conscious we try to be. *Heimarmenê* involves not only what individuals do, but also the choices that distant people have made on other continents centuries ago, which affect the course of history and in turn generate present consequences. We would go mad if we tried to encompass all of it in our minds.

Working with the composite

The zodiacal signs

Audience: Are the signs important in the composite chart?

Liz: There are astrologers who say the signs are not relevant. I believe they are. We need to remember that there are two midpoints for every pair of planets, and therefore we are really dealing with a polarity of signs. Every sign secretly contains its opposite But in practise I have found that the "near" midpoint signs are very visible in a relationship. If the composite Sun is in Scorpio, the intensity, depth, and seriousness of the relationship will often be very obvious, and very different from a composite Sun in Gemini, which has a lighter, more mental and fluid nature. If we look back on relationships which have been important to us, we can readily see that the composite signs are extremely important.

If a stellium appears in the composite chart, its sign will colour the whole ambience of the relationship, even if that sign doesn't appear in either individual's chart. We need to consider how this sign emphasis affects the two people. If one has little fire in the natal chart, and the composite has six planets in Leo, the relationship may prove both exhausting and inspiring. It not only makes up for what one personally lacks; it also generates energy of a kind that one may be quite unfamiliar with. In consequence, one will have to extend oneself in a way one would not have to do if the composite chart has six planets in Capricorn and one has a natal stellium in Taurus. In that case the relationship would harmonise with one's own values and goals, but it might not offer any challenge. Some relationships tax us because they require something from us that we are not accustomed to expressing. Sometimes it is the composite, rather than the other person, which is the more powerful source of attraction, impelling us into relationships which cannot be explained through synastry alone.

We can learn a lot about the zodiac by studying composites, because composite signs do not involve a personal expression of the energy. We can interview a hundred Capricorns, and discover that they all express their Capricorn Sun differently; so we see a hundred different sorts of Capricorn, including the materially ambitious Capricorn, the spiritually aspiring Capricorn who abjures material success, and the Capricorn who doesn't want to be a Capricorn at all and pretends to be a Gemini. Everything depends on how the person feels about being that sign. That, in turn, depends on the rest of the chart, and also on whether the family environment was sympathetic to Capricorn values and attributes. And if one believes in reincarnation, it may also depend on a much longer past. But a composite Sun in Capricorn is quintessential Capricorn, and we can see it expressed in a stark way that teaches us a lot about the fundamental nature of the sign. This will be clearer when we look at some examples.

Transits in the composite chart

We can interpret transits in a composite in the same way we would in an individual chart. When we read individual transits, we tend to pay the most attention to the heavy planets – Jupiter, Saturn, Chiron, Uranus, Neptune, and Pluto – which usually make several passages over a natal point. These are the deep, life-transforming transits. The same thing applies to a composite. The deep, life-transforming changes in a relationship take place under heavy planet transits.

Other transits, including lunations, eclipses, and stations of the inner planets, also trigger composites in the same way they do individual charts. They may kick a big transit into activity. We can apply everything we know about individual transits to composite transits. We can look at a transit through a given house. Let's say we are reading an individual chart, and we see that Saturn is moving through the 2nd house over a period of two or three years. Even if it is not aspecting any natal planets, it will quietly work away at the material foundations and underlying values of one's life. It prunes out all the dead wood, deflates all the fantasies, weeds out all the illusions, and leaves one with the stark reality of what one has actually built with one's innate talents and resources. We can apply that also to Saturn going through the composite 2nd house. It will work away quietly at the underlying resources, values, and security structures of the relationship, pruning out the dead wood and revealing the reality of the relationship's foundations.

The manifestation of a relationship

When an individual experiences a transit over the MC, there are many levels of meaning. For the moment, we will pass over the link between the MC and the mother-image – the deeper psychological level – and look at the more visible level. The traditional reading of a transit such as Saturn or Uranus conjunct the MC is a change in direction, goals, or social or professional position. Often such transits coincide with a critical moment in one's professional life. One may achieve something important in one's career, particularly if Saturn is involved. When transiting Saturn crosses the Descendant and begins its movement towards the MC, the person emerges into the world, and when Saturn reaches its culmination, potentials are anchored in form. Something is made solid and given visible shape. When transits go over the composite MC, the same meaning applies. How do you think this might be expressed?

Audience: The couple might get married.

Liz: Yes. Or they might meet for the first time. That is another thing we have to bear in mind with a composite chart. It will not tell us whether a couple have met, nor can it tell us whether they ever will meet. As I said earlier, we can do a composite with someone who has been dead for six hundred years. We can do one for ourselves and any public figure we have ever fancied, and while it may reveal the potential of such a relationship, it will not tell us whether the relationship will ever occur outside the realm of fantasy. Each of us has a composite chart with every single human being who has ever lived. That is absurd to think about, but the composite chart is an abstract entity, and does not indicate, in itself, the actuality of a relationship.

However, there are usually important transits and progressions in the composite when a relationship does manifest. We cannot tell what circumstances might be involved without knowing something about the reality of the situation, but we can see that something is happening. This can yield some very peculiar astrological pictures. If someone has been dead for six hundred years and we decide that we are going to write a book about the person, we might find that, when the book is published, transiting Saturn is on the composite MC. The relationship – and there is, indeed, a form of relationship, sometimes very deep, that occurs between a biographer and a long-deceased subject – has come into being in the world of form.

Synastry between the composite and the natal chart

Audience: Supposing the composite Sun is exactly on your own natal angle?

Liz: Your knowledge of synastry can help you to understand this kind of link. Hopefully it will become clearer when we look at some examples. Briefly, wherever the composite Sun of a particular relationship lands in our natal chart – including the natal house as well as aspects to a natal planet or angle – the life force and purpose of the relationship can invigorate and shed light on that particular dimension of our own nature and life. If the composite Sun lands on our MC, the relationship could enhance our standing in the world, and help us to focus our personal goals and professional aspirations. It may also trigger issues connected with the mother – the relationship may become a kind of mother, or may evoke or bring into consciousness childhood memories and emotional patterns involving the personal mother. It will have relevance to this level because it triggers the meridian, which is the parental axis. The same dynamic applies if the composite Sun falls on the Ascendant/Descendant axis. It may enliven and shed light on how we interact with the environment and in relationship with others.

Audience: So it is more dynamic on the angles of the birth chart.

Liz: It is dynamic if it conjuncts anything in the birth chart. There are relationships which we go into and come out of without any strong sense that there was a real point or purpose. In such cases, the composite Sun usually doesn't make strong aspects to the birth chart. There are other relationships which might be very brief but, if the composite Sun has a powerful impact on the birth chart, the relationship carries a sense of purpose which awakens some fundamental dimension of the individual personality and destiny.

Audience: What about the composite Sun conjunct your Moon?

Liz: How would you interpret another person's Sun conjuncting your natal Moon?

Audience: It's one of the classic indicators of a lasting relationship. It occurs in enduring marriages and friendships.

Liz: Yes. And why? What happens between you?

Audience: If someone's Sun is on my Moon, I instinctively feel sympathetic to who they are. I understand them. I usually like them. I feel comfortable around them.

Liz: Good. Now apply what you have just said to the effect a relationship would have on you, if the composite Sun is on your natal Moon. The relationship would probably have a powerful warming and energising effect on your emotional life. You would be sympathetic to the deeper purpose of the relationship, and would feel comfortable and "at home", even if the synastry between you and the other person was difficult. You might feel very protective of the bond, as well as experiencing a heightening and brightening of your emotional nature. You might feel you can "be yourself" in everyday ways. The relationship would probably give you a sense of "family". These kinds of contacts between composite and natal chart say a lot about why people often remain in relationships where they are not happy with the partner. There may be a lot of personal incompatibility – many squares and oppositions between the two birth charts. But then we might see the composite Sun right on somebody's natal Moon, and we can understand that, for this person, the relationship is home. It is going to take an awful lot to pry them loose, even if it is difficult from the point of view of mutual chemistry.

Naturally it works the other way as well. The involvement of composite planets with individual planets tells us a great deal about how the relationship affects the individuals. Equally, it tells us a lot about how the individuals affect the relationship. Synastry between composite and individuals may reflect the fact that the relationship is more important to one partner than to the other, or important in very different ways. The greater the interchange between the composite and the individual chart, the more the individual is likely to identify with the relationship.

Audience: I got the impression, from what you said earlier, that a relationship as such – a composite – doesn't have a consciousness of its own. Now you are saying that, if one of the partners is very bound up with the composite, he or she would have more of an input into the relationship. Would that mean more control over it?

Liz: A relationship has no consciousness of its own, but its inherent patterns are activated and animated by the two individuals. Input and involvement do not necessarily equate with control. Strong synastry links between two people don't indicate that they are controlling each other – they stir each other strongly on many levels. The same applies to the composite. I don't think important synastry contacts between composite and individual reflect a greater degree of control by that individual over the relationship. But I think they reflect a greater degree of intensity in the person's involvement with the relationship. This might mean that that individual acts out or embodies certain dimensions of the composite in quite obvious ways.

Let's go back to Arthur and Brenda. You may remember that Brenda has a Moon-Saturn conjunction in Cancer, and the composite Sun in Capricorn opposes this, while composite Uranus conjuncts it. Let's say that the composite Sun is on the composite MC, with composite Uranus at the composite IC. Brenda's Moon-Saturn therefore falls on the meridian of the composite chart, as well as landing on the composite Sun-Uranus opposition. It is clear that Brenda has a very powerful link with the relationship, through her natal Moon-Saturn. Her level of emotional involvement with the relationship is likely to be deep and complex. This relationship will matter terribly, far more than it might to someone whose natal chart is not affected so strongly by the composite.

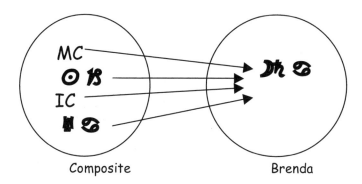

Composite   Brenda

This doesn't mean that Brenda can control the relationship. If anything, she may often feel controlled by it. It also doesn't mean that Arthur is uncommitted, or does not love her. But she may identify powerfully with the relationship, and feel both deeply emotionally contained and deeply emotionally threatened in quite compulsive ways. Because of this, she may invest a great deal of energy into maintaining the stability of the relationship. But Arthur, who may have no planets strongly aligned with the composite Sun-MC-Uranus-IC configuration, may feel, "Well, yes, I am in this relationship, and I love being with Brenda, but I am still myself. I have my own life and my own destiny." It is the degree of identification, rather than the degree of control, which is reflected by strong composite-natal links. The degree of identification can vary enormously between two people in a relationship. One partner may identify completely with the relationship, and feel as if they *are* that relationship. The other partner may feel the relationship is important, but their sense of individual separateness remains intact.

Transits which trigger both composite and natal charts

The transits which are most powerful in a composite are obviously the ones which also trigger the birth charts. There are usually points of strong contact, such as those in the example, between the composite chart and the two individual charts. When a relationship matters to us, we will always find that composite planets and angles land on our natal planets and angles. Usually there is at least one conjunction or opposition within a degree of exactness.

Audience: What orb do you use?

Liz: For synastry between composite and individual charts, I would use the same orbs as I do in ordinary synastry, and those are the same orbs I use for aspects in a natal chart. I allow 10° for conjunctions, oppositions, squares, and trines, and 6° for sextiles. As with natal aspects, the wider the orb, the greater the flexibility and room to maneuver. If composite Venus lands on one's Sun within 10° degrees, one will feel it, but it will be much more intense if the conjunction is within 1°. The effects of transits are also more obvious if the orb is tighter, because everything is set off at once. When a transit goes over such precise points of interaction, it is like a fuse being lit. We are activated, the other person is activated, and so is the composite, because these are the interlocking wires of the system. There is a birth chart here and a birth chart there, and the composite is the third entity. If there is a close overlap – something in the same degree in all three charts – that is a firing point. Any transit moving over that point will be very powerful, because it brings both individual and relationship issues out into the open.

The constant movements going on within a relationship are like a dance. We all know that relationships are not static. They don't remain the same, even if we wish they did. They ebb and flow, and one's role changes all the time. But the timing is quite extraordinary. Why should two people meet by apparent accident because someone happens to have missed a plane, or because they independently decided to book into that particular hotel in Panama City on that particular night because the other hotels were full? And lo and behold! they meet someone, and there is a transit of Uranus simultaneously conjuncting the composite Sun, one person's Moon, and the other person's Venus. Who arranges these things? It is a cosmic dance so huge that we cannot even begin to comprehend it. When these firing points in composites and natal charts are triggered, we may meet through activation of the linking wires; and when the firing points are triggered at another time, we may part.

Separations

A separation will also be reflected by appropriate transits and progressions in the composite, although these are sometimes indistinguishable from the movements which signify the beginning of a bond. Sometimes the separation is reflected, not when the couple physically part, but when the relationship is truly finished on the inner level. Sometimes the real separation occurs when one of the separated parties finds a new love. I have seen several examples where the composite of a divorced couple reflected a clear ending of the relationship – transiting Pluto, for example, over the composite Sun or Ascendant – when one of the partners became a parent through a new marriage. When one person decides to end a bond, this will usually be reflected by important movements in the birth chart. But sometimes we are disappointed to find so little. The event may show in the composite much more clearly than in the birth charts.

Audience: I had a transit like that in my composite with my ex-husband. The composite Sun is exactly on the Ascendant in Scorpio, with composite Venus also there. When we divorced, transiting Pluto wasn't yet on that point. Then, when he remarried, I checked and saw that it was right there.

Liz: This does raise the thorny issue of when a relationship really ends. When a separation is caused by the death of one of the individuals, that will usually also be reflected in the composite – although, once again, the astrological picture of the end of a relationship through physical demise may be indistinguishable from the picture of the beginning of the relationship, or the picture of the end of the relationship through other means. I can think of a number of examples of actual death reflected in the composite, and it does convey an eerie feeling of some fate at work, some *heimarmenê* which is beyond our ability to analyse or explain. There is an area here where our psychological knowledge begins to fails us. I do not believe we can foresee the death of a relationship, or the death of one of the individuals in a relationship, from transits in the composite chart. We don't really know whether a movement in the composite is reflecting the physical death of one of the partners, the metaphorical death of the relationship, the birth of the relationship, or a period of transition preceding a new phase in the relationship. The kind of transits and progressions which accompany death on the physical level might also describe other types of death on other levels. We only know that a major change is occurring.

Audience: If you did composites for yourself and members of your family, would you be able to find out when they might die?

Liz: We can see the timing of periods of upheaval, crisis, and change in the family. But we won't know whether there will be a literal death, or whether our relative will emigrate to Canada. The composite chart will not tell us the difference. It will tell us that something powerful and possibly irrevocable is happening to change the nature of the relationship. We can make educated guesses, in the same way we can with individuals. If one's grandmother is ninety-eight and ailing, it doesn't take a mind of great genius to work out that the approaching transiting station of Uranus and Neptune on the composite Sun will probably coincide with her death. Even then, we might be wrong; she might join a New Age spiritual cult.

Although there is a fated feeling around the timing in composite charts, the composite still cannot give us the thing that many astrologers wish they had – the ability to foretell the future in a concrete way. Transits in the composite describe the archetypal meaning of what is happening within a relationship, according to the nature of the planets involved. Pluto transits in a composite usually mean irrevocable change, but the nature of the irrevocable change can vary. The birth of a baby can mean an irrevocable change in a relationship. So can one partner having a love affair, because there may never be the same trust again, even if the relationship continues. A major move may constitute an irrevocable change. An in-law dying may signify an irrevocable change and a new lease of life for the relationship, if that parent has been a destructive influence.

Audience: So Pluto transits are not necessarily malefic, just irrevocable.

Liz: I don't believe any transit is malefic. Irrevocable changes, whether in an individual or in a relationship, can coincide with very happy events. But we can't go back to what we once were, and neither can the relationship. That may sometimes *feel* malefic.

The progressed composite chart

We can progress a composite chart just as we can an individual chart. We can use any method of progression – solar arc, primary progressions, secondary progressions, tertiaries, or diurnals. Progressing the composite chart is extremely simple in principle. The composite consists of the midpoints between each pair of planets in the two birth charts. For the progressed composite, we progress the two individuals' charts – by whichever system we favour – to a given date, and then find the midpoints between the two progressed Suns, the two progressed Moons, the two progressed Ascendants, the two progressed MC's, and so on. Calculating the progressed composite on a computer involves simply setting up the individual progressed charts and then getting the composite for them as though they were birth charts.

The real challenge is philosophical rather than mathematical. When we progress an individual chart, it "began" with the person's birth. There is a system known as converse progressions, but these still begin with the birth chart, although they move backwards. With a composite, we are not beginning anywhere. There isn't a time when it started because it has always existed, so we simply have to progress it to whatever date we are concerned with. We can progress it for the time of two people meeting, or a time when there is a major change in a relationship, or the time of the ending of a relationship. Or we can go deeper, and look at important progressed aspects occurring *before* the relationship manifested, to see what was happening in our own lives at that time, and what choices and consequences might have led to the relationship coming into being.

Progressed composite planets to composite planets

Please bear with me as we go through this theoretical material; we will look at an example soon. When we look at the progressed composite chart, we need to look at several different things. First, we view it in the same way that we view our own progressions: we consider the progressed planets and angles in relation to the natal ones. "Natal" in this case means the composite chart. Let's say that the progressed composite Sun is conjunct composite Mars. In an individual's chart, progressed planets aspecting natal planets describe an inner process of development. They are unique to the individual, in contrast to transits, which are in the same sign for everybody (although they affect each natal chart differently). Progressions seem to point to the meaning of the time in terms of internal growth and unfoldment of the "original" life-plan.

This inner quality also applies to the progressed composite chart. Progressed composite Sun reaching composite Mars may or may not not manifest as a specific event, but it points to a time when the passions and aggressive instinct inherent in the relationship are activated and need to be expressed. Transits, whether in the birth chart or the composite, are reflections of the cosmos impinging on the individual. Progressions are a purely symbolic motion. There is no astronomical basis for progressions. They seem to describe inner change, which is why they often tell a story quite different from how the person consciously feels and what he or she encounters in the outer world. This also applies to the composite. When we find progressed composite planets aspecting composite planets, we can read this as an internal shift within the relationship. Something inherent in the relationship's pattern of development has come to fruition, and now demands to be expressed in life.

When the angles are involved in progressed aspects, there is a tendency for inner changes to manifest outwardly, in the same way they do with individuals. When a progressed planet arrives at one of our natal angles, or a progressed angle arrives at a natal planet, it is usually acted out. These are the cardinal points in a horoscope, the skeletal structure of manifestation. The angles carry the same meaning in the composite chart as well. We might find, when a couple marry, that progressed composite Venus has reached the composite MC, or the progressed composite Descendant has reached the composite Sun.

Progressed to other progressed composite planets

We also need to look at progressed composite planets and angles making aspects to other progressed composite planets and angles – even if they make no aspects to the composite placements. This is sometimes overlooked when we work out the individual progressed chart. We are so busy looking at what progressed planets are doing to natal planets and angles that we may fail to notice important configurations such as progressed Sun arriving on progressed Ascendant.

Such configurations occurring within the progressed chart tell a story in themselves, and they are very sensitive to transits, which seem to "trigger" the progressed aspect even without a natal planet being involved. For this reason it is always a good idea to set up an entire progressed chart, complete with progressed angles and house cusps, rather than simply plotting the progressed planets around the natal wheel. The progressed houses are also important, because a progressed planet aspecting another progressed planet needs to be viewed in the progressed houses in which the aspect falls, as well as in the natal houses through which the progressed planets are passing. Transits to the progressed composite likewise need to be viewed in the progressed houses through which they are moving. In an individual chart, some progressed aspects have greater impact than others, and the same applies to the progressed composite.

I would like to quickly show you an example of the interweaving of transits, progressed composite placements, and composite placements for a major event occurring in a relationship – the death of one of the two people. I do not believe it would have been possible to foresee this death in the composite – especially since relationships, from the composite perspective, do not "die". They change form. But looking at the patterns at work at the time gives us a new perspective, not available from the individual charts alone. An event may hold a meaning for a relationship which is quite different from its meaning for the two individuals.

Here is the composite chart for John F. Kennedy and his wife Jacqueline. Following this is the progressed composite, set for time of his assassination in Dallas. The third chart is the transit map for the assassination. The transits in the composite are clearly relevant, but when we look at the progressed composite and the accompanying intense transit activity there, I think you will see why we need to include the progressed composite in our exploration of a relationship. You will have to do your own work on these if you want to go into them in any great detail. I just want to point out "highlights".

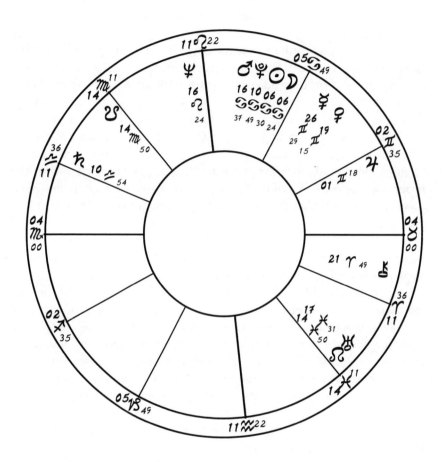

Composite for John F. Kennedy and Jacqueline Bouvier Kennedy

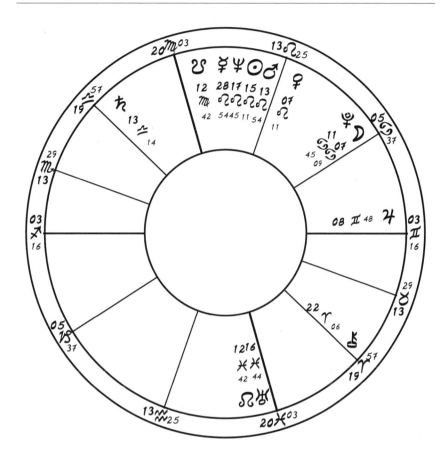

Progressed composite
John F. Kennedy and Jacqueline Bouvier Kennedy
Set for 22 November 1963, 12.30 pm CST

Most striking in terms of progressed composite to composite placements is the progressed Sun in 15° 11′ Leo, approaching a conjunction with composite Neptune in 16° 24′ Leo at the composite MC. Progressed composite Mars is following close behind. The implications are clear here of some kind of public sacrifice and the apotheosis of a myth (Neptune in Leo at the MC). We might also take note of the progressed composite Moon in 7° 09′ Cancer, right on the composite Sun-Moon conjunction – a composite lunar return, signalling the end of a cycle and the beginning of a new one.

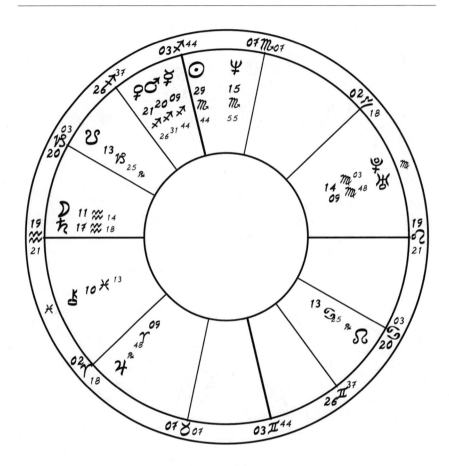

Assassination of John F. Kennedy
22 November 1963, 12.30 pm CST, Dallas

In terms of transits in the progressed composite and composite, one of the most striking is the transiting Saturn-Neptune square. Neptune in 15° 55′ Scorpio was within 1° of exact square to progressed composite Sun and composite Neptune. Transiting Saturn in 17° 18′ Aquarius was just past its opposition to progressed composite Sun, and was within 1° of exact square to progressed composite Neptune in 17° 45′ Leo. Transiting Moon and transiting Ascendant, both in Aquarius, are also part of this configuration. It may be worth pointing out, finally, that, in terms of the "firing points" which I referred to earlier, Jackie Kennedy had a Chiron-Node conjunction in, respectively, 14° 13′ and

17° 13' Taurus, and John Kennedy had Mars in 18° 26' Taurus. These natal placements link the individuals with the composite Neptune and, in turn, with the movements occurring in the progressed composite at the time of his death.

I do not believe we could look at this composite setup and say that John Kennedy would be shot. This event might be seen in his own chart, although that, too, is questionable. But we could say that something very big, dramatic, and perhaps tragic was happening in this relationship, on the themes of sacrifice and dissolution. The relationship had reached a critical point, reflected in progressed composite Sun's arrival on composite Neptune. If we step out of our ordinary human reactions of outrage at this murder, we can see something else portrayed here, something more impersonal and mysterious: the necessity of JFK's death as the ultimate act in an unfolding process that was meant to embody a myth to the outer world. That the aspect was 1° away from exact is not surprising; the actual moment of the shooting is not the issue here, but a profound and inevitable change and culmination of something concerned with the role of the relationship in society and in history.

Progressed composite planets to individual natal planets

We now need to look at the progressed composite in relation to the two individual natal charts. When a progressed composite planet arrives in exact aspect to something in our natal chart – and the conjunction and opposition are the most powerful aspects – we tend to be the one who acts out that progressed composite planet within the relationship. This is an extremely interesting dimension of the progressed composite. It is especially noticeable with the progressed composite Moon, which travels at roughly 1° a month by secondary progression, because that is the rate of speed at which the two individual Moons move.

Let's take another hypothetical example. A man has natal Mars in 3° Virgo, opposite Saturn in 3° Pisces and square Uranus in 2° Gemini. Now, that is obviously a pretty tense natal configuration. It suggests a good deal of self-will, but also some fear about his own effectiveness, and therefore a tendency to hold back just when he wants most to move forward. Thus he may often feel a lot of frustration and indecision alternating with impatience and aggression. He is in a relationship, and in the composite for that relationship, the progressed composite Moon has arrived at 2° Gemini. The relationship at this point in time is therefore activating this man's tense natal configuration. It is not a permanent situation; the progressed composite Moon will move on in a month or so. It is a phase. The emotional tenor of the relationship, as it is expressed at this moment in time, is going to trigger this man's inner stress. He may begin to behave in a particularly disruptive and aggressive way when he is with his partner, even though he may have no progressed aspects in his natal chart which reflect such behaviour. He is "plugged into" the progressed composite Moon because it has linked up with his natal chart, so he will probably act out his Mars-Saturn-Uranus in the relationship rather than in other spheres of his life.

Audience: And this happens even if there is no contact between the composite Moon and his Mars-Saturn-Uranus?

Liz: Yes, although it would be more powerful if there were an existing aspect between a planet in the composite and his natal T-cross. Then the progressed composite Moon would trigger both. An aspect between the progressed composite Moon and the man's natal Mars-Saturn-Uranus means that the emotional life of the relationship is now in a phase when it is confronting him with himself. It is acting as a mirror to his natal configuration, bringing it into awareness through the agency of the relationship, and inviting it to be expressed within the relationship.

     This is also a dimension of person-to-person synastry. If someone else's progressed planet arrives at one of our natal planets, that person, through the stage they have now reached in their development, is inadvertently confronting us with a piece of our own psyche. More often than not, our initial response is to project our natal planet onto the other person – especially if the natal planet is not expressed very well, or is quite unconscious. The only difference here is that it is the relationship itself, not another person, which is the agency of revelation. The relationship is triggering something in us which is likely to bring out a strong reaction because it was always part of our nature – part of our birth chart. This applies to benign configurations as well. The progressed composite Sun, or another progressed composite planet, may align with our natal grand trine in fire, or our natal Venus-

Jupiter conjunction. Then the reaction will be equally powerful, but very positive.

The progressed composite Moon

The progressed composite Sun moves at the same rate of speed as the individual progressed Sun. Even in a relationship of many years' duration, we may not experience many "big hits" from the progressed composite Sun to our natal chart. It is much easier to track the progressed composite Moon, which, as I said, moves approximately 1° a month. In an individual chart, the progressed Moon is the wanderer, the seeker, moving out into life and gathering experience through its emotional and instinctual perceptions and responses. The Moon is a vessel, a receptive faculty. It is like a bowl, longing to be filled, reaching out for connection with others and with life. As the Moon progresses around our birth chart, we go out and interact with life, encountering people and situations which personify the natal planets it aspects as it moves along. Each progressed lunar cycle of the Moon to its own natal place takes approximately twenty-eight years. The progressed Moon fulfills the purpose of its current cycle at the time of the opposition of the progressed Moon to the progressed Sun (a progressed full Moon), and begins a new "voyage" at the time of the conjunction of the progressed Moon with the progressed Sun (a progressed new Moon).

Thus we meet our destiny through relationship, and encounter our own archetypal patterns through the agency of others. We don't interact through the Sun – it is an inner thing, beyond the world of form, which depends on the Moon's incarnate encounters to take shape as "my purpose". The Moon is our attachment instinct. We get involved with others through the Moon. We meet significant people when the progressed Moon hits a natal planet, and they will be characteristic of, or carry the symbolism of, that natal planet. Things happen to us emotionally when the progressed Moon is making important aspects to our natal planets and angles.

Now, the composite Moon serves the same function within a relationship. It goes out and accumulates experience, and returns with a full bowl which is then processed by the composite Sun and turned into the "meaning" and "destiny" of the relationship. The composite Moon has to work through two humans, because the essence of the relationship itself – the composite Sun – isn't able to get on its bike and go out and have this kind of emotional interaction. So the progressed composite Moon will work through the two people involved.

When the progressed composite Moon arrives at something in our birth chart, we become the experience-gatherer for the relationship during that month, because it only stays for a month in that particular degree. When the progressed composite Moon conjuncts our Venus, we may be the one who brings harmony and pleasure and beauty into the relationship. When the progressed composite Moon opposes our Saturn, we may be the one whose withdrawal or defensiveness brings on an atmosphere of coldness. But when the progressed composite Moon conjuncts composite Venus, the relationship itself is passing through a phase of harmony and affection, and when the progressed composite Moon opposes composite Saturn, the relationship itself is cooling down or weighted with restrictions. Can you see the difference?

Audience: Yes, I think so. It's the difference between being aware of the ebb and flow of the relationship without feeling personally responsible or threatened, and getting plugged right in and reacting to whatever you feel is going on.

Liz: Exactly. And whatever you feel is going on is actually your own inner self, mirrored in the emotional tone of the relationship at that moment.

Audience: So if the progressed composite Moon hits your natal Mars, you are the one who is going to energise the relationship, through your anger or your passions, or through setting goals of some kind that will kick it into activity. If the progressed composite Moon hits your natal Sun, you are going to bring your solar light to bear on the relationship.

Liz: Yes, you have got the hang of it. The progressed composite Moon acts through the two people, according to what natal planet it happens to be moving over. If we are not conscious of this, we may find ourselves acting something out in the relationship without realising what on earth is going on. All of a sudden we start behaving in a certain way, and it seems to come out of nowhere. One does not have to be an astrologer to sense this process at work; one can observe and attend to it if one cares and pays attention to the way one feels in and about one's relationships. Lunar types tend to do this instinctively, with or without astrological knowledge. But this is one of the areas where, as individuals, we may have an important effect on the composite and the way the relationship develops.

The progressed composite Moon will carry whatever we put into it. As it touches off our natal chart, it is filled with experience which is coloured by what we offer of ourselves. Because the progressed composite Moon moves so quickly, it will make aspects of one kind or another to everything in our natal chart over a period of two and a half years. If one is in a long-term relationship, one has a chance to really see it in operation. Go back and have a look at what happened when the progressed composite Moon conjuncted your natal Uranus. What did you do? How did you feel about the relationship? What happened when the progressed composite Moon conjuncted your natal Saturn? How did you feel when it opposed your natal Neptune?

Audience: Would this kind of thing coincide with progressions or transits in the person's natal chart?

Liz: Often, yes. But they may say quite different things. Tracking the progressed composite Moon during a particularly critical time – doing it all the time can result in lots of information and no time for the relationship! – can give a different slant on what is happening in the relationship. This can expand our understanding of the progressions and transits in our own chart. Here a composite reveals most vividly that the relationship has its own dynamic. It can call things out of us even if an appropriate progressed or transiting aspect can't be found in the individual chart.

If an individual progressed planet triggers a natal planet, one's own issues are activated from within. It is *kairos,* the right moment for the emergence into consciousness of something belonging to one's own soul. If my progressed Moon goes over natal Saturn, I may get depressed and feel that nobody loves me. I may behave like that for the entire month the progression is operative. I may want to blame my relationship, or something in the world outside, but sooner or later I will have to start asking myself whether, and why, my own attitude is creating the neglect and isolation I am feeling. It is not that my partner, or the relationship, is making me feel like that; it is my own progressed aspect, even if external issues are serving as catalysts. My feelings are my own responsibility.

The progressed composite Moon may also go over my Saturn, and I may find myself behaving in the same way without my own progressed chart acting as a trigger. The relationship is making me aware of my Saturn, not because it is rejecting me, but because something about the current feeling tone of the relationship is pushing me into memories and experiences which call forth feelings of rejection and isolation. My feelings are equally my responsibility, even though I cannot attribute them to my own inner timing. Obviously, much depends on how connected I am with my Saturn. I might be able to respond in a creative way. Or I may just fall into the usual unconscious Saturnian negative space. Then I may turn around and launch my Saturn at the progressed composite Moon, which means I myself will stifle, chill, restrict, or withdraw from the emotional life of the relationship. Progressed composite planets can provoke strong reactions in us, both positive and negative. There are many relationship dilemmas where we may need to acknowledge the autonomous entity of the relationship itself. Something implicit in the relationship may act as a catalyst for both people's growth, suffering, and inner development, and neither individual is responsible for it. It is simply there, in the composite or progressed composite, although we are individually responsible for how we choose to work with it.

Audience: It is like a chemical reaction. Each substance has its own identity, but once you put them together, they create something quite different.

Liz: Anyone who has ever baked a cake knows that very important truth. We wind up with something that is totally different from the flour, eggs, sugar and yeast that we put in it. The heat and the chemical reaction have irrevocably changed the nature of the ingredients. We can't return those ingredients to their original state and make something different if we don't like the result; the cake is what it is. If we have baked a chocolate cake, we can't look at it and say, "I am going to take this apart and make a lemon cheesecake instead." It's a chocolate cake. Those were the ingredients that went into it. There is no way we can get another kind of cake.

Audience: But can't two conscious individuals do anything to change things?

Liz: I did warn you that this question would keep coming up. Two people can accept the fact that they have a chocolate cake, and stop whingeing because it is not a lemon cheesecake. That increases the enjoyment and alleviates a sense of disillusionment. They can serve it on a nice plate with a clean serviette, as a way of honouring what they have created. They can eat it slowly and enjoy it, rather than stuffing themselves and throwing up afterward. And if one of them develops an allergy to chocolate, there are two options: boost the immune system, or recognise that maybe this is not the right food, and look for something else. But the chocolate cake is what it is.

Audience: It's a field of experience we wouldn't enter without that relationship.

Liz: That's a very good way of putting it. A relationship often introduces both people to experiences they would not otherwise meet. If the composite has a powerful effect on the birth chart, it acts as a facilitator of one's development pattern. Often what we need for our development may not come from the other person's chart; it comes from the composite. I don't believe we enter relationships that we don't need, on some level. We pass them by. If someone is in our life, we need them there, at least for the time, although we may not always understand why. Sometimes it is the person we need, but sometimes it is the relationship itself.

Audience: What is the difference between a relationship where synastry gives the key to the attraction, and one where the composite is the real source of attraction? Do they serve different purposes?

Liz: I don't know. Strong aspects with a composite feel different from strong aspects with another individual. Of course, the two usually overlap; it is not so clear-cut as I have made it sound. But when there are powerful aspects between two birth charts, both people know that it is the other who exercises the fascination. We can work with it more actively, and make clearer choices. When it is the relationship itself, there is sometimes a strangely passive feeling. Both people feel caught in something. Without the clarity a composite can provide, it may be difficult to understand why one is with that person. The close links between composites and individual charts suggest to me that composites reveal a much larger pattern of interlocked humanity. Through relationships which make an impact on our individual charts, we are brought in touch with a huge system of evolving life, which moves forward through endless permutations of human interaction. It is much bigger than whether I love you or you love me. But that is as much as I can say about it.

An example

Now we can start grounding our theories. Here is a composite for a man and a woman. Later, I will put up the progressed composite for the date they married. We can also look at a few relevant transits, and some contacts between the composite and the two birth charts. First we need to get an idea of what this chart has to say about the relationship itself. Then we can look at all the other complicated bits. Does anything leap out and hit you about this composite?

Family inheritance in a composite

Audience: Jupiter and Chiron are right on the IC.

Liz: Yes. That virtually exact conjunction within 1° of the IC is very powerful. When composite planets fall on angles, it often means that the relationship embodies an archetype in some way, and personifies the qualities of the planet or planets in a very concrete fashion. If a planet is exactly conjunct any of the four angles in a birth chart, it is a focal point, because the angles "incarnate" us in earthly life along with any planets attached to them. We notice people with planets on the angles; they carry and personify the planet in a way that is not so apparent in other people. We notice composites with angular planets in the same way. This is obviously true with planets at the composite MC, but it applies equally to the IC, as we are always dealing with a polarity of midpoints.

What does this relationship embody? Look also at the aspects to the conjunction. Jupiter and Chiron trine the composite Sun in the 11th on the cusp of the 12th, and widely oppose Uranus at the MC.

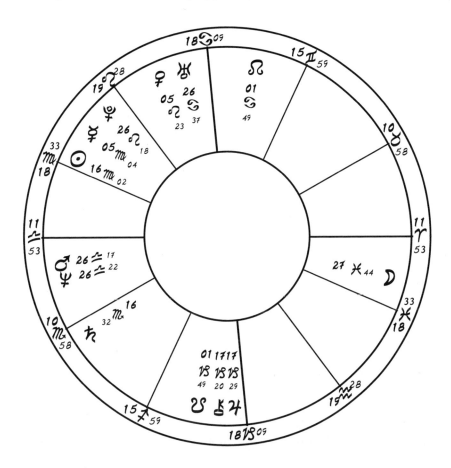

Audience: Could it be concerned with setting up a creative or healing centre? I was thinking about Chiron's connection with healing, and Jupiter having to do with expansion.

Liz: We could read it that way. But these planets are in Capricorn. Remember that the signs in composite charts are more literal. If these planets were in Scorpio or Pisces, I would take your point and think,

"Yes, maybe that is appropriate." Let's consider what we know about Capricorn. What is this sign about?

Audience: Hard times.

Audience: Sorrow.

Liz: You are all being rather depressing about poor Capricorn, aren't you? Capricorn's symbolism concerns status, position in society, hierarchy, and authority. Jupiter is concerned with expansion and benefits. Chiron is concerned with damage from the past. The IC is concerned with roots and origins and ancestry. Try to think in a more fundamental astrological way for the moment.

Audience: An angular Jupiter is very theatrical.

Liz: Yes, but, in this case, in a formal and subtle way. Jupiter is in Capricorn, not Leo, and it is at the IC, not the MC.

Audience: It's very businesslike.

Audience: It may be a couple who are involved in politics behind the scenes.

Liz: That might be more along Capricornian lines.

Audience: Is it Bill and Hilary Clinton?

Liz: No. But try to understand more of the chart before you start guessing.

Audience: Uranus is on the MC, widely conjunct Venus in Leo, which is the chart ruler. I'd say these people have a very public, very glamorous, and very unconventional life.

Liz: Yes, Venus-Uranus would suggest that. But for the moment, try to stay with the conjunction at the IC. We know that Chiron is concerned with wounding of a very special kind. It describes wounds which are inflicted by the collective, which arise because of the flawed nature of human beings and of society. Chiron wounds through the sign in which it is placed. What are Capricorn wounds about?

Audience: The father-principle. Authority. Would it mean that there is something wounded about the relationship itself? Something that cannot be healed, because it is part of the past, and part of the world in which the relationship exists?

Liz: Yes. This relationship is rooted in ancestral wounds (Chiron) as much as in ancestral privilege (Jupiter). It is wounded by something from the past, something concerned with society and with the family line – something unhealable. Capricorn as well as the IC is related to the father-principle, so we have a double statement about the parental past.

Audience: I was thinking that Britain itself was born under Capricorn. Is the wound something to do with class, with inherited position?

Liz: Yes, you are thinking along the right lines. You have also touched on a very interesting point. The birth Sun of the United Kingdom is in 10° 11' Capricorn, and that Sun in Capricorn conjuncts this couple's composite Jupiter-Chiron-IC. This is what I meant when I said the synastry between the composite and the individuals can be very revealing. Here we are looking at the synastry between the composite and the country in which the couple live. The effect this very public relationship has had on the nation is both expansive and fortunate, and deeply wounding.[2] You can now work out whose composite this is without a lot of effort.

Audience: Charles and Diana.

Liz: Congratulations. Do you see what I mean by "literal"? Here is the most public relationship in the world, with a composite Jupiter-Chiron conjunction on the IC, trine an 11th/12th house Sun.

---

[2]This seminar was given in April 1997, five months before Diana's death. The discussion in the seminar about the marriage of the Prince and Princess of Wales has not been altered to accommodate this event. However, the progressed composite chart and transits to the composite at the time of Diana's death are included in the Appendix to Part One.

The purpose of the relationship

Let's consider this composite Sun. What is the purpose of this marriage?

Audience: A symbol for society.

Liz: Yes, the purpose of this relationship is the provision of a symbol for the collective. That is why it exists. If we find the Sun in the 11th in an individual chart, we might interpret it as a need to provide leadership for the group. 11th house Sun people often find themselves an example to others. This marriage came into being to offer an example to society. Initially everyone thought the example would be superhuman and flawless. It has turned out to be a truer example of ordinary flawed humanity than anyone could possibly have imagined, and has perhaps fulfilled its real purpose because of that. The example has been a profound teaching instrument for many people, although perhaps not in the way they wished. This is also a 12th house Sun, so what else is it for?

Audience: Service and sacrifice for the collective.

Liz: Yes. The Sun's trines to the conjunction at the IC suggest that it is meant to serve the ancestors, to serve tradition, as well the collective. Its purpose is not a love-match. The 12th is the house of the ancestral collective psyche, and the composite Sun on the cusp reflects many generations of relationships, and all the myths which surround relationships in this family and this nation. We cannot really know the eventual impact of this relationship. But we can see how literal a statement the composite makes. Whatever these individuals might feel personally, this composite Sun serves a greater, invisible entity. That "destiny" would ultimately subsume whatever either party attempted to make of the relationship. Now, what does the composite Moon in the 6th in Pisces suggest to you?

The emotional life of the relationship

Audience: An emotional life which is bound by duty.

Liz: Yes, the emotional life of the relationship is circumscribed by ritual and the necessities of everyday mundane life. We might also say that a 6th house Moon finds its security in ritual and routine. An individual with the Moon in the 6th is often a "workaholic", addicted to his or her daily tasks because that is where safety seems to lie.

Audience: Could you also say there is emotional security in service of some kind? The relationship has certainly brought about involvement in many charities and public "good works".

Liz: Yes, that is a good point. The composite Sun describes the purpose of the relationship, the core of its being. What is the composite Moon about?

Audience: The emotional life of the relationship.

Audience: The everyday. It would describe the way the relationship functions on a day-to-day level.

Liz: It is the everyday emotional anchoring of the relationship. The composite Moon in the 6th describes an emotional life that is rooted in the orderly functioning of the material environment. This is the case with an individual as well as with a relationship. If there is any interference with this orderly functioning, an individual may develop "illness", that is, a somatic expression of unease or dis-ease. On the other hand, this Moon is in Pisces, which is anything but orderly. The quality of feeling in the relationship is romantic, dreamlike, full of fantasies and unreal expectations. It is poetic, chaotic, unformed, and unusually receptive to outside influences. There is a sadness about this watery, vulnerable Moon trapped in the house which is naturally ruled by the opposite sign.

Let's consider the composite Moon's aspects. It is trine Uranus and Venus in the 10th, and forms a yod with the Mars-Neptune conjunction in the 1st and Pluto in the 11th.

Audience: The composite Moon trine Uranus might mean there is a need to detach and live separate emotional lives.

Audience: Venus conjunct Uranus often means a separation or a divorce.

Liz: You are running ahead too quickly. Let's stay with the Moon. Composite Moon trine Uranus implies that there is something quite independent and detached about the emotional life of the relationship, the Moon in Pisces notwithstanding. That might not be entirely comfortable for the individuals concerned, but the relationship itself requires an element of emotional freedom. We will look later at how these placements affect the two birth charts. There is potential for both affection (Moon in Pisces trine Venus) and independence within the relationship. Whether both parties are capable of living this, and in what way, is another matter.

Composite Moon in a yod

Now, what about the yod? Remember Howard's description of a planet "caught" in a yod?[3] He compared it to a calf which has been caught by two ropes, and can't pull in either direction. This composite Moon is "caught" between composite Pluto in the 11th and composite Mars-Neptune in the 1st in Libra.

Audience: That Pluto in the 11th makes me think of the way in which people project all sorts of things on the relationship. It is a real "outsider". When anything goes wrong, everyone hears about it and blames them, even though people might be behaving the same way themselves.

Liz: Yes, that is an astute observation – the relationship is a "loner", a transforming agent, and also a kind of scapegoat for the collective. It carries the collective shadow. This obstructs the Moon, which is already hemmed in by being placed in the 6th.

---

[3]See Howard Sasportas, *Direction and Destiny in the Birth Chart*, CPA Press, London, 1998.

Audience: In an individual chart, the Moon would describe something about the mother. How do we look at the mother in a composite? Whose mother is it? His or hers?

Liz: The composite Moon does not describe the mother of either person. It describes the relationship's emotional colouration and requirements. The Sun describes its purpose. The Sun and Moon reflect the masculine and feminine dimensions of the relationship, rather than specific parents. Nor do the 10th and 4th houses describe specific parents, although these houses do say something about the family inheritance. We can't look at Uranus at the MC and say, "That's the Queen." Perhaps the Moon and the 10th house describe both mothers, all the mothers, going back into both maternal lines.

The Moon in Pisces in the 6th suggests emotion made martyr to duty, and this could be said of all the women on both sides of the family. Uranus on the MC suggests something powerful and unconventional, and this too could be said of the women on both sides. Diana's mother ran off with another man, and the Queen, ruling in her own right with a consort rather than a King, is Uranian in role, although not in personality. Uranus in the 10th in a natal chart often suggests a "trapped" mother, an independent woman unable to live her free spirit, who may seem cold, distant, or erratic to her children.

The composite Moon may say something about inheritance from the feminine line on both sides of the family, but we need to avoid getting too personal. Although we can read family complexes in the composite, we need to think in terms of maternal and paternal lines rather than individual parents. The archetypal principles inherited from the family line are certainly portrayed in the composite 4th and 10th. If these houses are emphasised, as they are in this composite, family complexes may form an important part of the relationship. But the composite won't tell you whose in-law it is.

The "vocation" of the relationship

Let's briefly consider the Venus-Uranus conjunction. You have already mentioned the public image of glamour and unconventionality, and the association of Venus-Uranus with separation and divorce. What is the "task" of the relationship in the world, reflected in these placements? We would generally read planets in an individual's 10th house as the vocation, or the kind of role the person needs to play in society.

Audience: I think there is something interesting about Uranus being in Cancer at the MC. I know the composite is not a "real" chart, but when you have talked about the generation of people born with Uranus in Cancer, you have said that they carry new ideals about family life. They are a generation which is looking for a different kind of family, maybe not so bound up with blood ties. Maybe this relationship serves the same purpose.

Liz: Yes, I think it does. Although the marriage was meant to carry on the royal family line, it is likely do something quite different in the end. In a way, this relationship is "anti-family" because of composite Uranus in Cancer at the MC. We might even say that this revolutionary spirit has been brewing in the family line for a long time. The relationship has "inherited" its Uranian proclivities from the maternal line, and sooner or later it would have to erupt.

Audience: I would like to hear more about Jupiter-Chiron at the IC. That surely says something about the father. Charles has a father who was unfaithful to his wife.

Audience: Prince Philip had a French mistress, who is now dead.

Audience: On what authority do you get this? Kitty Kelly?

Audience: I have a lot of friends in Fleet Street. So there's probably a certain amount of truth in it.

Liz: I said earlier that it is unwise to get too personal with a composite. I don't believe composite Jupiter-Chiron at the IC says Prince Philip had a French mistress. But there is the suggestion of great privilege and status (Jupiter in Capricorn) in the paternal heritage, as well as deep wounding and a mistrust or misuse of authority (Chiron in Capricorn).

Audience: Prince Philip is Greek, and I think Diana's mother eventually married an Argentinian. The royal family is actually

German, but the name was changed to Windsor because of the First World War. That's all very Uranian.

Liz: Yes, I suppose it is a very mixed ancestry. No pure British blood to be found here![4]

Audience: I can't quite get my mind around the idea of a relationship being wounded. Does the relationship "feel" hurt like a person?

Liz: This is an important point. We cannot attribute human feelings to the composite. Chiron on the IC says something about wounding by, and to, the authority principle, and this lies at the root of the relationship and is an inheritance from the past. But the presence of a wound in the composite is a statement of fact, not of feeling. What, in fact, is a wound? The *Chambers Twentieth Century Dictionary* defines it as "any division of soft parts produced by external mechanical force, whether incised, punctured, contused, lacerated, or poisoned." A natural pattern or innate state of being has been forcibly interfered with in some way; something has been penetrated, broken, or maimed without consent. Humans feel pain when they are wounded, physically or psychologically. Any entity can be damaged or wounded, but if it is not an organic life-form, it does not "feel" pain at the wounding. A building may be badly damaged by a hurricane, but it does not "hurt" in any sense we humans can understand. The owner may hurt, especially if he or she has no insurance; but the building does not.

We experience Chiron's wounding as painful because we know there is something within us which has been "incised, punctured, contused, lacerated, or poisoned", and we feel we have not deserved the damage imposed upon us. We are conscious of what we might have been without the wound, and this hurts. But a relationship does not react with a sense of frustration, pain, and anger. This relationship does not say to itself, "It isn't fair that I should have such a complicated family past." Composite Chiron on the IC simply makes a statement that there are unalterable limitations in this relationship. It is bound by the family history in a way that is inconceivable to most of us. There are inherent limits of a Capricorn kind – traditions, rules, laws – which help

---

[4] A recent article in *The Times* has suggested that there is also a black ancestor in the royal family.

to support the purpose of the relationship (composite Chiron trine composite Sun) but may block its natural expression (composite Chiron square composite Ascendant).

The "damage" of composite Chiron is not related to some abstract "norm" for all relationships. There are no "norms". Composite Chiron's damage needs to be measured in relation to the "norm" potentially possible for that particular relationship. This composite placement is not saying that the relationship is good or bad, nor that it is in pain. It is merely stating a fact: the full potential of the relationship can never be reached because something was irrevocably damaged long before the two individuals were born.

The meaning of the composite Sun

Audience: I would like to understand more about the sacrificial aspect of the Sun in the 12th. If the composite Sun is the purpose of the relationship, then in the 12th its purpose is sacrificed.

Liz: No, its purpose is *sacrifice*. That is a different thing. In the 12th, the Sun cannot function solely for itself. Its light cannot shine for the joy and benefit of the relationship alone. Its light must be given out to the larger entity of which it is a part. This relationship cannot exist solely for the pleasure and satisfaction of the two individuals. Personal happiness and fulfillment are subsumed in a greater whole, which reflects not only the ancestors, but also the national collective psyche. The relationship must give up something that most people take for granted when they enter relationships. Once again, we need to think about whether either of these people is personally equipped to cope with a relationship with these requirements. Unless something similar appears in the individual charts, there may be great resentment, because the life force of the relationship cannot be used to nourish the two people. It is there to nourish everybody, and perhaps also to redeem the past in some way. That is the sacrificial element. As with Chiron at the IC, this placement of the composite Sun doesn't say it is painful or not painful, because this is not the chart of a person. It simply states a fact about the relationship. It is the individuals who may suffer the pain, if they are unable to accommodate the purpose of the relationship.

Audience: You have sometimes said that the 12th house is mediumistic.

Liz: Planets in the 12th are mediumistic. By this I don't mean seance-type mediumship. When something is in the 12th, it is receptive to the deeper levels of the collective psyche. The innate urge which the planet represents cannot be expressed without bringing everyone else with it. The individual with the Sun in the 12th may find it hard to express individuality, because he or she is so attuned to the collective psyche, including the family past. The "purpose" is not to avoid developing individuality, but to develop it as an act of devotion to that larger psyche. That is why service and spiritual commitment are so often the themes of the 12th. So is the artist's inspiration, which draws on deeper and older sources than mere personal experience. Planets in the 12th need to reflect what the collective unconscious requires. They serve a greater whole.

Audience: The composite Moon is in Pisces, which has a 12th house kind of feeling, and it is in a yod with Neptune. That's a hell of a lot of collective service, isn't it?

Liz: Indeed. Therefore we should not be surprised at the muddle which this marriage became. It mirrors our own muddle back to us.

Audience: Could it mean that this relationship has to carry the mantle of the archetypal royal marriage?

Liz: It has to carry all the unconscious dreams, fantasies, yearnings, sufferings, and redemptive hopes of the collective. What you call the archetypal royal marriage is a collective vision of redemption. The failure of this vision was inevitable, because fairy-tale marriages are always doomed to humanisation outside the realm of fairy tales. As a relationship, this royal marriage has had to carry impossible collective expectations. Charles and Diana as individuals may pursue their own development, together or independently, but the relationship itself serves a collective function. It also carries an archetypal persona described by Uranus in Cancer at the MC. This composite Uranus describes something new and innovative which needs to be offered to society. Uranus always breaks all the rules, and in Cancer it breaks all the rules of "normal" family life. When we put all these factors together, it is hard to imagine that this relationship could ever have developed in the nice, problem-free, happily-ever-after way which everyone hoped for.

Audience: It is interesting to note that Charles' natal Saturn is in Virgo.

Liz: Yes, I want to talk about that in a moment. The synastry between the composite and the two birth charts is extremely revealing.

Audience: What is the Sun actually saying in a composite chart? I'm still having some difficulty grasping that.

Liz: The composite Sun describes the purpose of the relationship. Just as the individual Sun says something about the mystery of why a unique individual is alive, and what their purpose and destiny involve, the composite Sun says something about why this unique relationship has come into being. There is a very impersonal feeling about the composite Sun. We do not necessarily recognise it when we are in a relationship. It is hard enough to recognise the Sun in our own charts. We can easily identify our personal needs, but it takes a deeper and broader perspective to gain a glimpse of who we are meant to be. The composite Sun will tell us what a relationship is meant to be. What is its function? Why does it exist? What is it here for?

The composite Sun also points to what constitutes the highest value for the relationship. The Sun in an individual chart describes what is of the highest value for that person. Many people never become conscious of this. They never fully live the Sun, and identify with the collective values around them. They don't discover individual values. It is possible that many relationships also do not fulfill their purpose – they do not embody the highest value of which they are capable – because the individuals cannot find a way to provide the right vehicles, or give up before the relationship comes to fruition. How many of you believe you are conscious of and express your highest values? Well, at least some of you have your hands up. The composite Sun is not guaranteed fulfillment any more than the individual Sun. It is a potential and a path.

When Charles and Diana married, they knew, at least on an intellectual level, that their marriage was meant to serve a greater whole. Emotionally, it is likely that Charles could cope with this because he was raised to do so, but Diana has not coped with it at all well. Most of us don't even have an intellectual concept of what our relationships are meant to become, let alone the emotional wisdom to accept it. We think we are involved with someone because we have fallen in love. When we find ourselves dissatisfied or unhappy, we blame the other person, or our circumstances. But the composite Sun makes another statement. It says, "This is the nature of the life force in this relationship. This is what it is for. Whatever your individual hopes and potentials might be, this is the potential of the relationship. Make the best of it, and contribute what you can as an individual." Remember, we can set up a composite with anyone, and this abstract potential may never manifest. If the relationship does materialise, it may not last long enough for its solar purpose to be fulfilled. These are things the composite cannot tell us.

The meaning of composite Saturn

Perhaps we could have a quick look at composite Saturn in Scorpio in the 2nd. This Saturn makes quite benign aspects – it is exactly sextile the composite Sun on one side, and closely sextile the Jupiter-Chiron conjunction on the other. What do you make of this?

Audience: It is very binding. Saturn sextile the Sun could mean something enduring. Even a divorce can't make the marriage go away. It has entered history, especially because of the children being heirs to the throne.

Audience: It can also mean a lot of difficulty in their sex life.

Liz: Perhaps. Let's think about what Saturn means in the individual chart. It describes an experience of lack or deprivation, where we feel something deeply important to us has been denied. Eventually we have to build it ourselves. We may feel limited, fearful, and inadequate, and we struggle to compensate, or we avoid the sense of limitation altogether and project it elsewhere. The sign in which Saturn is placed tells us something about the qualities we feel we lack or have been denied, and the house placement will tell us something about the sphere of life through which we experience the denial. It can also tell us where, if we are honest about our fears and are prepared to work for what we want, we can build solid foundations and a sense of self-sufficiency and competence.

We can also apply this to the composite. We know that the 2nd is concerned with values, with resources and substance, with security, and with what we need in order to feel we have a strong base in life. Saturn placed here suggests that there is a deep instability in the relationship, a denial of some fundamental ingredient needed for firm anchoring in the physical world. Scorpio, being a water sign, is connected with emotional and sexual intimacy and honesty. These things are desperately important to the relationship, but they are lacking – perhaps, in part, because emotional honesty is alien to the family background of both people. Hard work is required to compensate for the sense of limitation and create a solid, enduring emotional foundation for the relationship.

Neither individual can be blamed for this. It is inherent in the relationship. Every composite chart has a Saturn. The message here seems to be that a real sense of intimacy and stability must be built brick by brick, with consciousness and commitment. Money is also an issue with the 2nd, and in this case there is too much of it. So much wealth and property can mask a lack of genuine emotional exchange. Money is used as a substitute for intimacy. This is often the case with individuals with natal Saturn in the 2nd. Sometimes they come from materially deprived backgrounds. Equally often, they come from backgrounds where material possessions were used in place of genuine affection and valuing of their identity. If I saw Saturn in Scorpio in the 2nd in an individual chart, regardless of aspects, I would say that the person needs to build a sense of confidence through learning to relate to others deeply and honestly. Emotional intimacy was probably lacking in early life, and mistrust and secrecy could become a bad habit. Something similar might be said of this composite.

Audience: I think it does describe the powerful material inheritance from the family. As you say, great wealth makes it possible to hide a lot of things. You can go on shopping sprees to make yourself feel better. You don't have to face the real issues that people have to face if they live in a one-bedroom flat and have to cook the dinner.

The meaning of composite Mars

Audience: It seems to me there is some connection with the Mars-Neptune conjunction in the 1st. I think that also has something to do with sexual issues.

Liz: This Mars-Neptune is a subtle and complex aspect. I think we can all see the glamour and external beauty reflected by the Libra Ascendant, and Mars-Neptune has a reputation for being enchanting and seductive. It is a placement which we might expect to find in the chart of a film star. But there is also a statement here about the quality of energy in the relationship, and the dissipation of energy in dreams and fantasies. Mars in Libra is a highly civilised Mars, so the relationship expresses its energy in a decorous and mannered way. And there is great receptivity to the feelings and fantasies of the collective, because of the conjunction with Neptune. The natural energy and assertiveness of Mars cannot express itself without tremendous inhibitions. In a sense, the relationship cannot "act" for itself, but can only make an impact when it reflects a collective need or serves a collective purpose. We are back again to the theme of sacrifice and service to the collective.

Audience: Might it describe the sexual deception which has gone on in the relationship? Would that be a possible interpretation?

Liz: Would you say that about a person with this placement?

Audience: No, I wouldn't.

Liz: What would you say?

Audience: There is a conflict between action and passivity. A person with Mars-Neptune rising would try to act and be decisive, and then wind up doing nothing because they needed to please other people so much.

Liz: Composites do not describe the actions of the two individuals. This Mars-Neptune does not say, "Charles and Di will cheat on each other." But Mars is in the sign of its detriment in Libra. This is relevant in a composite as well as in a natal chart. Mars in detriment loses its cutting edge, and struggles with ethical inhibitions and anxiety about pleasing others (Libra) or with self-indulgence and resistance to change (Taurus). Mars in Taurus or Libra gains many fine sensuous and aesthetic qualities, but loses some of its capacity to fight. Mars in Libra strives to harmonise with others according to an *a priori* ethical framework. Neptune in Libra is a romantic idealist, steeped in collective dreams of perfect love in a perfect, beautiful world. This interpretation applies to a composite as well as to an individual belonging to the Neptune in Libra generation group.

This relationship has a mode of expression which is gracious, reasonable, civilised, and in harmony with others' fantasies and expectations. That is the "personality" of the relationship. It would be hard for the two individuals to express unruly emotions directly in such a relationship, because there is something about the relationship which requires a lovely outer image. It "dresses well", as it were, and can never allow itself to be seen without makeup. It is not surprising that important emotional issues were avoided for so long, or that such rage erupted behind the scenes. It is very hard for a couple to present anything other than civilised behaviour in public, with a composite Ascendant and 1st house like this. One cannot blame the royal family for this, although most people do, including Diana herself. Yet it is inherent in the composite.

Audience: I would have expected some kind of theatrical quality. They aren't free to express themselves on stage in the way actors and actresses can, but a rising Mars-Neptune is very theatrical.

Liz: And you don't think they are performing? I think they are acting all the time, in both comic and tragic parts. And look at the friends the relationship attracts – show business people and mystics. The ambience of this relationship is a cross between a Walt Disney film and a tragedy by Aeschylos.

Audience: Mars-Neptune is squaring Uranus, as well.

Liz: Yes, and it is an exact square. The anarchic Uranian social "role" of the relationship is in intense conflict with the "perfect romantic couple" image of Mars-Neptune rising in Libra. The Uranus-Neptune square from Cancer to Libra is, of course, a generation marker. It occurred during the 1950's and reflects an innate conflict in a whole generation of people, between romantic idealism and revolutionary attitudes toward family. Because of their age difference, Charles and Diana have this aspect in the composite, although neither has it in the birth chart. The 1st house of the composite may also say something about why the relationship has had such problems with the press, which is forever invading their privacy. There have always been "leaks". Their antagonism toward each other is exhibited in indirect ways.

Audience: Constant evasive action has to be taken.

Audience: Or their evasiveness makes them act that way.

Audience: But you are saying this is something inherent in the relationship.

Liz: Yes, that is what I am saying – not that trouble with the press is inherent in the composite, but that there is something in the quality of the relationship which makes honesty difficult. Both Charles and Diana have fire signs rising, and Leo and Sagittarius are not known for evasive tactics. It is the nature of fire signs to be straight and open. Although their backgrounds inhibit such openness to a great extent, nevertheless they are, as individuals, temperamentally both inclined to express who they are. But something else is happening here which pervades the energy field of the relationship itself, and influences the couple whenever they are together. It is what I was trying to describe at the beginning of the day. We find ourselves behaving in certain ways in certain relationships, and those ways may be quite out of keeping with who we believe ourselves to be and how we behave in other relationships. I am not suggesting that a composite with Mars-Neptune rising in Libra is "bad". This composite placement has many beautiful qualities. But if there are difficult issues between two people, then such an aspect may make it very hard to tackle those issues honestly. Subterfuge may then become habitual.

It is also interesting to consider what others notice about the relationship. That is also reflected by the composite 1st house. The outside world seems to be obsessed with one thing only. They don't want to know about Charles' philosophical views; they want to know about his mistress. They don't care about Diana's opinions about the world; they want to know whether she has a lover. There is an incessant emphasis on the sexual and emotional side of the relationship which is somehow drawn out of the environment by the relationship itself. There is nothing new about royalty having illicit love affairs; it is, in fact, difficult to find a member of the royal family who hasn't had any. But the public and the press are always on the hunt for erotic snippets about Charles and Diana. There is a kind of prurience, a snooping, peeping mentality, which appears to infect any journalist who comes within a hundred yards. There has always been a climate of mystery and mistrust around this couple, which I believe is connected with the rising Mars-Neptune. No one quite believes what is said or presented, and this also applies to the couple themselves. We all respond to this composite Mars-Neptune rising in Libra, and sometimes fail to see anything else about the relationship or the two individuals.

Audience: The potency of the relationship is in the hands of the collective. That is how I would understand Mars-Neptune.

Audience: Is this the dark side of the archetype that we have tried to project onto them, the "Happy Ever After" Prince and Princess?

Liz: It is one dimension of it. The composite Ascendant describes the "personality" of the relationship and its impact on the environment. Photographers do not lurk in the bushes waiting for the Queen of Spain to be caught in bed with her groom. There is something about this relationship that attracts such antics. I am not suggesting that the press are blameless, or that there are no other factors involved. But this composite carries certain ambiguous qualities which provoke an ambiguous response from the environment. It is up to the individuals to work consciously with this. Sadly, there seems to be a good deal of unconsciousness displayed here, so we often see a rather unattractive expression of the rising Mars-Neptune.

Saturn's limits

Audience: If this were an individual chart, over time the 2nd house Saturn could be expressed much more positively, couldn't it?

Liz: If an individual has Saturn in Scorpio in the 2nd, he or she can explore the issues around emotional or sexual blocks. Enormous inner strength could develop over time as emotional and material self-sufficiency and honesty yield greater self-confidence. There might always be a certain restraint with this placement, but that is not a bad thing. Self-knowledge and increased self-esteem could loosen up many of the emotional inhibitions. Unfortunately, this relationship seems to be stuck with a rather literal rendition of the limitations Saturn describes.

Audience: Do you say that because it is a composite chart?

Liz: Yes, in part. This is not a "bad" Saturn, and it is well aspected in the composite. But the relationship cannot undergo the kind of deep self-analysis which is often needed to unlock Scorpio passions. Only individuals can. And an enormous amount depends on how well the individuals cope with composite placements. A composite with Saturn in Scorpio in the 2nd will probably always carry certain emotional and sexual inhibitions. This is no worse than inhibitions in any other area of life. Limits are not in themselves necessarily negative; they create a pressure-cooker situation which, handled well, can vastly improve quality while it inhibits quantity. Think of the analogy of pruning roses. If one hard-prunes a rose bush, it compensates for the curtailment of its natural growth by producing larger and more beautiful flowers. The 2nd house and Scorpio describe the sphere in which this particular relationship experiences Saturn's hard pruning. This placement does not say, "The sex will be terrible," or, "You will never feel close." But real intimacy may come intermittently and only with effort, although it might be well worth waiting for. Some people might accept this, recognising that one cannot have everything and that there are many compensations. Others are unable or unwilling to accept such restraints.

Composite planets to the natal chart

Now let's look at the interaction between the composite and the birth charts. As we might expect, there are a number of striking contacts. One of the most striking is composite Venus exactly conjunct Charles' Ascendant. But first, let's look at composite Saturn's interaction. Someone earlier mentioned that Charles' Saturn is in Virgo. The orb is too wide for it to conjunct the composite Sun. But Charles' Sun is in 22° Scorpio, and is therefore within orb of conjunction with composite Saturn. This suggests that he would feel the relationship as a responsibility and a burden. The relationship restricts him. Its emotional and sexual limitations, described by composite Saturn – which we cannot blame on either him or Diana – might make it difficult for him to feel he can be a deep, intense, passionate Scorpio. He would experience a lot of frustration trying to express who he truly is within the limits of the relationship.

This cross-aspect also has a positive side. No doubt the frustration has helped to discipline him, and without this restraint he would be less self-aware. The relationship pushes him into introversion and robs him of confidence. Yet it also focuses him, shapes him, and impels him to become himself. He in turn brings light to composite Saturn, because his Sun energises it. He has done this in a rather problematic way, but nevertheless he has exposed this composite Saturn's hidden difficulties through his own behaviour. In terms of what a relationship is "for", perhaps this exposure has helped to fulfill the ultimate 11th/12th house purpose of the marriage, through making the collective more conscious of the hidden dimension of human relationships.

His Saturn in Virgo trine natal Moon allows him to understand a relationship based on duty and obligation, so he is, at least in part, in harmony with the purpose of the relationship as described by composite Saturn sextile composite Sun in Virgo. But composite Saturn is also exactly square his natal Pluto, which is in 16° Leo. In fact, composite Saturn triggers his natal Sun-Pluto square. He would not only suffer from the lack of real emotional intimacy in the relationship; he would probably also experience it as a power battle, and his survival instincts would be mobilised.

Composite Saturn is also uncomfortable in Diana's chart – more so than in Charles'. First, her Venus, which is in 24° Taurus, is 8° degrees away from exact opposition with composite Saturn. That has clearly been very painful for her, although the aspect is not close. The emotional and sexual limits of the relationship undermine her confidence in her feminine worth, and trigger her T-cross involving Moon in 25° Aquarius, Venus, and Uranus in 23° Leo. This triggering of her T-cross would occur whether or not Charles had been faithful to her. Although composite Saturn is well aspected in the composite chart, its effect in Diana's chart is to stir up a painful natal configuration and confront her with her own internal difficulties.

Audience: Charles has Mars-Jupiter in the 5th in Sagittarius, opposition Uranus at the end of Gemini.

Liz: Yes. And?

Audience: These planets square the composite Moon.

Liz: Go on. What does that say to you?

Audience: Would that mean that his independent, adventurous side would find it hard to be with the soft, Piscean feeling tone of the relationship? Would he reject the emotional life of the relationship?

Liz: Yes, I think so. When this couple are together, an emotional quality comes into play which is gentle, clinging, receptive, romantic, and needy. He would find that hard because, as you say, he has a very independent side to his nature, and can be extremely self-willed. His Uranus square the composite Moon suggests that, in response, he might simply cut himself off from the emotional life of the relationship. Also, it would make him angry. Something about it makes him irritable and abrupt, and he may behave in an unfeeling way which might not be the case in another relationship.

Playing out the composite: division of roles

This raises another important point about composites. Two people will often divide up the conflicting dimensions of a composite. In other words, where there are dichotomies – and there are in every chart, composite or individual – one person will align themselves with one side, and the other person with the other side. This composite has some tough, strong, cool, restrained aspects – Sun in Virgo sextile Saturn in Scorpio, for example, and Chiron in Capricorn trine the Sun. It also has some very soft, receptive, romantic aspects – Mars-Neptune in Libra and a Pisces Moon quincunx Neptune. Charles appears to have acted out the harder contacts, and Diana the softer ones. This may not be the truth about them as individuals. What we see of a relationship is often not the individuals, but a mutual acting out of different dimensions of the composite.

In terms of who acts out what, we can get some insight from aspects like the one you just mentioned – the composite Moon in Pisces square Charles' Mars-Jupiter-Uranus. He is temperamentally unsuited to identifying with the composite Moon. He is probably repelled by it, although he is a water sign with a Venus-Neptune conjunction. He acts out something much harder and more unfeeling than he in fact actually is. But Diana is more aligned with the composite Moon by virtue of her grand water trine, particularly since her Sun trines Neptune. Although her Moon in Aquarius opposite Uranus, her Pluto-Mars-Uranus conjunction, and her Sagittarius Ascendant describe qualities as ferociously independent as anything in Charles' chart, she seems to act out the Neptunian side of the relationship, and appears to us – and probably feels, when she is with him – far more Neptunian than she in fact is.

Audience: So he gets to play composite Saturn in Scorpio sextile Sun in Virgo, and she gets to play composite Moon in Pisces quincunx Neptune.

Liz: In effect, yes. Relationships can emphasise sides of us which might otherwise be more balanced or not so overtly expressed. The composite requires us to live within it as long as we are in that relationship, and so we gravitate toward those parts of the composite which are most congenial to our natures and easiest to live out.

Composite Mercury

Now let's look at another important contact between the composite and the two birth charts. We can't cover everything, but this one is quite striking. Composite Mercury is in 5° Virgo in the 11ᵗʰ house. Diana has Mars in 2° Virgo and Pluto in 6° Virgo, so composite Mercury is right on this conjunction in her chart, falling in her 8ᵗʰ house and opposing her Chiron in 6° Pisces. Charles, in turn, has natal Saturn in 5° Virgo, so composite Mercury is exactly on that. Composite Mercury triggers not only the two individuals, but also a complex cross-aspect between their own charts – his Saturn on her Mars-Pluto-Chiron. This is clearly a firing point, in the same way composite Saturn is a firing point because it falls on his Sun and her natal T-cross and sets off the cross-aspects between them. Now, what do you make of it?

Audience: Composite Mercury in the 11th has something to do with how they communicate to the public.

Audience: I think composite Mercury in Virgo in the 11th says the relationship needs to have communication with the people. They have to go out and communicate. They can't hide at Balmoral, or behind some mystique of royalty.

Liz: Good. The relationship needs to communicate its values and purpose to as wide an audience as possible. It is meant to be a "people's marriage", conveying ideas to the collective. The question is, what does it communicate? This is where the firing point becomes relevant. This composite Mercury receives its information from his Saturn and her Mars-Pluto-Chiron. It is being fed by both of them, and in turn conveys their messages to the public. And it also receives information from the collective and feeds it back to the two individuals, making them feel Saturn and Mars-Pluto respectively.

Audience: So he feels rejected by the people, and she feels violated and persecuted.

Liz: Exactly.

Audience: This must be one of the reasons why the press have always been so involved with this marriage. It's as if they have to be. Everyone always blames either the press or Charles and Diana for leaking things to the press. But you are saying that this composite Mercury is a kind of lightning rod. It gives and takes messages. The relationship is a communicator.

Audience: The relationship has also given her a vehicle to communicate. She has learned to become a public speaker about Virgo issues – healing and service. That is the positive side.

Liz: Now you are getting the hang of it. As with everything else in astrology, composite Mercury's links with the two birth charts work in both positive and negative ways. We could say that this composite Mercury is a mouthpiece for both of them, allowing them to make direct practical contributions to the public and influence public thinking in ways which other royal couples have not been able to do. We could also say that the constant interchange with the public, which knows far more about them than it ever has about any other royal couple, has an undermining effect on Charles' confidence (Saturn in Virgo in the 2nd) and stirs up deep fear, rage, and pain in Diana (Mars-Pluto in Virgo in the 8th opposite Chiron in the 2nd).

Mercury in a birth chart has many levels. One of its most basic meanings is that it describes the kind of things one thinks about. If one has Mercury in the 2nd, one thinks about money and security. If it is in the 10th, one thinks about one's work in the world. If it is in the 1st, one thinks about oneself and the impact one has on others. Mercury is where our perceptions are focused. Relationships as independent entities do not think in the human sense, any more than they feel wounded. But there is a focus of interest described by composite Mercury in the 11th, and it is the collective, the people "out there". What the people think matters enormously to the development of this relationship. So does the welfare of the people, and the necessity of educating them. The role of friends has also always been extremely important; friends wield great influence over the relationship. Most of what we hear of the couple's personal life has been communicated through friends. Composite Mercury describes all these things.

This composite Mercury triggers hidden and very difficult issues in Diana's birth chart. She has made personal dilemmas, such as her bulimia, public. As you say, she has become a mouthpiece for the cause of AIDS patients and the dangers of land mines, both of which may be seen as a Mars-Pluto-Chiron-8th house thing. That isn't quite what people expected from Diana. Initially she just seemed like a nice girl who loved children. But she has publicly aligned herself with 8th house causes, as well as revealing 8th house secrets. This reflects the "lightning rod", as you put it, of composite Mercury in the 11th landing on her natal 8th house conjunction. She has also been forced into thinking about her own problems. The relationship not only makes her look at her psychological difficulties, but also impels her to talk about them in a very public way.

Audience: Because it triggers her natal 8th house, it may bring up sexual issues.

Liz: Those, too. The relationship, through composite Mercury, pushes her into confronting her Mars-Pluto-Chiron issues. She can't get away from them. She has publicly blamed Charles for the eruption of her bulimia. But it might be fairer to say that the relationship itself has brought the problem out into the open. It was there before she met Charles, of course, but it flared up badly at the beginning of the marriage. His Saturn falls on her Mars-Pluto, so her feeling of being rejected has undoubtedly triggered her inner compulsions. The relationship, however, has impelled her to think and talk about them. She seems to have come very close to healing many of these inner demons, and the "public confessional" generated by the relationship – composite Mercury in the 11th – has, in large part, facilitated that healing process.

We haven't talked about composite Venus on Charles' Ascendant, nor about the composite Ascendant on his Venus-Neptune. These contacts suggest that it was not Diana herself – his Venus has little contact with her chart – as much as the magnetic attraction of the relationship which made him decide to choose her as his wife. Nor have we touched on the composite MC and Moon's Node in Cancer conjuncting Diana's Sun. These are all very powerful links, and they are not uncommon when one looks at composites in relation to the individual birth charts. I believe invaluable insights can be found in studying, not only the composite itself, but its effect on the people concerned. We have left out a lot about this composite, but I am aware of the time passing, and I think we should move on to the progressed composite, set for the time of the wedding.

The progressed composite

Charles married Diana on 29 July, 1981. The progressed composite Sun at the time of the wedding was in 12° 11' Libra, and was within a quarter of a degree of exact conjunction with the composite Ascendant. Do I need to explain this? It is so glaringly obvious that it is downright awesome. This progressed composite Sun arriving on the composite Ascendant states that the relationship has been born in the world. It has manifested in outer reality.

The progressed composite Sun was also within 1° of Charles' IC in 13° Libra, so he created a new home and family as well as perpetuating his own family line. In other words, the progressed composite Sun activated his IC. "It's time to settle down," he said to himself. The relationship itself helped him to feel this. It was not just public and family pressure – that had been going on for years. *This* relationship invoked a definite decision at *that* moment in time.

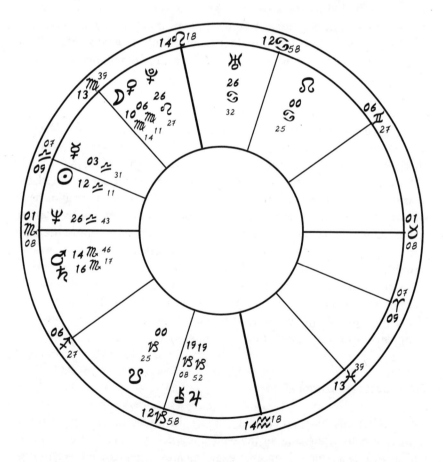

Audience: What about the Sun in the 4th in a composite chart? Would people want to root?

Liz: I would be careful of putting it that way if I were you. It means something else in Australia. I was told the following joke: Why is a wombat like an Australian male? Because it eats roots and leaves. You don't get it? Ask one of the Australians in the group.

If the composite Sun is in the 4th house, the relationship's purpose may involve creating a home and roots. Usually, when the composite Sun is in the 4th, people have a tendency to want to settle together. The relationship itself motivates them this way, even if both of them have been raving *puers* for the last twenty years. They get into a relationship with the Sun in the composite 4th, and suddenly they start thinking about mortgages. Of course, the 4th house is not just about home and family, but also about the psychological inheritance and the search for an inner source. Composite Sun in the 4th can impel one or both people to look within and begin an inner journey of a psychological and/or spiritual kind. In our example chart, it is the progressed composite Sun which seems to be provoking a 4th house response in Charles' chart. This is a vivid example of a progressed composite planet aspecting both the composite chart itself and the natal chart of one of the individuals.

Now have a look at progressed composite Mars. It was in 14° Scorpio at the time of the marriage, not quite conjunct composite Saturn, but very close. You can see that progressed composite Saturn and composite Saturn are virtually the same. That is because his Saturn went retrograde after his birth and hers was already retrograde, so the two Saturns have not moved much by individual progressed motion. Therefore progressed composite Saturn has not moved much either. But progressed composite Mars has moved along at its usual rate of motion, and was creeping up to composite Saturn at the time of the wedding. The relationship seems to have gone through a particularly nasty phase during the two or three years following the wedding. This is when Diana's bulimia erupted, and when all the anger and suspicion and jealousy and frustration began to take root.

This is very sad, because this aspect from progressed composite Mars to composite Saturn suggests that there was a kind of inevitability about the emotional and sexual alienation and deep, unforgiving anger which was generated so early in the marriage. Looking at this aspect, I find it hard to assign blame to either person for what happened. It has the kind of unrelenting momentum of a Greek tragedy. The progressed composite MC had reached 16° Leo as well, exactly square composite

Saturn and conjunct Charles' natal Pluto in the 1st house. This aspect did not help matters, since it no doubt increased the sense of limitation within the relationship as well as stirring up Charles' most primal survival instincts. These two people went into a marriage with this progressed aspect building up. It is a hard, painful cosmic statement: "Lovely wedding, nice dress, lots of potential, but the two of you are going to come face to face with the limits of this relationship very quickly – perhaps too quickly to build a foundation which could withstand the disappointment."

Now have a look at progressed composite Venus. The relationship's expression of harmony and pleasure, represented by composite Venus, had progressed from 5° Leo to 6° Virgo. You can see that it had reached not only composite Mercury in 5° Virgo, but also, Charles' natal Saturn, in the months before the wedding. They became engaged under this aspect of progressed composite Venus to composite Mercury. Progressed composite Venus at the time of the wedding was exactly on Diana's natal Pluto and opposite her natal Chiron. It had reached one of the firing points. Like progressed composite Sun to composite Ascendant, this aspect is downright awesome in its precision. Any comments?

Audience: I feel quite breathless looking at this. Also very sad. I can see what progressed Venus to Mercury might mean – flirtation, romance, announcement of the engagement. Maybe its conjunction with his Saturn says something about his formal commitment to marriage. It made him think of security and stability. Also, there is a massive change of values for both of them, a complete change in their value structure.

Liz: In one sense, progressed composite Venus activated their "karma". It stirred up all kinds of deep unconscious conflicts in both of them. It attracted them to each other and to the promise of the relationship, but it also stirred up all the hidden compulsions and inheritance from the past. This progressed composite Venus on Charles' Saturn must have made him feel not only quite insecure, but also determined to have the marriage. He needed to give the relationship form. When our natal Saturn is activated, we may react not only with anxiety, but also with intense possessiveness, because the thing that is threatening is also fascinating. Saturn always involves an element of envy, because it is where we feel deprived or inadequate. When we see someone who appears to be expressing the envied thing freely, we are often deeply attracted to them, but we may also resent them because they remind us of our own inadequacy. Very powerful ambivalence may be stirred up when one's natal Saturn is triggered. Here the trigger is not only Diana's natal Mars-Pluto, but also progressed composite Venus. Some glimpse of beauty and innocence and purity (Venus in Virgo), offered by the relationship itself, drew him to taking on a cross-chart synastry aspect that is, by anyone's standards, extremely difficult.

Audience: What did progressed composite Venus do to her Pluto, then? And to her Chiron?

Liz: It must have awakened quite unfamiliar feelings of passion. At the same time, it would have triggered her sense of being damaged, wounded, and unlovable. There is a great deal of ambivalence in this natal opposition being activated by progressed composite Venus. Pluto would have made the marriage seem an absolute necessity, a compulsion. Chiron would have made the marriage seem a potential threat, something which would activate old wounds – as indeed it did.

Audience: When they married, progressed composite Moon was in 10° Virgo. When did it reach composite Mercury and progressed composite Venus, and go over her Mars-Pluto-Chiron and his Saturn?

Liz: The progressed composite Moon moves roughly 1° per month. It reached 5° to 6° Virgo in February 1981.

Audience: That is when they got engaged. It was a pretty fast romance. It probably kicked into life when the progressed composite Moon hit composite Pluto in 26° Leo. The courtship started in September 1980.

Audience: This is actually getting quite creepy.

Audience: Relax, everyone keeps telling us astrology is a load of bunkum anyway.

Liz: The progressed composite Moon moved over Diana's fixed T-cross, Charles' Sun-Chiron, and composite Pluto, during the initial stages of the courtship. It triggered the major synastry contacts between the two birth charts like a pinball machine. It *is* a bit creepy, since this is merely an abstract entity comprised of midpoints. But abstract entity though the composite might be, you can see that it packs a powerful punch.

Now let's finish this part of the seminar by taking a brief look at some relevant transits. Transiting Uranus was in 26° Scorpio, exactly square composite Pluto (and right on the midpoint of Charles' Sun-Chiron conjunction) at the time of the marriage. Transiting Pluto was in 21° Libra, and moved over composite Mars-Neptune in the year or two following the marriage, at the same time progressed composite Mars reached composite Saturn. This emphasises what I said earlier about the inevitability of the emotional and sexual mess which ensued so early in the relationship. Transiting Saturn was in 5° Libra, and in the months following the wedding moved over the progressed composite Sun as well as Charles' IC and the composite Ascendant. This seems to have crystallised the relationship in the world of form.

When does it begin?

Audience: Would there be a case for beginning a composite from the time that two people met, in the sense that that would be the birth or beginning of the relationship?

Liz: We can set up a horoscope based on the time of first meeting. We can also do an individual progressed chart for that moment. Likewise, we can set up a progressed composite chart for that moment, by doing the two individual progressed charts and finding the midpoints. But we can't "begin" a composite from that moment, because it has always existed.

Audience: It seems logical to begin at the beginning of the relationship.

Liz: We can't begin the composite at that moment, because we can't begin a composite. It is not a birth chart. It has no time orientation, in the sense of starting or ending. It has always existed. It will always exist. Even if one had never been born, it would still be possible to do a composite between every moment in time and every other moment in time, including the moment which became one's birth moment. I know it's hard to get one's mind around this. But composites do not map the birth of anything, nor are they anchored in time and space. They describe a field of interaction between two things which have been born in time and space.

Composites make us think about time in new ways. We have seen that there are usually important transits or progressions occurring in the composite when a relationship begins. But often the transit or progressed aspect has begun before the couple have actually met. The heavy planets generally make three passes over a particular zodiacal degree. I have seen cases where a planet has made two passes over the composite Sun, and it is on the third pass that the two people physically meet. What was going on during the previous two passes? Because of the precision of transits in a composite, I thought it would be worth finding out. I discovered that, although the relationship had not yet begun, the arrangement of circumstances that led to the meeting began under those first two passes.

For example, a man might apply for a job at a new company at the time transiting Pluto makes its first conjunction to the composite Sun. Although he doesn't know it, the woman he will fall in love with works for that company. They have not met yet, but the groundwork is being laid, and the composite for the yet-to-be relationship has already been activated. Then, the second time transiting Pluto moves over the composite Sun, these two people meet briefly in the company car park and exchange a few words. When Pluto makes its final pass over the composite Sun, they get emotionally and sexually involved.

This makes me think again of *heimarmenê*, the Stoics' chain of cause-and-effect which works its way invisibly over the world and through aeons of time. If one hadn't been in London at such-and-such a time to do the CPA course, one wouldn't have met so-and-so, who introduced one to the person whom one married. When we start tracking the seeds of relationships back over time, we find that the stage is already being set for the eventual emergence of the relationship under the initial phases of these transits and progressions in the composite.

We cannot "begin" a composite, not only technically, but also because we don't know when a relationship really begins or, for that matter, when it really ends. We looked at this issue earlier in the day. Two people might get involved, separate, and never see each other again. Six years later, one of these people gets married to somebody else, although the earlier lover knows nothing of this. In their composite chart, transiting Pluto is exactly conjunct composite Ascendant. Even though the couple have not been in contact for many years, the marriage of one of them to another person signifies an irrevocable change in the relationship. Or a woman divorces her husband, meets another man, and has a child by him. Her ex-husband knows nothing about it because they have not been in contact. But the progressed composite Sun has reached composite Neptune in the 5th house by exact conjunction. Or an old friend that we haven't seen for twenty years dies, and we hear about it through the grapevine, and we look at the composite chart and see progressed composite Sun opposite composite Uranus. We might not have had what we ordinarily think of as a relationship with that person for a long time. Yet composites teach us that, at some level, all relationships continue to exist, even if we feel nothing for the person any more.

Audience: It makes you wonder who's the puppeteer.

Liz: Perhaps "the creator of the software" might be a more up-to-date way of putting it. I do often wonder who or what arranges these things. Perhaps it's Bill Gates. Composites raise a profound problem about what we define as the beginning and ending of things. We are rather narrow in terms of how we look at our lives. We connect a sequence of events together and say, "This relationship started on such-and-such a date, followed a course of A, B, and C, and then ended." But we don't look at the much broader backdrop of the vast chain of contacts and life circumstances that eventually contributed to the formation of that tie, and all of the consequences that arise from it later, even if we never see the person again.

Audience: Then there is the issue of one composite having an effect on another.

Liz: Yes, that is another path to madness. When we were looking at the composite for Charles and Diana, perhaps we should have compared it with the composite between Charles and the Queen, and the composite between Charles and Camilla.

Audience: And the composites between the Queen and each of her corgis.

Audience: Then we really would go mad.

Liz: There is a school of thought which suggests that we are already. However, the family is an interesting place to experiment with comparing composites. For example, we can compare the composite between a father and his son and the composite between the mother and the son, and explore how the two relationships affect each other. Or we can compare the composite for a man and his lover with the composite for the same man and his marriage partner. This is just as valid as exploring the interaction of two people, and it gives us a different perspective from traditional synastry.

Audience: Now that we have looked at the composite for Charles and Diana, I take your point about a chocolate cake being a chocolate cake.

Audience: Would you say that to him?

Liz: Say what? That a chocolate cake is a chocolate cake? I expect he has already worked that out.

Audience: I keep thinking that there must be ways to work with composite Saturn and composite Chiron that can make them more positive. Does it really have to stay a chocolate cake?

Liz: Saturn and Chiron are not negative in the composite. They symbolise inherent limits in a relationship, just as they do in an individual. The two individuals can do a lot to give composite Saturn and Chiron constructive rather than destructive channels. Limits can generate very creative responses. But the limits are inherent and will not go away. I know what you are asking for, and I would love to be able to say we can change anything if we work hard enough. But I don't believe we can, even though I also believe we must try. We can go a long way in our inner work. But if composite Saturn is in the 2nd in Scorpio, it is always going to be composite Saturn in the 2nd in Scorpio. It will not magically become composite Jupiter in the 2nd in Sagittarius. To achieve that, you must find another relationship which *has* composite Jupiter in the 2nd in Sagittarius.

Everyone has a composite Saturn in any relationship they are in. There is always going to be a composite Saturn, just as there will be a

Saturn in every birth chart. None of us can be whatever we wish, and none of us can alter what we fundamentally are. We are all limited in some way. We can react in many different ways to Saturnian limits, and they may bring the very best out of us, but the limits will not go away. It is our attitudes toward them which change. Every relationship is likewise limited, and we should probably be grateful that this is so, for otherwise we would have nothing to strive for or dream about. It all depends on how you look at it.

Hard aspects in the composite

Audience: I have a question about aspects in the composite chart. A transiting square in an individual chart is usually difficult. Is a transiting square in a composite necessarily going to be difficult, since composites don't "feel" as people do?

Liz: A square describes a situation of tension or friction between two principles. Both vie for the position of power. Neither wishes to compromise, so a struggle ensues. When two principles are in conflict, they generate an erratic and uncomfortable energy which requires effort and action, so something "happens" – something new tries to emerge which is a resolution of the conflict. A transiting square, whether in a birth chart or in a composite, requires effort and action in order to release energy. A "third" thing, a new way of seeing or being, tries to emerge from the battle of warring principles. The square, in its most profound meaning, is the aspect of creation. It brings new life into being. The natal or composite planet is forced to change, to regroup, to find a new way of expressing itself.

However, we often react to squares badly, because the ego does not like conflict and finds it hard to contain paradoxes. We don't cope well with two things that are disparate yet equally valid. Faced with two warring principles, we feel we have to choose between them. One must be right and the other wrong. We have difficulty in containing the conflict until the struggle produces its new "third" thing. We cannot bear the tension, so we try to evade the struggle. We often react to squares in a defensive way, by projecting or stifling one end, which is why they sometimes lead to so much trouble and suffering.

A transiting square in the composite may not mean pain, but it does mean conflict. Something in the relationship is required to change and create a new way of expressing. The relationship does not "hurt" in the human sense. But the two people need to be able to contain the struggle in order for the new thing to emerge. The new thing may, of course, be the end of the relationship. But if this is genuinely the new thing, and not a reflection of panic on the part of one or both individuals, then it will be experienced as a "right" thing – even if it causes pain to both people on the emotional level. If one or both individuals cannot tolerate the tension in the relationship, then a transiting square in the composite may cause a lot of destructive acting out, just as a transiting square in an individual chart might. But it is a herald of something new emerging in the relationship.

Composite Nodes

Audience: What about the Nodes in the composite?

Liz: The Nodes are very odd animals to explore in composites. They seem to have the same mysterious implication of an intersection between solar meaning and lunar embodiment that they do in an individual chart. They are entries into manifestation. There is a feeling of fate around the houses in which the Nodes are placed, and the agency is usually relationship. Transits and progressions to the composite Nodes seem to trigger events. Also, the synastry between composite Nodes and natal planets is often quite startling. The composite north or south Node will usually be found conjuncting something important in one or both individual charts. Or one of the individual's Nodes conjuncts something in the composite chart. And the progressed composite Nodes also seem to be sensitive points, especially when they aspect something in the composite chart. Charles and Diana have the composite north Node in 1° Cancer in the 9th house. It conjuncts Diana's Sun and Mercury.

Audience: What does that point to?

Liz: The composite nodal axis lies across the houses of communication and knowledge. This is the sphere where the meaning of the relationship manifests most powerfully, because the Nodes combine the Sun's purpose and the Moon's direct emotional experience. The decisive events in the relationship pivot on what is *said* and *known* – what they say to and know about each other, what they say to the public, and what the public says and knows about them. Also, the world-view of the relationship matters – what they believe in as a couple, their moral and philosophical attitudes, and, in the most traditional sense of the 9th, what the law and the Church of England have to say about the relationship. Divorce and remarriage are, of course, relevant here, with all their constitutional challenges. The north Node in Cancer and the south Node in Capricorn suggest that there is a need to develop more emotional openness in communication, and less reliance on tradition and traditional opinions. Or, put another way, this relationship requires the formulation of a global world-view, a philosophy of life which can lift the relationship out of the personal realm and into the universal.

The north Node conjunct Diana's Sun and Mercury suggests that this emphasis on a global world-view, which is inherent in the relationship, will encourage her to develop her individuality and her powers of communication. As her natal Sun and Mercury are in the 7th, the relationship would also impel her into greater contact with the public. She, in turn, would give life to the composite north Node through her work with international charities. She is more linked with this composite Node than Charles, which may mean she is more instrumental in opening up this dimension of the relationship. It may also mean that the relationship has a greater impact on her individual growth than it does on Charles'. Do you get the idea?

Audience: Yes. Thank you.

Audience: Do you use Juno and Vesta in composites?

Liz: No. I am sure the asteroids have validity. But I have enough trouble with ten planets plus Chiron. At a certain point I draw the line, to avoid overload of information and keep the main themes clear. There are over three thousand asteroids. They have very peculiar names, because after the first thousand, the astronomers got pretty desperate. They named a lot of them after their wives and children. I could plot all three thousand in a chart, and think, "Oh, that's interesting, Diana's Lithuania is on Charles' Tin of Sardines." But with three thousand of the little buggers, the likelihood is that everything will be aspecting everything.

Audience: Is there really an asteroid called Lithuania?
Liz: Yes, and there is one called Austria, but I wouldn't swear in court about the Tin of Sardines.

A composite from the group

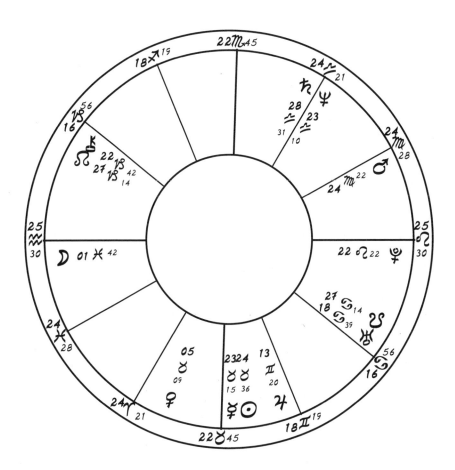

Pat and Phil

Shall we try exploring a composite given to me by a couple in the group? Let's look at the composite first, and then see how it interacts with the two birth charts. Both Pat and Phil are here today, so they can give us whatever feedback we need. Later we can look at some of the transits in the composite.

Audience: There's a 1st house composite Moon in Pisces.

Liz: Yes, the composite Ascendant is 25° 30' Aquarius, and the composite Moon is conjunct the Ascendant in 1° 42' Pisces.

Audience: I was thinking earlier about a rising composite Moon needing to establish some kind of home base together.

Liz: Can you tell us about that, Pat? Was there a strong impetus to build a home together?

Composite Sun at the IC: settling down

Pat: Yes, there was. Earlier, I didn't feel like settling down. I never thought I would want to. But I was only nineteen when I got married. It sounds silly, but I never thought it would happen. When I met Phil, it all happened very quickly. I knew right from the start. I didn't see him for a while. Then, when we started seeing each other again, we got engaged within a couple of months, and about five months later we got married.

Audience: Did you get a home together?

Phil: Yes. As soon as we realised we wanted to get married, we bought a house and got cats.

Liz: The rising composite Moon in Pisces certainly suggests an atmosphere of emotional closeness, but I think the composite Sun in this chart makes a much clearer statement about anchoring the relationship in marriage and a home. The composite Sun is in Taurus at the composite IC. It suggests a very powerful drive toward material security, roots, and the building of a home. We might even say that the purpose of the relationship is, in part, to create these things. A couple with this placement are not likely to run an erratic love affair from opposite ends of town, unless the composite Sun is conjunct Uranus, in which case they would probably both own houses with cats, and keep sets of good quality clothes in both homes.

The interaction between the composite and the two birth charts is extremely interesting. There is no room to put all the charts up on the overhead projector, but I will mention a couple of relevant points. Pat's Ascendant is 22° Taurus. The composite MC/IC axis runs exactly along her Ascendant/Descendant axis, and the composite Sun and Mercury are on her Ascendant. Composite Mars and Chiron, which are part of a grand earth trine with composite Sun and Mercury, are both trine Pat's Ascendant. The relationship has obviously had a profound impact on you.

Pat: Yes.

Audience: Does that mean that she would feel more herself than before?

Liz: I believe so. The "purpose" of the relationship (composite Sun), and its style of communication (composite Mercury), are activating her natal Ascendant, bringing light to it and waking it up. The relationship brings life to a side of Pat which may not have been conscious or easily expressed, but which is the means through which her inner development is enacted in the world.

Audience: She would be very identified with the relationship.

Liz: Yes. I think you said, Pat, that you believed you would never settle down.

Pat: Settling down is something I never had in mind. I liked being free and single.

Liz: And yet you have a Taurus Ascendant. The natal Ascendant is often an image of something which we need to develop, in order to provide a means of expression for the Sun and the other planets. Although the Ascendant is how we perceive the world and express ourselves in it, we often project it and believe that it is the world that is like that, not ourselves. It seems that your Taurus Ascendant was not entirely acceptable to your conscious values, yet sooner or later you would have to recognise and develop Taurus values. The composite Sun and IC have activated a side of you that you didn't know about. You probably knew some of your more fluid qualities, but you weren't familiar with the Taurean side of yourself, and the relationship suddenly triggered your Ascendant into awareness. I would expect a very powerful identification with the home that you and Phil have created together. I would also expect the family inheritance, both material and psychological, to play a large part in the relationship – although not always a happy part. In past seminars you have talked quite a bit about the family background of both of you. Because of the composite Sun in the 4th, the family history becomes terribly important.

Pat: It wasn't easy when we got married. Phil's Mum and Dad didn't want him to marry me.

Phil: She was banned from the house when we got engaged.

Pat: I don't think it was personal. They didn't want him to get married to anyone. I feel as though I have had to prove myself to them as the years have gone by. I think I am accepted by them now. There was a point where I decided I wouldn't put up with what they said to him about me. I just put a stop to it – I refused to see them. That went on for four years. In that time Phil was quite ill and was off work, and I just carried on working. I think they were really surprised. It showed them something about me that maybe they didn't see was there. Since then, they are very different with me. I feel I have proved myself. I wonder if it's got something to do with the composite Sun square Pluto.

Liz: Yes, I think it does – although what you are describing may also be the effect of the composite Sun on your Taurus Ascendant. The relationship, with its legacy from the family past, has pushed you into recognising your own strength, endurance, and patience. These personal qualities feed back into the relationship in turn, and help to give it life. But as you say, it is also a Sun-Pluto relationship, and it must struggle for survival in order to fulfill itself. One of the areas of struggle described in the composite seems to be other people – composite Pluto is conjunct the composite Descendant. It is not really individuals one by one who appear to be the enemy, but a kind of instinctive collective pressure which feels as though it is mobilised against the relationship.

Composite Chiron in the 12th in Capricorn, conjunct the composite north Node, also attracts my attention, because of the implication of some kind of hurt or wound from the past, from the ancestral psyche. This wound seems to be concerned with misuse of authority and tradition. It suggests that there is an inherent sense of isolation in the relationship – isolation from the family group, and mistrust of collective authority. You have proven yourself to the family, Pat, but as a couple I doubt that you and Phil feel you belong.

Phil: That is true.

Liz: Composite Chiron's trines to composite Sun and Mercury may reflect the fact that, as a couple, you have been able to resolve some of the difficulty through empathy and understanding. The composite Sun benefits from many positive qualities. Being in Taurus, it expresses stability and endurance. The trine to composite Mars in Virgo describes a dynamic relationship, full of energy and determination. We would say something similar about a person with the Sun in Taurus trine Mars in Virgo – here is someone who has a lot of tenacity, who will keep on going, despite any amount of obstacles, until they get what they want. There is a will to work at things which is inherent in the relationship.

There is also a capacity to be philosophical about suffering, which is reflected by composite Sun trine composite Chiron. The relationship has been wounded by the family past, and the fact that both of you have had to deal with these issues binds you together. A composite Sun-Chiron aspect suggests a potential strengthening of the relationship through shared wounds. A similar aspect exists in the composite between Charles and Diana – in that case, it is composite Sun in Virgo trine Chiron in Capricorn – but the potential binding seems not to have been sufficient to save the relationship.

Chiron's wounds can generate tenacity and commitment in a composite. This relationship has great staying power, even against very heavy odds. Since composite Chiron also trines your natal Ascendant, Pat, it too has brought out your innate Taurean strength and commitment. The opposition from the family made you determined to get on with it and prove them wrong. Many people might not have been able to stay the course.

Composite Sun square Pluto: They're out to get us

Now, what would you say about a person with Sun square Pluto?

Audience: They are obsessive.

Liz: Yes, the person may be obsessive, because there is an intense awareness of the need to survive. Everything seems to be a life-or-death struggle. Everything matters terribly. Because many things are perceived as a threat to survival, an individual with Sun-Pluto may frequently engage in power battles. That is also a characteristic of this relationship. It may sometimes feel like an "us against them" scenario – the two of you as a couple must survive against the world's opposition. Sometimes power battles may flare up within the relationship itself, because both of you may be affected by the general "they're out to get me" Plutonian paranoia. The two of you may fight for the position of control, even if neither of you is a particularly controlling person in other situations.

Pat: Would it have anything to do with health matters? I am saying that because composite Pluto is in the 6th, and Phil was ill for a long time.

Liz: It is in the 6th, but conjunct the composite Descendant, so we need to consider it in both the 6th and 7th houses. "Fated" dilemmas – situations which require a struggle to survive – tend to erupt in a relationship around composite Pluto's place, and the difficulties bring about profound changes in the relationship itself. But the composite 6th will not describe your or Phil's health. It is concerned with the relationship's integration into everyday life – *its* health, rather than that of the two individuals. Daily routines and the ordinary rituals of the relationship are some of the areas which the composite 6th covers. Work is relevant, but not yours or Phil's individually. What "work" does the relationship do in the world? What "service" does it offer? Composite

Uranus is also in the 6th, which suggests many changes and upheavals in the sphere of the everyday functioning of the relationship. It has "special needs" in terms of how it is anchored in the mundane world. It will not be "healthy" if it is imprisoned within a "normal" marital routine. Composite Pluto on the Descendant also describes a relationship with a proneness to head-on confrontations with the outer world – and perhaps, eventually, a position of power or influence in the world as well.

Pat: Work has always been an issue in one way or another, ever since we were married. We always discussed whether or not we should work together. Last year we finally had the opportunity to buy a second-hand bookshop. We are working together in this, with me doing astrology on the side.

Liz: The importance of working together may be reflected by several things in the composite, and also in the way the composite affects the natal charts. Composite Sun trine composite Mars in Virgo puts an emphasis on joint goals and material achievements; this relationship "wants" to work hard, to fulfill specific mundane aspirations, to be "useful". I would also like to mention a link between the composite and Phil's chart which may be relevant to the issues of work and illness. His Ascendant is 28° Scorpio. The composite Sun therefore conjuncts his Descendant, but falls in his 6th house. Because the composite Sun activates his 6th, the relationship makes him more aware of health and work issues. The Sun's light is not always comfortable, because it may illuminate a hidden conflict in the individual which then comes to the surface. The end result may be extremely creative, but if there is a prior lack of integration in the individual, the composite Sun can stir up some very uncomfortable experiences. This may be connected with Phil's period of illness, although I am sure there are personal issues involved too, connected with separation from the family matrix.

Phil: What would the composite Sun mean on my Descendant?

Liz: The relationship makes you aware of your need for stability and security through others (Taurus at the Descendant), and helps you to be more conscious of your effect on them and theirs on you.

Pat: My health hasn't been good ever since I got married. But I have also had transiting Pluto going through my 6th ever since I got married. I have been more aware of my health during that time. At one point I actually told Phil I was allergic to him!

Liz: With composite Pluto and Uranus both in the composite 6th, it may be that the relationship itself is allergic to anything which tries to coerce it into being "normal".

Audience: I think there is a struggle shown in this composite, between a powerful vocational urge and the need to keep the home together. You have to be at home with Taurus, the great Earth-mother, but the square from Pluto in the 6th can create problems if there isn't some sort of shared work commitment.

Composite Saturn in the 9th: moral and religious issues

Liz: We could spend a lot more time talking about these placements, but the afternoon is passing. Shall we look at composite Saturn in the 9th?

Audience: Could that be Pat's in-laws?

Liz: That is getting extremely literal. Also, traditionally, the in-laws are described by the 4th and 10th. One's partner is the 7th, and the partner's mother is the 10th from the 7th, which is the 4th, and the partner's father is the 4th from the 7th, which is the 10th. In-laws and parents are part of the same meridian soup, which is not surprising from a psychological perspective, since we tend to be attracted to those who share similar family complexes. On the other hand, composites *can* sometimes be very literal. The 6th house is the house of small animals, and Pat and Phil have cats.

Pat: We've always had cats, ever since we got married, and we've got a goat.

Phil: In fact, we've got a sexually questionable cat.

Liz: I won't ask in what way it is questionable. Perhaps this is a new interpretation of composite Pluto in the 6th. Anyway, let's go back to composite Saturn in Libra in the 9th. There are limits suggested around the moral/religious background of the marriage. The relationship has a highly developed moral conscience, and there may be conflicts of a religious nature, or some irreconcilable religious difference.

Pat: My parents are Catholic. We wanted to get married in a registry office. We wish now that we had just gone off and got married on our own. Instead, we got married in the Catholic Church, purely because of my Mum and Dad. It sounds awful, but neither of us enjoyed our wedding day.

Liz: What are the implications for the relationship?

Pat: We would have to bring our children up as Catholics.

Liz: Is that a problem for either of you?

Pat: We don't want any children.

Liz: It does seem there is a nice Saturnian dilemma around this religious background. Deciding not to have children is, of course, contrary to Church teaching. I won't even bother to mention the additional offence of studying astrology. As a couple you have already offended Phil's parents, and if you choose not to have a family you will offend your parents as well, not to mention the God you were brought up to believe in.

Pat: It has been a big problem. Over the years I have been working through that doctrine. I gave up Catholicism when I was sixteen or seventeen, and just went my separate way. I didn't realise the profound effect it had on me until I went into analysis. I think it has affected the relationship, from the point of view of what I believe to be right. We both have strong principles, and they have changed over the years because we have seen that sometimes we can get very dogmatic, with each other and with other people.

Audience: With composite Neptune conjunct composite Saturn, the beliefs you develop in the relationship would be very idealised. But transiting Uranus and Neptune were squaring that conjunction for a long time, so your ideals have probably changed a lot.

Phil: They have. Both of us have become a bit more cynical about things in the last few years.

Liz: That may certainly reflect transiting Uranus and Neptune, which were also moving back and forth over composite Chiron and setting off the composite T-cross of Chiron, Uranus, Saturn, and Neptune. I would like to spend some time later on the current transits in this composite. But for the moment, let's continue with the composite Saturn-Neptune conjunction.

Composite Saturn conjunct Neptune: the quest for the ideal

In an individual chart, a Saturn-Neptune conjunction is intensely idealistic. Yet there is always a tempering process which compels the ideals to adapt to reality. This conjunction in the composite falls in Libra, which emphasises the perfectionism inherent in the aspect. Saturn tries to ground Neptune's boundless vision in form, so there is a ceaseless movement toward trying to find, or create, a perfect model of beauty and order in life. This conjunction in Libra is also a generational aspect which was operative in the early 1950's. Couples born within a few of years of each other and within range of this Saturn-Neptune conjunction will therefore have it in the composite, even if they have just missed it in the natal chart. Phil has the conjunction in Libra, but Pat was born after the conjunction passed, and has natal Saturn in Scorpio.

An aspect like this in the composite is no less important because it is generational. It makes the same statement about the relationship as it does about an individual who has it natally. The relationship is a mouthpiece for this visionary generation, and is impelled to ground the vision of a perfect world through the composite house in which the conjunction is placed. In this composite, the conjunction straddles the 9th house cusp, with Neptune just into the 8th. Do you have any feeling of what that might imply?

Audience: There is a lot of romanticism, and maybe a strong spiritual emphasis. But Saturn sits on it, or makes it hard to express in some way. As you say, it tempers it.

Liz: Yes, there is enormous romanticism, and a kind of mysticism – a yearning to touch something "higher". This is held in check by Saturn, which imposes certain moral and intellectual limits. These limits also describe the effect the outer world has on the ideals inherent in the relationship, and over time, some disillusionment and cynicism may result. There is a great emphasis on understanding the "why" of life, which would challenge and deepen both Pat's and Phil's thinking. Saturn tries to get Neptune to ground itself in some kind of philosophy or code of ethics which pulls it out of the purely emotional, intimate realm and into the realm of knowledge. Saturn makes Neptune work for the vision of perfection through disseminating ideas. It blocks Neptune, but also forces it to materialise, challenging Neptune's vague mysticism through the moral and philosophical precepts you espouse as a couple.

Audience: Composite Saturn squares the composite nodal axis, so they can't get away from that moral code.

Audience: I think the composite Moon in Pisces close to the Ascendant is also very romantic and emotional.

Composite Ascendant in Aquarius: an eccentric couple

Liz: Do either of you have a sense of how other people see the relationship?

Pat: I don't think people see the Taurean side. We appear to be more of an Aquarian couple. People often find that we don't tend to conform. We never have done. We don't do things at the times when everybody else does things.

Liz: So they see you as an eccentric and unconventional couple.

Pat: I think they do, even though we are not really like that when they get to know us. When people are going out, we are coming home, and when people are coming home, we are going out. It's that kind of thing.

Liz: There is also the fact that you married very young but have no children. There is a powerful "nesting" instinct yet you haven't wanted a family. That might also be seen as very eccentric, because it doesn't follow a conventional pattern. There seem to be very strong ideals motivating the relationship – the composite Saturn-Neptune conjunction in Libra trines the composite Ascendant in Aquarius – and the two of you follow those ideals and don't really pay a lot of attention to what other people expect of you as a couple.

Composite Moon in the 1st: playing to the audience

Let's look at the rising Moon in Pisces. What would you say about a person with a 1st house Moon?

Audience: The emotions are reflected in the body.

Audience: The emotions are in the shop window.

Liz: The Moon in the 1st house is a mirror for the immediate environment. I have known many actors with this placement. A person with a rising Moon has the instinctive ability to pick up unspoken emotional currents and atmospheres and play to the audience. The Moon appears to become whatever other people expect it to be, and it is constantly changing. It is a form of camouflage as well as a form of contact.

The Moon is changeable and reflects the situation of the moment. Here we are looking at a relationship, not an individual, so the feeling life of the relationship is constantly mirroring the environment, shifting and fluctuating according to the immediate situation. It is not the same from one week to the next, or one month to the next. The emotional atmosphere keeps changing. The core of the relationship is stable and rock-solid, but the feeling life is in a constant state of flux, and is easily affected by what is going on in the environment.

Audience: What is the meaning of the 1st house in a composite? In an individual it would be your image of yourself.

Liz: It is the image the relationship expresses to the outer world. It is how the relationship "behaves". The natal 1st house describes how a person expresses what is inside the chart. It is the doorway to the chart. It is not the public image – that is the 10th. The 1st describes expression in the immediate environment. But the Ascendant has other levels. It is also a mode of perception. The doorway to the chart is our own doorway, and when we look through it, we perceive the world outside as having a certain colouration. We believe – at least in the first part of life – that the colouration belongs to the world, not to ourselves. We think we are reacting to the environment when we behave in certain habitual ways, but the environment we see is the one we see through the lens of our own perceptions. Jung once said that one sees what one sees best oneself. That describes the 1st house nicely.

The Ascendant also describes qualities that need to be owned and developed, because everything in the chart – including the Sun – must pass through the doorway of the Ascendant in order to express in the outer world. If the Ascendant remains projected "out there", then there is no conscious cooperation between it and the internal dynamics of the chart. One feels life is forcing certain experiences down one's throat, when in fact these experiences are required by the Ascendant to give shape to what is within the chart. That is why Pat's Taurus Ascendant, which didn't seem to be in evidence until this relationship came along, suddenly emerged into her life with great power. She needed to learn to express Taurean qualities and values, because these provide the "right" vehicle through which the rest of her chart can express.

The same thing applies to the composite Ascendant, which needs to be expressed consciously by both people, rather than projected or acted out blindly. Often other people see it before the couple themselves do. It is the form the relationship takes in the outer world. The natal Ascendant says a great deal about what someone looks like, how they dress, how they move, what facial expressions they adopt. It reflects personal "style". It is why we can often "guess" somebody's Ascendant when they come in through the door. The natal Sun-sign is harder to recognise, and we need to know the person or see them at a moment when they are expressing what they believe in most strongly.

Usually the Sun-sign is apparent only over time, but the Ascendant makes its impact immediately. The composite Ascendant is the same. It describes how the relationship "looks" and "dresses". This relationship looks like an Aquarian relationship – it appears very eccentric. People say to themselves, "Do they really have a goat? And have you heard about that sexually questionable cat? Are they really married? How come they don't have any kids? And just look at the funny subjects the two of them study!" Underneath is a very stable Taurus Sun, but what shows is the Aquarius Ascendant, made even more unpredictable by the ebb and flow of the rising composite Moon in Pisces.

Phil: I suppose we give the impression of a sort of "New Age" couple. I don't think either of us really feels like that, but I am sure it is what people think.

Liz: People who come in contact with you as a couple may also think you are more detached with each other than you actually are. The emotional ambience of the relationship is described by the dreamy and romantic composite Moon in Pisces, but usually, when a planet is in the 1st but in a different sign from the Ascendant, it takes time for it to show itself. And the Moon throws up camouflage mechanisms as well. Only if people are around the two of you long enough would they see the emotional closeness that exists within the relationship. If the two of you are together, I would guess that you don't look at each other much or hold hands – you are too busy chatting with other people. You could just be good friends who happened to meet each other at that particular dinner party.

Pat: It's true. We never refer to one another as husband and wife. It is something we have never done. When Phil introduces me, I am always just Pat. He doesn't say, "This is my wife."

Liz: And you don't say, "This is my husband."

Pat: No. I say, "This is Phil." I think it is only when people get to know us that they see what is underneath.

Liz: And this is something which has just arisen naturally in the relationship, not something you have had a discussion about?

Phil: We never discussed it. We never sat down and said, "I won't say this and you won't say that." It just happened.

Liz: The relationship itself has dictated its own image.

Audience: Isn't a Pisces Moon in a composite very emotionally needy?

Liz: Yes, although I wouldn't put it quite that way – the relationship itself isn't "needy", but when the couple are together they may experience a breaking down of emotional boundaries and a feeling of being merged. As we have seen, the composite of Charles and Diana also has a Pisces Moon, and the breaking down of boundaries may have been one of the main problems between them because it is so antithetical to qualities in Charles' natal chart. But this composite Moon has a strong trine to Saturn. The trine is out-of-sign but is nevertheless a trine, and there is a very structured, self-contained quality which holds the emotional fluidity of the relationship together. The ethics and ideals of the relationship give strength and self-sufficiency to the composite Moon, just as they would if this were a natal configuration. Whatever "mood" the relationship passes through, composite Saturn whispers to the Moon, "Just hang in there and keep going. No excessive self-indulgence on display, please."

Audience: I hope Pat and Phil don't mind me saying something personal.

Pat: No, carry on.

Audience: I sometimes sit with them in the refectory before a seminar starts, and the impression I get of them as a couple is a very close, warm feeling. They seem very much together, as if they are fused.

Liz: You have by-passed the Aquarian Ascendant and are tuning into the Pisces Moon. Maybe this is because you often sit with them in a relaxed situation. If they had just walked into a party and you had never met them before, perhaps you would not get this impression. But this also may have to do with how the composite affects your own chart. Do you have any natal placement that plugs into this composite Moon in Pisces?

Audience: I have Sun in Pisces conjunct their composite Moon.

Liz: Then it is obvious why you are so attuned to the emotional life of the relationship. Many other people might miss it. Someone else might have natal Sun in Libra on their composite Saturn and think, "These people are heavy to be around. They're always broadcasting their philosophical opinions." Other people's relationships affect us in the same way other individuals do. And we, in turn, bring things out of a relationship. Probably Pat and Phil enjoy sitting with you, too, because you bring their composite Pisces Moon alive.

Audience: Do you have lots of fun, with composite Jupiter in Gemini?

Pat: We play a lot.

Liz: It is highly appropriate that you have a bookshop, because of composite Jupiter in Gemini in the 4th. The bookshop is both a material and a spiritual home to you. Contrary to what we might expect, I have noticed that, in an individual chart, Jupiter in the 4th may have some resistance against having a family – perhaps because Jupiter is the *puer*, the free spirit which needs unlimited possibilities to explore. This is especially the case when it is in Gemini. The urge to expand, to develop ideas, is very powerful in this relationship, and a family may seem too limiting. Composite Jupiter seems to be saying, "Don't tie me down. Create some other kind of family, an intellectual or a spiritual one, but don't be in too big a hurry for a corporeal one. My vision and enthusiasm might be stifled."

Bonds that endure

Audience: Would you expect to see a strong Saturn in the composite chart of a stable relationship?

Liz: Not necessarily. All planets have their own form of stability, according to their natures. Even Uranus can display absolute loyalty to an ideal, and Uranian relationships, although often eccentric on the concrete level, can remain enduring and stable friendships based on a shared belief-system. However, if "stable" is interpreted as a capacity to remain together through material bad times, a relationship *is* helped enormously in that way by a strong Saturn or Chiron. The capacity to endure difficulties is often reflected by composite Sun-Saturn trines, sextiles, and conjunctions, or by Moon-Saturn aspects like the trine in the composite for Pat and Phil. Sometimes Saturn is on the Ascendant or MC of the composite.

The squares and oppositions of composite Saturn can also be very binding, but may create a feeling of great restriction in the relationship. While this can still provide a glue which binds the relationship, it depends on how well the individuals cope with the sense of limitation. Even a composite Sun-Saturn sextile can feel restrictive to an individual whose nature is strongly Jupiterian. The same applies to composite Chiron. Chiron's aspects in the composite may reflect a capacity to philosophically endure suffering and unhappiness. But a romantic idealist may find even a composite Sun-Chiron trine very heavy going.

Saturn and Chiron are the two realists of the planetary pantheon. They both know that life is tough, and that there is no such thing as a free lunch. They also both know that searching for the perfect love is a fruitless exercise. They are often strong in a composite when a relationship must survive many hardships and practical problems, and they may describe a deep sense of responsibility which affects both people. Many relationships endure without these aspects, but they endure for other reasons. Relationships may endure because of compulsive passions (these are the Plutonian composites) or because there are shared moral, political, or spiritual beliefs (these are the Neptunian and Uranian composites). Powerful composite Venus and Moon placements tend to reflect stability because they feel good, or because they convey a sense of "coming home". Or the relationship may endure because it is just too much trouble to leave. With a strong composite Saturn, one gets the feeling that, while there may be serious problems in the relationship, it would take something truly momentous to part the couple. There is something extremely tenacious in the relationship, even if neither individual is very Saturnian, and even if both of them often feel they want to get out.

It is interesting to see two quite flighty individuals bound by a strong composite Saturn. Two *puers* may easily fall in love, but usually they are looking for romance rather than stability, and when it starts to get a bit rough, they are out the door. Then they enter a relationship where composite Sun conjuncts Saturn, or composite Saturn sits on the Ascendant; and whether the glue comes from external responsibilities or newly discovered security needs, they simply cannot make the usual quick exit, however much they bleat and whinge. This can also happen when the composite of a parent and child has a strong Saturn. Some people do not feel deeply committed to any living thing until a child is born, and then they experience something so binding that they are quite transformed. I do not believe every parent feels this way; many certainly do not behave as though they do. In the animal world, the young are abandoned as soon as they are self-sufficient. A parent can love a child deeply, yet not experience that irrevocably binding and often very heavy Saturnian feeling. The parent-child composite in such a case may have an angular Saturn, or Saturn aspecting the Luminaries. Or composite Saturn conjuncts the individual's natal Sun or Moon, or composite Sun or Moon conjuncts the individual's natal Saturn.

Audience: If composite Moon conjuncts composite Saturn, isn't it a dampener?

Liz: Yes, in the sense that the relationship won't be an endless Dionysian carnival of emotional ecstasy. But Moon-Saturn can describe a very enduring emotional bond. Moon-Saturn individuals do not have the spontaneity of emotional expression that a Moon-Jupiter person has. A relationship with composite Moon conjunct Saturn has inherent restraints placed on the emotional life of the relationship. These restraints might be material or psychological, but easy emotional expression may be difficult. I have sometimes seen this in composites where the couple have to work very hard, or have important shared responsibilities. There may not be a lot of money around, or they have to live with their parents. Sometimes the aspect is expressed on the emotional level. There are inhibitions of one kind or another, perhaps from the social background or from family attitudes. I have also seen it when one of the people is married to someone else, and the existence of another relationship creates the emotional restriction.

Composite Moon-Saturn can be very binding. That is the "up" side. And not everyone wants an endless party. If the individuals are earthy, or have natal Moon-Saturn, Sun-Saturn, or Venus-Saturn contacts, they may deeply appreciate the tenacity and restraint of this composite aspect. It can help to foster a sense of mutual responsibility in two people who might not ordinarily be so inclined. For the people born before World War II, there was a collective assumption that one stuck with a marriage. This was not just because of religious or financial reasons. It is also part of the survival instinct of the generation born with Pluto in Cancer, for whom strong family bonds often matter more than individual happiness. If a marriage is bad, one puts up with it, because it is the family, and the security that families provide, which ensure survival. That feeling is often strong in Moon-Saturn people: one gets on with it and stops whining, because there is an awful lot worse out there. It is better to have stable unhappiness than happy instability. Indeed, Moon-Saturn in the composite can be a dampener, like Moon-Chiron, but it can also help to make a relationship endure through hardship.

Audience: What about Saturn-Venus?

Liz: The same. The orb is wide in Pat's and Phil's composite, but there is an operative opposition between Saturn and Venus. This aspect may be connected with what Pat has said about the way religious and philosophical issues have affected the relationship. Composite Saturn dampens the expression of composite Venus, but it is also very binding, and there is a strong sense of loyalty and responsibility.

Audience: It is a very sensual composite Venus.

Liz: Yes, and it is also very security-orientated. Composite Saturn's restrictions may create some difficulty – the relationship may generate a sense that there is too much hard work and little time for pleasure. But as I said, this aspect can also give a very binding quality to the relationship, a joint sense of wishing to make something last.

Composite Mars-Saturn aspects

Audience: What about Mars-Saturn in a composite? Is that binding?

Liz: Mars-Saturn does not bind emotionally, because Mars is not concerned with attachments. Mars-Saturn in a composite can be very frustrating. A great deal depends on how it affects the two birth charts.

The hard aspects in a composite may provoke a lot of anger in one or both individuals, if their own charts are triggered. Composite Mars describes the energy of the relationship – how it moves forward. The Sun in an individual chart says, "I want this in order to fulfill myself," and Mars then serves the Sun by going after the thing that is desired. The same applies to the composite; composite Mars serves the composite Sun's goals. Composite Mars describes the manner in which the relationship asserts its presence in the world. Composite Mars in Libra, for example, is highly reactive to how others respond to the relationship. Goals are pursued diplomatically, not aggressively. The composite for Charles and Diana, with composite Mars-Neptune in Libra, is a good example of this. Other people's opinions make an enormous impact on the energy flow of the relationship. The "will" of the relationship is not expressed directly.

If composite Saturn challenges composite Mars, there are inherent restrictions which obstruct the dynamic energy of the relationship. This might describe something as simple and natural as the presence of children frustrating the sexual expression of the couple. Saturnian restrictions may also take the form of material difficulties or important work commitments which thwart the spontaneous expression of energy. Or the psychological or material baggage which the couple have inherited from the past may inhibit the energy flow. The relationship achieves its goals slowly, and only with a lot of hard work. We saw an example of this in the applying conjunction of progressed composite Mars to composite Saturn at the time of the marriage of Charles and Diana. As I keep saying, much depends on what it touches off in the individual charts.

Audience: Could it be an indication of violence in a relationship?

Liz: A relationship does not become violent. Individuals do. If we see this composite aspect, we could say that the energy of the relationship is held back in some way. There are inherent limits placed on any forward movement, any urge for progress, any expression of passion. Energy must be disciplined and expressed within limits. The limits will be described by Saturn's house and sign placement. But hard aspects between composite Mars and composite Saturn do not indicate that violence will erupt in the relationship, because relationships do not "feel" enraged when they are thwarted.

If composite Mars-Saturn triggers something potentially explosive in one of the natal charts, the person might react by trying to break through the obstacles in a violent way. But the aspect in a composite simply says, "There is a restriction on the speed at which this car can move, no matter how hard you put your foot down on the accelerator." As you may know, there are certain luxury cars which have their maximum potential speed restricted by built-in mechanical inhibitors; these cars can never be driven at their full power. This does not make the car less worthwhile, unless one is determined to do 250 kilometres an hour down the motorway, in which case one should clearly be on the race track and not on the motorway. Relationships with composite Mars-Saturn are a bit like that.

Composite Uranus-Chiron

Audience: Could you talk about composite Uranus opposite Chiron? It is in the composite for Pat and Phil.

Liz: This is a generational aspect. Because Chiron has an elliptical orbit like Pluto's, it moves very slowly through Capricorn, and many people were born under the opposition with Uranus in Cancer. The idealistic vision of a world made more perfect through the transformation of traditional family ties (Uranus in Cancer) is challenged by a sense of irrevocable damage through misuse of authority and a world-weariness and disillusionment generated by a society focused on class, materialism, and hierarchy (Chiron in Capricorn). Because Pat and Phil were born fairly close together, the relationship embodies one of the chief conflicts of their generation group. There is, in fact, a T-cross here – composite Chiron is opposite composite Uranus from the 12th to the 6th, and both are square composite Saturn-Neptune on the 9th house cusp. That T-cross is part of the challenge and task of this generation, of which the relationship is a part.

Audience: Uranus also sextiles Mercury, Sun, and Mars.

Liz: Yes, it forms a "kite" with the grand earth trine in the composite. Why don't you try interpreting this?

Audience: I think composite Uranus probably does reflect the Aquarian Ascendant of the composite, with the "New Age" tone of the relationship – working together in a bookshop and doing astrology. That's a very good use of it. It helps focus the purpose of the relationship, and makes the 4th house composite Sun more spiritual and less conventionally domestic, if you see what I mean.

Liz: Yes, I see what you mean. Composite Uranus, the composite chart ruler, gives support of an innovative and unconventional kind to composite Mercury and composite Sun. It brings an element of creative inspiration through some kind of shared work (6th house) – the "work" the relationship "does" in the mundane world. This not only focuses the composite Sun, but also kicks composite Chiron into consciousness. Otherwise Chiron might disappear into the family soup that a 12th house placement implies, and could make a lot of trouble later. It is as if something constantly forces Chiron out into the open, so Pat and Phil have to discuss it, look at it, work with it. It isn't allowed to simply lie there.

Pat: There are issues that Phil has had to work out with his family, and issues I have had to work out with mine, and we do talk about it a lot. Since we got the shop, we have an outlet away from family. We have an excuse now.

Liz: It is worth noting that composite Uranus is within 1° of conjunction of Pat's natal 3rd house Sun. This relationship wakes you up, Pat. It inspires your thinking, your communication, and your self-expression. It has motivated you to try to understand a lot of new things. You have gone into therapy, and now you have bought a bookshop. Composite Uranus has woken you up on a mental level, and has brought your 3rd house Sun alive.

The composite chart aspects Pat's Sun and Ascendant with virtually exact conjunctions. The aspects to Phil's chart are also strong, but these exact contacts to Pat's chart are particularly striking. This is usually the case in important relationships. We saw it earlier in the composite for Charles and Diana. At the moment I am looking at what the composite does to Phil's chart. Composite Mars in Virgo is exactly on his MC. The energy of the relationship focuses his worldly goals and stimulates his desire for professional achievement. And composite

Chiron is on Pat's MC. The unhappy inheritance from the past gives Pat a worldly focus as well, and demands that she do something with her life that makes a concrete impact on the world. There is a powerful stimulus from the composite to the natal MC in both charts. This underlines the importance of your work, together and independently.

Audience: What if there were squares instead of conjunctions?

Liz: Then the effect would be more uncomfortable. If composite Uranus were exactly square Pat's Sun, it would still wake her up, but it might do it in a rather edgy way. She would feel it as a conflict. The relationship would be going one way, and she might try to go another, and she would probably fight it. Then it could manifest in a way she experienced as painfully disruptive. That is not necessarily a bad thing, but it would generate more tension and anxiety.

Audience: There are so many strong aspects between composites and individuals. How do you evaluate them? By size of orb?

Liz: Aspects between the composite and the natal charts reflect the impact the relationship has on the individuals, and the degree of involvement and impact the individuals have with and on the relationship. Whether the aspect is a sextile, trine, conjunction, square, or opposition, if it is within 1° of orb it is going to be very powerful. If we were doing conventional synastry, we would look at close aspects first, because the wider the orb, the less powerful the energy. But we must also look at the planets themselves. An exact sextile between composite Neptune and someone's natal Pluto is unlikely to activate fireworks, because a sextile between these two planets has been operative in the heavens for most of this century, and we will find it in many composites and, in turn, aspecting many individual charts. But when composite planets trigger natal angles or personal planets such as Sun, Moon, Venus, or Saturn, then we should pay careful attention to any major aspects, even if the orb is wide.

Audience: Could you say a bit about how you think Pat and Phil might work together? Sometimes you can have a great relationship, but you can't work together. But these two seem as if they could.

Liz: The composite grand earth trine activates both natal MC's, so the relationship could stimulate and give shape to both their professional lives. That doesn't necessarily mean they should work together. The composite itself has nothing in the 10th, so this relationship is not focused on making an impact on society. Some composite charts do have a busy 10th house. I think it is clear, in that case, that the relationship needs to establish something in the world – practical, in the case of earth signs, or on the level of ideas, in the case of air, or creatively, in the case of fire, or through human interchange, in the case of water. A 10th house relationship has the potential of making an impact on the *status quo,* and it often has "status". There usually needs to be joint work of some kind, particular if the composite Sun, the purpose of the relationship, is in the 10th. Even if the relationship has started as an intense romantic bond, its deeper purpose is to leave a lasting legacy to the world.

Audience: So if you have a composite chart with planets on the MC, that means these planets need to be manifested somehow?

Liz: Yes. Composite planets in the 10th indicate a relationship that needs to incorporate something tangible in the outer world. Relationships with 10th house planets are showcases, and they are noticed by others. They have a role in the world, and something to contribute. Pat's and Phil's composite isn't clear about joint work in this sense, because there are no composite planets in the 10th. But there are problematic issues indicated around work. Either Pat and Phil go completely separate ways, in which case their separate routines may begin to conflict with the home life they are trying to build (composite Sun in the 4th square Pluto in the 6th), or they incorporate this tension in some kind of joint work which is unusual and unconventional (composite Uranus in the 6th) and involves a struggle (composite Pluto in the 6th). There is some choice in this matter. The fact that they are trying to build something together means the intensity of composite Sun-Pluto could be expressed through this channel. If they don't provide a channel, their working lives could conflict with the relationship.

Pat: That has happened in the past.

Audience: What about a composite with mainly trines and sextiles? Would you read that in the same way as a natal chart?

Liz: Yes. There is an innately harmonious energy in the relationship, and mutual agreement might come easily, even if the two natal charts show a lot of hard aspects. The same applies to an individual with a very "triney" chart. Inner harmony and many natural gifts are often characteristic of the person's nature. But it may be difficult to cope with the challenges reflected by transiting hard aspects, because the natural response is to think of nicer things and hope that it will all go away. People with many hard aspects feel they always have to struggle with life, but they are used to battle and less inclined to back off from difficulties. A "triney" relationship can prove difficult when heavy transits to the composite come along. It can be hard to muster the necessary fighting spirit because the relationship does not possess that kind of innate combative energy.

Audience: But what if Saturn is well aspected to the Sun or Moon?

Liz: These aspects suggests a strong drive toward stability, and a willingness to endure difficulties. They might also describe a relationship in which the discipline of necessary restrictions helps to build a solid and lasting foundation. But Sun-Saturn and Moon-Saturn trines and sextiles, in an individual or a composite, are not energetic fighters. They plough on doggedly, persisting in the same course and hoping that their efforts will eventually win through. Sometimes that works. But if commitment alone is insufficient, and real creative change is required, they may give up the struggle.

The tension generated by squares and oppositions gives not only stamina, but also initiative. This can even be true of hard aspects to Neptune, provided the other planet can stand its ground and is not overwhelmed or undermined by Neptune's longing to go home. Life's difficulties may require a more creative response than doggedly sticking with something. A preponderance of hard aspects in a composite does not mean that it is a "bad" relationship, or that it will end at the first difficult transit. In fact, it may call a level of energy and creative opportunism out of both people which they didn't know they had. But there may be a lot of bewilderment and disappointment and anger if the individuals are themselves very "triney" and have expected something lovely and easy.

It is interesting to see how relationships react to crisis. Individuals react in a whole range of individual ways, according to their natal charts and the degree of consciousness they bring to the situation. But when a relationship is in trouble, the individuals may abandon their habitual responses and react according to the tone of the composite. A composite lacking hard aspects, like an individual lacking hard aspects, may not always have the resilience to cope well with a difficult transit or progression. Because the general tone is comfortable and easy, it can feel like an awful shock when life intrudes. Once the crisis ends, things may be fine again. But there are relationships which collapse simply because neither the composite nor the individuals can muster the toughness and initiative which hard aspects contribute.

The composite Sun in the houses

Composite Sun in the 7th

Audience: What about the composite Sun in the 7th house?

Liz: What would you say about an individual with the Sun in the 7th?

Audience: They are looking for another person through whom they can find themselves.

Liz: Yes, a 7th house Sun individual needs others to serve as a mirror in order to experience a sense of identity. One is real only in relation to others. One's potential can only be expressed through and for others. That is where one comes alive, and also where one can best give one's life force. This is why a 7th house Sun person will often feel fulfilled working with others as a vocation. It is a frequent placement in therapists' charts. Both Freud and Jung had the natal Sun in the 7th. One feels real through the mirroring of other people, and in turn one helps others to feel real by acting as a mirror oneself. A relationship with a composite 7th house Sun needs other people to stimulate its life force. It exists through and for others. It also has a great deal to give others. A 7th house composite Sun may describe a couple who need a circle of friends around them, or a joint work environment with colleagues who can give the relationship a sense of identity through what it has to offer others. If there is no mirror, both people may wonder: "Who are we? What are we together for?"

Audience: What about having children? Would that provide what it needs?

Liz: Not really. Children are not "other" enough. The composite Sun in the 7th looks further afield than the immediate family. Of course, no relationship exists in a vacuum. Every relationship involves some interaction with others. Most often the interaction is with family members and friends. There are always other people in the life of any relationship. We don't enter a relationship and then disappear into a cave somewhere. Possibly, if a composite had all the planets in the 12th house, the couple might enjoy living on a desert island.

But with the composite Sun in the 7th, it is different. Involvement with others is essential and total. The relationship receives its energy, in both a positive and negative sense, through the intrusion of the outside world, and its energy only flows outward effectively if it can participate in the outside world. If the composite Sun or composite ruler is in the 7th, other people are especially important for that relationship. As with any other placement, a composite 7th house Sun is neither "good" nor "bad". It simply makes a statement about the purpose of the relationship. There may be a compulsive need to have other people around, which one might not experience in another relationship. Other people tend to get involved with the relationship in very obvious ways. The fulfillment of the relationship's purpose depends on others, so the major events and experiences which shape the life and direction of the relationship usually come through the agency of others, rather than from the two individuals themselves.

Audience: Would a 7th house composite Sun be concerned with how the relationship appears in the world?

Liz: That is more typical of the composite Sun in the 10th, where the image in the eyes of the public matters. The 7th has more to do with the necessity of mirroring by others. This is Libra's natural house. It is as though one doesn't really feel one has a relationship unless there is someone out there who says, "You are a couple."

One of the things Rob Hand points out in his book is that the composite Sun in the 7th predisposes the couple to marriage. From what I have seen, I think this is true about love relationships with the composite Sun in the 7th. But I would not stop at that interpretation, because it is describing the result rather than the motivation; and also, many 7th house composite Sun relationships are not love relationships. A 7th house composite Sun requires other people to recognise the relationship. Other people are the focus and purpose of the relationship. Marriage is, amongst other things, a way of getting people to acknowledge that we have created a relationship. It is a social statement as much as a personal one. If we are drifting in and out of a love affair, or living with someone with no formal arrangements, other people might not recognise the relationship as a real, valid entity. A 7th house composite Sun's requirement for marriage is not really based on romantic reasons. It springs from the requirement that the relationship be acknowledged by others.

Audience: Then a couple without that need for marriage might have something like a 5th house Sun.

Liz: Possibly. Many people feel they are part of a couple whether they have a marriage certificate or not. The opinions and input of others make little difference in terms of how they see the relationship. The identity and purpose of the relationship do not depend on feedback from outside world. But some people don't feel like a couple unless others validate their bond. Relationships are all different, just like individuals. There are some relationships which are absolutely solid, but both people may have quite independent lives. They go their own ways intellectually, creatively, and even sexually, yet they know they are a couple, and they have no question about the stability of the relationship. Other relationships need a lot of feedback. The couple need to be seen by and interact with others as a couple before they feel real together. The composite Sun in the 7th can indicate that predisposition.

Composite Sun in the 10th

Audience: The 10th has to do with public image. Isn't that concerned with other people?

Liz: Yes, the 10th is connected with public image. But more importantly, it is the house of goals and aspirations. One's public image is the result, not the cause, of those goals and aspirations. Planets in an individual's 10th describe not only how the person appears to the world, but what he or she seeks to contribute to the world. The composite 10th is the "vocation" of the relationship. It is Capricorn's natural house, and composite planets placed there strive to manifest potentials in a visible form in the outer world. A relationship, like a person, can carry a requirement of producing something concrete, something useful that is acknowledged in the world. A composite 10th house Sun may convey a powerful public image because the relationship generates the impetus to become an effective couple, a contributing couple.

This composite Sun must make its mark on the world. It is an ambitious relationship – not in the personal, human sense, but in the sense of driving toward a specific goal in society. Feedback, for a composite 10th house Sun, lies in the respect and recognition of others for what the relationship has been able to produce in the world. But even without the feedback, the impetus to produce will still be there. It may therefore bring ambition, skills, and a desire to contribute out of both individuals, in ways which they might not develop independently.

Composite Sun in the 8th

Audience: How is an 8th house composite Sun different from a 7th house composite Sun?

Liz: An 8th house Sun in a composite is very private, just as the 8th house in a birth chart is very private. People don't broadcast what is in their 8th house; it goes on behind closed bedroom doors. One level of the 8th is connected with the unconscious dimension of life, the hidden wellspring that draws from inherited emotional patterns. The 8th is also the gateway into the underworld, the transitional place where we discover that we are not masters of our lives, but must bow to more archaic, primal needs and patterns that are larger and older than any individual. The meaning is the same in the composite chart. The purpose of an 8th house composite Sun is concerned with bringing light into the underworld, and making a connection with the hidden side of life where the patterns of necessity operate beneath the surface of "normal" relating. A relationship with the composite Sun in the 8th must co-exist with this other realm, just as an individual with the Sun in the 8th must. He or she is pushed into becoming conscious of the invisible side of life, and may eventually act as its medium or mouthpiece, being transformed in the process.

If one has an 8th house Sun natally, one has probably experienced one's share of characteristic Plutonian eruptions, particularly through emotional crises which alter one's perception of reality and connect one with a deeper intelligence at work in life. The Sun's purpose in the 8th, individual or composite, is to explore that realm and be irrevocably changed by it. A relationship with an 8th house Sun often begins innocently enough, and is then compelled into a different awareness through crisis. Both people are usually required to become aware of this realm through the relationship, whether or not they are natally predisposed in that direction.

Audience: Could it be a hidden relationship?

Liz: It can be. So can the composite Sun in the 12th. But the feeling is different. The 12th house does not present us with Pluto's array of primal experiences – power struggles, the desire to destroy, overwhelming emotions, compulsive passions. The 12th also does not force us to let go in the same way as the 8th. In the 12th, things dissolve. In the 8th, they are wrenched away, and one must be either humble or humiliated. The composite Sun in the 8th may generate compulsive patterns that force the two people to deal with emotional issues that they might not otherwise have looked at. Shared resources in the form of money may come into this, but usually the important thing is the emotions rather than the money itself. A relationship with a composite 8th house Sun can certainly be secret. The composite Sun in the 8th and the 12th are two classic indicators of a secret relationship. So is composite Sun conjunct Neptune. But secrecy in the 8th feels different from secrecy in the 12th. Neptunian secrets have a bittersweet, poignant quality, a sense of something being sacrificed. Plutonian secrets have a suspicious, "outlaw" quality which feels subtly explosive and threatening.

Audience: A composite placement in the 12th or 8th might bring in spiritual themes.

Liz: If other factors suggest it, yes – perhaps composite Sun conjunct Jupiter in the 8th in Sagittarius, or composite Sun in Pisces in the 12th trine Uranus or Neptune in the 9th, or composite Jupiter conjunct Uranus straddling the 8th/9th cusps. The 12th house in itself is not necessarily spiritual. In fact I have found quite the opposite – what we call spiritual is often more connected with Uranus and Jupiter than with Neptune. Neptune can be extremely tricky, and has as much to do with fusion and a uroboric longing to return to the womb as it does with aspirations toward the divine. A lot of people call Neptunian longings spiritual because such longings are a way of escaping life. But you can escape life by getting stoned or roaring drunk as well, which is equally Neptunian. A 12th house composite Sun does not necessarily connote a spiritual relationship, unless the signs and other planets point that way.

Audience: What about the 8th, where Plutonian transformation happens? Wouldn't that be a spiritual relationship?

Liz: I am exceedingly mistrustful of that word "spiritual" at the best of times, and especially when it is applied to Pluto. The term "spiritual" is rather like the word "love" – people use it to conceal a multitude of sins. Since the 1960's it has become a kind of buzz-word, and very often, when it is used, one really means, "I can't cope with this awful incarnate world. I just want to go home." The kind of transformation that occurs under Pluto aspects, or with planets in the 8th house, may not look like anything spiritual in the sense of merging with a higher, transcendent source. Very often it is the opposite – a collision between the ego and the darkest, most chthonic dimensions of reality.

Pluto is transformative because the ego has to relinquish control. Pluto breaks down our identification with objects and external appearances, revealing the secret patterns underneath. That also happens to planets in the 8th. Don't forget that the 8th is the opposite of the 2nd, and there is no house more concrete than the 2nd and no sign more earthbound than Taurus, its natural ruler. When we move into the

8th, everything that we thought was real and immovable – the body, personal values, personal possessions – begins to waver and shake and break apart in the hands of the unseen. Things start happening that point to another reality, invisible on a material level and far greater and more powerful than any individual's personal wishes and will.

That reality may not be what we like to call spiritual. It may be the most rampant Oedipal feelings, or all sorts of quite ferocious passions that are very destructive, compulsive, or primitive in nature. The transformation takes place because one's whole view of reality is forced to change. One has to recognise that human beings are far more complex than one thought they were. One discovers the depths, which reveal a multi-dimensional reality. And one comes face to face with what the ancient mind perceived as Moira – the intrinsic law of Nature that apportions just and irrevocable allotment to all living things. That in itself is profoundly transformative. But it may not have anything that we would call spiritual in it, unless, of course, we recognise the essential divinity of Nature itself.

Audience: You have to transcend the darkness in order to get to the light.

Liz: That is a perfectly valid philosophical point of view. Many people espouse it. I can only say that it is not my philosophical point of view. I don't believe we transcend anything. To me, life is full of paradox, and darkness contains its own light, just as light contains a hidden darkness. I believe we become more whole. Talking about transcendence in relation to Pluto and the 8th house always makes me uneasy. My analytic work has taught me that, whenever there is a strenuous attempt to transcend Pluto, there is invariably an awful explosion later – or someone else, usually a partner or child, gets to carry the can. If a relationship has an 8th house composite Sun, attempting to "transcend" may provoke the less attractive dimensions of Pluto's realm. This kind of approach to Pluto tends to make boils break out, because it is *hubris*. Pluto is very definitely part of our animal nature, our link with the greater life of Nature. Are we so arrogant that we believe we can transcend this? Why should it not be recognised as divine in its own right?

A composite 8th house Sun does not mean that the couple are going to have a spiritual experience, or that they should learn to transcend something. It means that, sooner or later, all hell is going to break loose, because the doors to the hidden realms stand open. Then everything depends on what the two people do with it.

Audience: Could it be a *Who's Afraid of Virginia Woolf* kind of relationship?

Liz: It could be that. More often, it is a lot lower-key on the surface. But there are generally strong compulsions or dramatic emotional experiences involved. The relationship may generate a kind of death in both people – they are irrevocably changed.

Plutonian composites

I was thinking about a couple for whom I did a chart interpretation quite a few years ago. The composite did not have an 8th house Sun, but it was very Plutonian. Both natal charts had a Scorpio Ascendant, around 15° apart, so in the composite, the Ascendant was, of course, Scorpio. Composite Sun in Aquarius was opposite composite Saturn and Pluto in Leo. There were a lot of sexual difficulties and power battles and emotional struggles in this relationship. When transiting Pluto came within range of the composite Scorpio Ascendant, the man developed lung cancer. He had smoked when he was younger, but had quit some years before. Pluto was within orb of the composite Ascendant during the whole time he was ill, performing its inevitable three passes. It was already well past his wife's Ascendant and had not yet reached his Ascendant. But when it went over the exact degree of the composite Ascendant for the third time, he died.

He went through extraordinary experiences in the time leading up to his death. So did his wife. I would not say that either of them had a spiritual experience, except insofar as death is itself a spiritual experience. The transformative agent in the relationship was the inevitability of death and the powerlessness of the individual ego. The Plutonian emphasis in the composite, as well as other factors, ensured that the intimate side of the relationship was quite fraught. The wife had an affair with someone, and the husband found out, and then he left her for another woman, and then he went back again. Neither of them understood why all this was happening. By the time they began to explore it, it was too late; he was already ill. I would hardly describe what they went through as a transcendent spiritual experience, in the sense such experiences are usually defined. But they came to terms with something through it.

He came to terms with death in a way which is rare when one is dying slowly and young. Not everyone dies gracefully, but this man did. He made peace with a lot of things. It is a difficult business when someone dies with so much unlived. He was in his forties. On the other hand, what is a well-lived life? Does it depend on length, or is it the ability to make peace with what one is? It might be that the latter is very important, and if that is the criterion, then he managed it. She also made peace, not only with his death, but with the marriage itself. There could have been a lot of bitterness and lack of forgiveness and self-forgiveness; she could have blamed herself. They both changed, in an irrevocable and, I believe, positive way. I don't think we would hear either of them talking about transcending anything. The word "spiritual" was not part of their vocabulary.

One encounters a different level of life when a composite chart is very Plutonian, either through the planet, the sign, or the house. The relationship may create a profundity of experience and understanding which is not available to many people. Death on the literal level may not be involved, but death on some level usually is. One is never the same afterward. Life is bigger, deeper, richer, and more awesome, although not necessarily prettier. One makes peace with things; one accepts things in a way that makes one feel as if one has been really arrogant up to that point. With a composite Sun-Pluto, the relationship will have depths which we might not ordinarily encounter. Depending on what is in one's own chart, one might or might not cope well with it. Both people I mentioned had the equipment to cope, because they both had Scorpio Ascendants. There was something in both of them that could comprehend what Plutonian reality entailed.

With some relationships, neither person has this Pluto component. Only the composite has it. The relationship may then invoke things that neither person would ordinarily dream of going near, and it may be quite awful for a time. There may be very difficult experiences to go through. I don't think the issue here is that the couple must transcend something, although they clearly must go through something. Pluto is not malevolent. It is only from a certain human perspective that it looks malevolent, because its instinctive wisdom may not accord with what we aspire to individually. There is a fated quality about Sun-Pluto relationships. Yet they may be very enduring, and even indestructible.

Audience: My colleague and I have the composite Sun opposite composite Saturn-Pluto. Each of us was born with it, so it is in the composite as well. We have been working together for seven years. It is very intense.

Liz: If you have this in your composite, you will have it in your life as long as you work together. The fact that both of you have it natally means that, as individuals, you have always experienced it on an inner level, so it should not prove that difficult to accept the power battles and mutual mistrust. You can't expect this to be a light, fun relationship all the time. It might be sometimes, especially intellectually, but it will also demand a lot from you.

Audience: Pluto is conjunct the Ascendant in the composite. Would that be transformative?

Liz: It would suggest profound changes in the outer shape and expression of the relationship. It begins as one thing and then becomes something else. Nothing is left of the past. At some point there is a breaking down of the existing form of the relationship. Then it takes a new form, utterly different from the old. There is often a compulsiveness about this, as though it cannot in any way be avoided. Individuals with Pluto rising often have a series of incarnations. Their lives fall into distinct chapters, each of which has a recognisable beginning and ending. They are one way for a few years, doing a particular profession, wearing a particular kind of clothing, exhibiting a particular kind of personality, espousing a particular set of values. Then something happens – not always visible – and they become somebody completely different. They build a new personality out of the ashes of the old. The former life is gone forever, and something new starts which may go on for five or ten or twenty years. And then the same thing happens again.

A relationship with composite Pluto on the Ascendant has the same tendency to fall into distinct chapters. Whatever form it has for a time, it reaches a certain point of ripeness, and there is a complete dismantling and a recreation of the relationship in an entirely different form. A marriage may end and become a friendship, or a friendship transforms into a marriage, or a business partnership becomes a compulsive love affair. Then, at some future point, it may change shape again. The reasons for this are usually inexplicable. One cannot say, "The marriage ended because we weren't getting on, so we decided to remain friends," or, "The business partnership developed because we discovered when we were lovers that we had mutual professional interests." There is quite a different feeling. Something powerful and compulsive makes it impossible for things to be any other way. Personal feelings do not matter to Pluto. Some deeper pattern is at work and we may never know what ultimate purpose it serves, except that it is for the collective rather than the individual. Something says, "Time's up. You've done that one." This is often the way people feel who have natal Pluto rising.

Audience: I have Pluto rising. The other day I had to fill in my CV for a job application. I have changed my occupation five times. Each one was like a different incarnation. I didn't know what to write.

Liz: Just write, "Pluto rising", and they can work it out. Pluto represents a powerful instinctive drive to destroy the old and create something new – to end chapters of life and begin new ones on the ashes of the old. It is connected with survival, although the survival may be that of the group or species rather than that of the individual. There is a dramatic quality about Pluto on the Ascendant. This drive to destroy and renew its outer form exists in the relationship itself if composite Pluto is on the Ascendant. Do any of you have a relationship with this composite placement?

Audience: Yes. I married my best friend. We were best friends for years. Then suddenly we became something else. It was as if we saw each other for the first time.

Liz: Pluto's impetus for change comes from such a deep place that usually neither person knows why it has happened. It is not voluntary or based on conscious choice. There is a sense of compulsiveness, of fate, of necessity. It simply has to be this way – everything has changed and one cannot ever go back again. Then you both have to rearrange everything in your lives, because everyone – including you – perceived the two of you as one thing, and then, suddenly, you are something else.

Composite Sun in the 1st

Audience: Could you say something about a 1st house composite Sun?

Liz: A 1st house composite Sun describes a relationship that has a strong and catalytic effect on the environment. It has enormous "personality". Relationships, like individuals, come in a whole variety of guises. There are some people whom one doesn't notice, and other people who stand out. There are also some relationships which one doesn't notice, and some relationships which stand out. This has to do with energy, not appearances. There are couples who walk into a room and immediately, magically, create an effect around them. They haven't done anything, but there is something about the energy which attracts notice. Everybody looks at them, and people gravitate to them, and wherever they go, they generate a feeling of something exciting happening. They make a very strong impact, and act as catalysts for change.

A 1st house composite Sun carries that kind of feeling, although the couple may not be conscious of it. The purpose of the relationship is very simple and direct – to bring light into the immediate environment. The two people may not make this kind of impact individually. But the relationship does. The 1st is Aries' natural house, so think about the unique quality of Aries energy. Wherever it is unleashed, things begin to move. The spring equinox, when the Sun enters Aries each year, is a time when the life force of nature bursts forth from the regressive apathy of winter. T. S. Eliot wrote, "April is the cruelest month, breeding lilacs out of the dead land." Aries can't leave anything alone. It is dynamic and innovative, and acts as a catalyst in the environment. The composite Sun placed in Aries' natural house, whatever the sign, also has this effect. The relationship itself may be stable and peaceful, with composite Sun in Taurus sextile composite Moon in Cancer, but all the energy of the Sun is right up front, generating movement wherever it goes.

Audience: My and my husband's composite Sun is in Capricorn in the 1st, so it's toned down, and isn't very visible.

Liz: Perhaps. But your impact as a couple may be more powerful than you realise. There is a kind of chemical reaction in the environment when the composite 1st house is emphasised. People open up in ways they might not do around others. Sometimes this can be disruptive. A couple walk through a room and suddenly somebody starts a punch-up in the corner, and that happens to be the moment that the lights blow. Maybe, with the composite Sun in Capricorn, the impact is made in a low-key way. But things tend to get activated in the environment when there is a couple with a 1st house composite Sun around. Light is cast into dark corners, and things are energised which might otherwise remain asleep.

Audience: It's true that people are always coming up to ask for advice. It happens a lot. They seem to think we look wise and have answers, or something. It's very funny sometimes. I hadn't thought about it that way before.

Composite Sun in the 6th

Audience: How about a 6th house composite Sun? It's difficult to get very excited about it.

Liz: Ah, the poor old 6th house. It's always sadly underrated.

Audience: It must be more important than Rob Hand makes out.

Liz: It is not an obvious house. The composite Sun doesn't shine as overtly as it does on the composite MC or Ascendant. The energy of the relationship usually flows into everyday life. This composite Sun requires living in the moment. The core of the relationship is rooted in the reality of the world here and now, and the everyday tasks of living and creating order and harmony on the earth plane. This is also called the house of service, and often the relationship serves others in some practical way. I am thinking of a couple I know with a 6th house composite Sun, and both are doctors and share a deep commitment to helping others. The 6th is also known as the house of healing, and the relationship may serve to heal not only others but the couple themselves. Also, there may be a shared love of skill and craft. The 6th does not necessarily involve boring responsibilities; don't forget that this is Mercury's natural house. You may see couples like the one I mentioned, where both are involved in healing or helping others. Or both may be craftsmen and have a studio together. Or they may live the composite Sun by creating an orderly and serene ambience in their environment.

With this placement there is an implication of working together. The composite Sun in the 6th suggests a relationship which needs to "do" something useful in life. It is not focused on making a lasting impact on the world, like the composite Sun in the 10th, but often there is enormous satisfaction in creating something together that makes everyday life better and more rewarding. That is lovely, unless you have got two people who are individually very fiery. They may find the world of the 6th house elusive or oppressive, and they may not understand why they are being brought down to the earth plane all the time by everyday, ordinary tasks and challenges. The composite Sun in the 6th is neither unimportant nor boring, but it does not offer all its wares in the shop window.

Audience: A friend of mine and her husband have the composite Sun in the 6th, and she is nursing him now. They did work together, but now he's ill.

Liz: It is hard to fully appreciate the gentle rewards of a composite 6th house Sun unless you are one of the people in the relationship, because its life force is expressed in the here and now, moment by moment, and there isn't always a lot to show the outside world.

Audience: What you are saying about living from day to day is interesting, because it was a day-to-day thing whether they were going to get married at all. They were living together for years and suddenly one day they went off and got married. It was a spur-of-the-moment decision.

Audience: The 12th house is also a house of service. With Charles' and Diana's composite Sun being 2° away from the 12th, would that apply to their relationship?

Liz: Not in the same way. "Service" has a different meaning in the 12th, and rarely consists of practical tasks in the here-and-now. Their composite Moon is in the 6th, but that does not describe the purpose of the relationship. I think we have already discussed this. There are clearly 12th house elements in that composite – we spoke about the issue of sacrifice and the relationship being a mouthpiece for collective aspirations and a repository for the ancestral inheritance – but it is really an 11th house Sun. The relationship needs to serve a purpose in helping collective consciousness to evolve. Both houses are important, but I would give the main focus to the 11th.

      I fear we are running out of time. Unfortunately it is too late in the day to look at the transits in the composite for Pat and Phil, which I had wanted to do. Perhaps there are some final questions or comments?

Audience: The midpoint of my parents' Ascendant is in Libra, and yet the nearer midpoint of the MC's is in Capricorn. How do you sort out a chart like that?

Liz: Occasionally this happens. You will need to choose one – the MC or the Ascendant – and build the rest of the map around it. I would look first at what houses their two Suns are placed in natally, because if they both have the Sun above the horizon, it would make more sense for the composite Sun to also be above the horizon.

Audience: I think the Capricorn MC is the right one. That is certainly the image they present.

Liz: Then Aries would be on the composite Ascendant. You can use the composite Sun as a monitor. If both natal Suns are in a certain hemisphere, then the composite Sun ought to be in the same hemisphere.

Audience: They both have 10th house Suns.

Liz: Then the composite Sun should be in the 10th as well. And that should give you the MC sign which would be most appropriate to use.

Audience: A Capricorn MC puts the composite Sun in the 10th. I also think it is correct that Aries is rising, not Libra. They fight a lot, quite openly, although not in public. And they run a business together.

Audience: I find this whole business of the progressed composite terribly interesting, especially for the time of meeting.

Liz: I find it terribly interesting as well. The progressed composite portrays the nature of the movements within the relationship that have brought about the actual meeting. Naturally the transits and progressions in the individual chart are equally important, because they will describe what is happening within each person. But the relationship itself has its own agenda and timing. We can take any relationship and progress the composite for any critical point – the first meeting, the first sexual encounter, the time when people marry or decide to live together, when they have a child, when they break up, when one of them has an affair, when they move, when one of them dies. We will usually learn a lot, and gain a new perspective.

Important shifts in parent-child relationships are also fascinating when viewed in the progressed composite – when a sibling is born, when there is a death or separation in the family, when the child leaves home. It is worth looking at many periods in the life of a relationship, because they are all likely to be revealing, and to give insight into the deeper nature and development pattern of the relationship. First meetings often look very surprising in the progressed composite. They may not look like what we would expect. Where a strong Venus aspect might appear in the individual progressed chart, we may see Uranus, Chiron, or Saturn activated in the composite. These emphases will show what factors within the relationship have impelled it into manifestation.

Now we have reached the end of the day. Thank you all for coming and for contributing so much.

Bibliography

Hand, Robert, *Planets in Composite,* Para Research, Gloucester, Massachusetts, 1975.

Reinhart, Melanie, *Incarnation: The Four Angles and the Moon's Nodes,* CPA Press, London, 1997.

Sasportas, Howard, *Direction and Destiny in the Birth Chart,* CPA Press, London, 1998.

Appendix to Part One

The following charts may be useful to anyone who wishes to study in detail the composite of Prince Charles and Princess Diana at the time of her death.

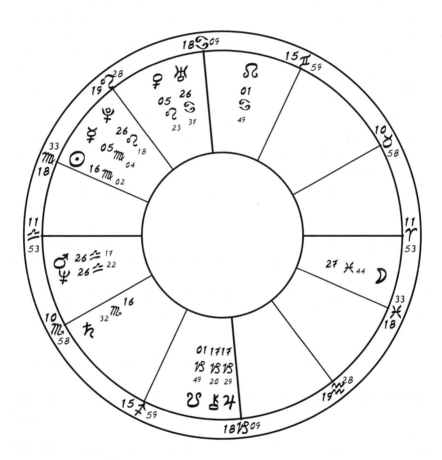

Composite chart for Charles and Diana

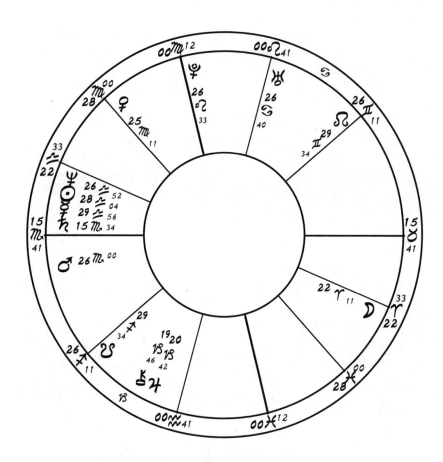

Progressed composite for Charles and Diana
Set for 31 August 1997, 12.15 am CED

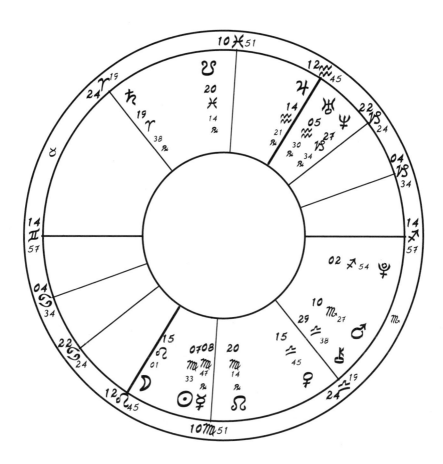

Transit chart for the time of Diana's death
31 August 1997, 12.15 am CED, Paris

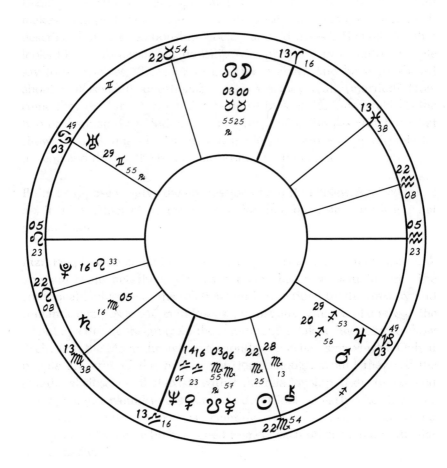

Prince Charles
14 November 1948, 9.14 pm GMT, London

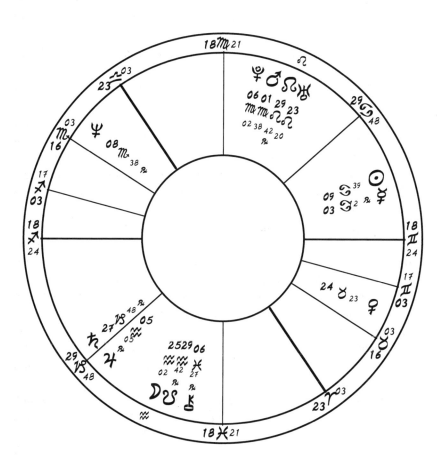

Princess Diana
1 July 1961, 7.45 pm GMT, Sandringham

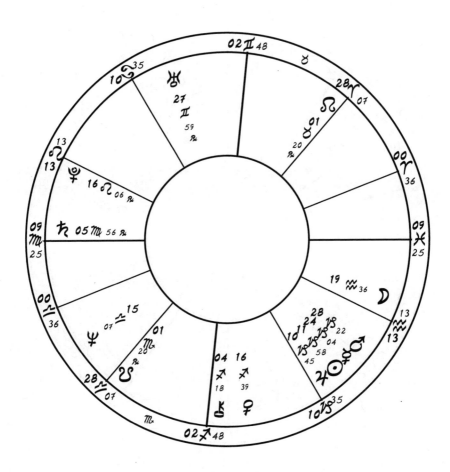

Prince Charles
Progressed chart for the time of Diana's death

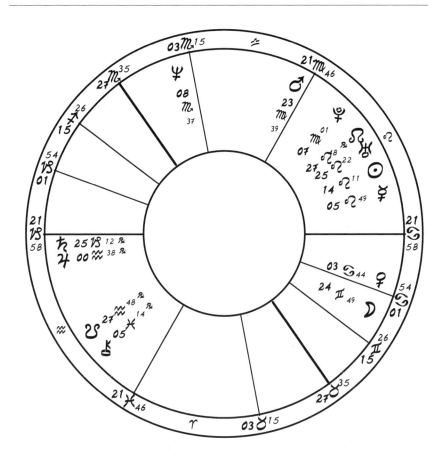

Princess Diana
Progressions for the time of her death

The most striking feature of the progressed composite in relation to the composite is that progressed composite Ascendant in 15° 41' Scorpio reached an exact conjunction (within 7' of arc) to progressed composite Saturn in 15° 34' at the time of Diana's death. This could carry the implication of an ending, and in a very literal way, considering Scorpio's traditional associations with death and the 2nd house association with the physical body (in this case, of the relationship). Progressed composite Mars in 26° 00' Scorpio was trine composite Uranus in 26° 37' Cancer, and was square (18' of arc) composite Pluto in 26° 18' Leo. The Mars-Uranus trine suggests a freeing of energy, while the Mars-Pluto square suggests some kind of struggle or fate which is imposed by collective forces on the "will" of the relationship. Both aspects, because they affect composite 10th and 11th house planets, may also relate to the way in which the event of Diana's death was received by the public.

Transits to the composite are not as striking as progressed composite to composite placements. Transiting Uranus in 5° 30′ Aquarius was opposite (7′ of arc) composite Venus in 5° 23′ Leo in the 10th house. Although there were no transits across the composite angles, Venus is the ruler of the composite chart. 5° 23′ Leo is also the degree of Prince Charles' Ascendant; transiting Uranus over the Descendant in a natal chart often reflects a sudden separation of some kind, and this transit needs no elaboration. Transiting Neptune was retrograde in 27° 34′ Capricorn, within 1° of exact opposition to composite Uranus in 26° 37′ Cancer, triggering the grand trine between composite Moon in 27° 44′ Pisces, composite Uranus, and progressed composite Mars in 26° 00′ Scorpio. This strange configuration, close to exact at the time of the accident, hints at a dissolution and the fruition of some kind of collective fate.

Progressed composite Ascendant in 15° 41′ Scorpio was square Charles' natal Pluto, setting off the square between his natal Pluto and composite Saturn. It could be said that the end of the relationship, even more than the marriage itself, forced him into a radical change of personality and personal image (natal Pluto in the 1st house).

Progressed composite Sun in 28° 04′ was in exact sextile to Diana's natal north Node in 28° 10′ Leo, placed in her 8th house. Another interesting configuration is the progressed composite MC in 00° 12′ Virgo, lining up to her natal Mars in 1° 38′ Virgo in the 8th house. I would not presume to pretend I know what these aspects mean, although they are highly suggestive. It is as though the point that the purpose and direction of the relationship had reached (progressed composite Sun and progressed composite MC) were in some way connected with her death. That is an obvious conclusion, since the demise of one meant the demise of the other, but it is eerie to see it portrayed astrologically in this way.

Prince Charles' progressed Venus in 16° 38′ Sagittarius was square (36′ of arc) the composite Sun in 16° 02′ Virgo. This suggests that he had arrived at a point in his life when his need for freedom and exploration in love was colliding with the nature of the relationship itself and all its attendant sacrificial, duty-bound (composite Sun in

Virgo in the 11th/12th) connotations. Diana's progressed Chiron in 5° 14' Pisces was in exact opposition (10' of arc) to composite Mercury in 5° 04' Virgo. As progressed Chiron was retrograde, this opposition was applying. Since Prince Charles' Saturn is in 5° 16' Virgo, this triggers the synastry between his Saturn and the composite Mercury, suggesting that something about her suffering and victimisation at the time of her death stirred not only his discomfort and sadness, but also the manner in which the relationship communicated with the public. It is not surprising that rumours abounded and are still abounding about the cause and nature of the death.

There are many other links between the composite, the progressed composite, and the natal and progressed charts of Charles and Diana, which the reader may explore *ad nauseam*. Many of the connections are obscure and only seem to hint at some mystery which we do not fully understand; other connections seem quite obvious and reflect the nature of the events which occurred. One thing emerges clearly from the material given above: the precision and intricacy with which composites and natal charts are interlocked opens our eyes to a vast web of human connections which, if nothing else, must leave us in awe of the greater design of which we are a part.

Part Two: The Eternal Triangle

This seminar was given on 15 March, 1998 at Regents College, London, as part of the Spring Term of the seminar programme of the Centre for Psychological Astrology.

The universality of triangles

The large number of people attending today's seminar demonstrates rather dramatically the universality of the theme we are dealing with. John Etherington has done a chart for the beginning of the seminar, and he has pointed out that Venus is in 8° Aries, exactly sextile Mars in 8° Aquarius and exactly trine Pluto in 8° Sagittarius. He suggests that this describes passion, rape, and assault. Hopefully these things will remain on the level of discussion, and not manifest in the seminar.

It would appear that relationship triangles are an archetypal dimension of human life. We don't ever really get away from them. We also tend to handle them rather badly when they enter our lives. That is perhaps understandable, because triangles can be evocative of very painful emotions, regardless of the point of the triangle on which one finds oneself. We may have to cope with feelings of jealousy, humiliation, and betrayal. We may have to cope with the sense of being a betrayer, of being dishonest, of injuring someone. We may feel all these feelings at once, as well as the conviction of being a failure. The emotions involved in triangular relationships are often agonising and cut away at self-esteem. Because triangles confront us with very difficult feelings, we often try to blame someone for the presence of a triangle in our lives. Either we blame ourselves or we blame one of the other two people. But triangles are indeed archetypal. If we have any question about their universality, we need only read myth, never mind the literature of the last three thousand years. Anything archetypal presents us with a world of purposeful patterns and intelligent inner development. Triangles are one of our most powerful means of transformation and growth, unpleasant and painful though they are. The experience of betrayal, whether one is the betrayer or the betrayed, does something to the individual which could potentially be of enormous value.

Because we handle triangles so badly, I thought it would be worth exploring whether there is such a thing as a pattern in the horoscope that is conducive to triangles. I would also like to consider what deeper reasons, perhaps unconscious, might impel any individual into a triangle. Then there is the thorny question of why some people are more prone to triangles than others. Certain individuals seem to lurch from one romantic triangle to another, caught in a compulsive pattern not of their choosing. I would also like to examine what possible approaches we could take to working with triangles more creatively than we usually do, which will involve looking at them psychologically and symbolically. This kind of exploration will inevitably open up a large area of extremely sensitive stuff. Therefore, when we get around to looking at example charts in the afternoon, I will not be surprised if nobody wants to offer his or her chart for discussion.

Adult sexual triangles

There are many kinds of triangles, not all involving an adult sexual relationship. Even if we were to restrict ourselves to sexual triangles, we would find many different varieties. Sexual triangles are not always made of the grand dramatic stuff of Arthur, Lancelot, and Guinevere. There are adult love triangles where all three points are fixed. One partner in a relationship is involved with a third person, and there isn't any movement in the triangle. It is static and may go on for many years, until one of the three participants dies. There are other love triangles where one of the points is constantly changing. One can have serial adultery, rather than one consistent lover. But both these situations are triangles, even though we tend to accord a higher romantic value to the first and usually condemn the second; and both can evoke the same spectrum of feelings.

Other kinds of triangles

Apart from adult love triangles where a sexual involvement exists between any combination of the two sexes, there are many other kinds of triangles. The most fundamental are triangles that involve parents and children. There are triangles which involve friendships. And there are triangles which involve non-human companions. One partner may feel betrayed because of the other partner's dedication to work or artistic involvement or spiritual development. Such triangles can evoke exactly the same feelings as the sexual variety. Any of you who do creative work may know that when one withdraws into a creative space, one has somehow "left" the person one lives with, and it can stir up great insecurity in one's partner. I see that some of you are nodding. The creative process is an act of love; that is why the 5th house is traditionally said to govern both. If one loves one's work, it may evoke enormous jealousy.

There are even triangles involved with pets. You may think this is funny, but one partner can feel extremely jealous, hurt, and neglected because the other partner is deeply attached to his or her cat or dog. All these different kinds of triangles may seem unrelated. The one thing they have in common is the component of one or another variety of love which, in a triangle, is no longer exclusive. And when we must share someone's love, whether with another person or with something ineffable like the imagination, we may feel betrayed, abandoned, and bereft.

We have a huge subject to cover today. I want to talk first about the different kinds of triangles that we may become involved in, and what their psychological dynamics might look like. We can explore possible astrological correlations, and also, if there is time, look at some mythic material which illustrates the workings of different kinds of triangles. Once we have gone through this material, I would like to look at how we could work with our triangles differently, and cope better with the typically primitive, unconscious reactions that most human beings have. The object of all this is to explore the deeper meaning behind triangles, psychologically and astrologically, and the possible reasons why they appear in our lives.

I don't believe that anything enters the individual's life that is not in some way connected with the individual's journey. This does not imply blame or causality, but it does imply a deeper meaning which may be transformative for the person who is prepared to seek that meaning. However painful these issues may be, if a triangle enters one's life, it is there for something. We may choose to react with rage, self-pity, bitterness, or specious rationalisations. We may prefer to believe the situation is someone's "fault". But we could also choose to make the triangle a springboard for some real soul-searching. This is particularly difficult because the experience of humiliation usually invokes all the defence systems of infancy, and it is very hard to move beyond such primal responses to a more detached perspective.

The points of the triangle

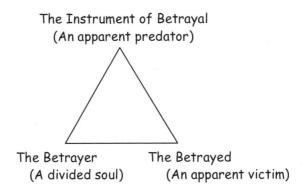

The Instrument of Betrayal
(An apparent predator)

The Betrayer   The Betrayed
(A divided soul)   (An apparent victim)

The Betrayer, the Betrayed, and the Instrument of Betrayal

Here is a little diagram which can give us a starting point. For the moment I am going to ignore the astrological significators, although no doubt you will all think of various links as we go on. This is a very simplistic picture of the three points of the triangle. Some people experience only one of these points in a lifetime, and some are experienced in all three.

The Betrayer is the person who apparently chooses to get involved in the triangle. I use the word "apparently" because unconscious compulsion often overwhelms conscious choice; and also, one cannot be sure how much secret collusion exists between Betrayer and Betrayed. But whatever might be at work beneath the surface, the Betrayer is a divided soul. There is a love, passionate attraction, or need for two different things. Most of us carry the assumption that love should be exclusive, even if on a conscious level we profess a more liberal perspective. Because of the values of our Judeo-Christian heritage, we are brought up to believe that if our love is not exclusive, it is not love, and we are no longer "good" people. We have failed, or we are selfish and unfeeling. When we experience this kind of deep inner division, it can be very hard to bear. It is much easier for the Betrayer to come up with a list of justifications for why he or she is committing the act of betrayal. We don't often hear the Betrayer say, "I am divided. I am torn in half." More commonly, what we hear is: "My partner is treating me very badly. He/She is not giving me sex/money/affection/attention/children/hot meals. I am unhappy. Therefore I am justified in looking elsewhere."

At the next point of the triangle is the Betrayed, who is apparently the unwilling victim of the Betrayer's inability to love exclusively. I have used the word "apparently" here, too, because, as I said, there may be unconscious collusion involved in this role. You will see, as we go along, that all three points on the triangle are actually interchangeable. They are not as different as they might first appear. But the Betrayed generally believes that he or she is loyal, and it is the other person who is disloyal. It is someone else who has initiated the triangle. Usually we think of the Betrayed as having the hardest time in a triangle, because this is the person who generally acts out all the rage and jealousy and feelings of humiliation.

Finally, at the third point of the triangle, there is the Instrument of Betrayal. This person enters an already existing relationship between two people, and apparently threatens to destroy or change it. This point of the triangle usually gets rather a bad press, being seen as "predatory" or a taker of someone else's beloved possession. If we happen to occupy this point, we may receive only limited sympathy, and none at all from those in established relationships who feel the cold wind of their own possible future. The Instrument of Betrayal may, however, feel himself or herself to be a victim, and may perceive the Betrayed as the predator. We can begin to glimpse the secret identity between these two points of the triangle.

There are people who move around the triangle and try all three points during the course of their lives, sometimes many times. There are other people who stick with one point exclusively, and always get betrayed in their relationships, or always wind up playing the Betrayer. Or they are always the Instrument of Betrayal, invariably involved with people who are attached elsewhere. This is one of the things I would like you to contemplate as we go on. From your own experience, think about which of these points you tend to favour – if that is indeed the right word. Have you moved around the triangle, or have you stuck with one point? And do you have particularly strong moral convictions about any of these three roles?

Types of triangles

I would like to explore four different groups of triangles. This grouping is, of course, quite arbitrary. We could approach the different kinds of triangles from many different perspectives. I am really trying to give some kind of initial structure to a very emotive and amorphous mass of material. In the end, the four different kinds of triangles end up, like different rivers all flowing into the sea, as "Triangles which reflect unlived psychic life". But the triangle which life first presents us with is the family triangle, so we are going to start off looking at that one in more detail.

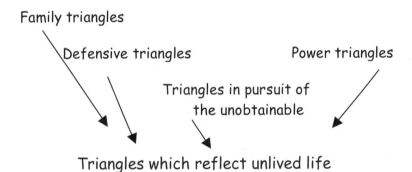

Family triangles

Defensive triangles   Power triangles

Triangles in pursuit of
the unobtainable

Triangles which reflect unlived life

Of course we have Freud's inspired concept of the Oedipal triangle to kick us off. But looked at closely, this concept is not what it initially appears to be. Family triangles have repercussions throughout life. They don't just happen in childhood. They keep repeating when they are unresolved, and they will usually find their way into adult relationships. Where there is a repeating pattern of triangles in adult life, there is often an unhealed family triangle. Because it is unresolved, we recreate it, once or many times, hoping on some deep and inaccessible level that we will find a way to heal it. We need to look at the family triangle in quite a lot of depth, because it is so compulsive and so fundamental.

You will also see "Power triangles" and "Defensive triangles" in the diagram. These kinds of triangles are very similar, although there are some differences which are apparent astrologically, as we shall see later. But they both have a particular odour about them, and the reasons for their entry into one's life may not be entirely rooted in the family background.

What I am calling a defensive triangle would be, for example, a man or woman who needs to form an additional relationship outside their established partnership because of feelings of deep inadequacy. They may be plagued by great insecurity, and may feel very frightened that, if they put all of their emotional eggs in a single basket, they will be too vulnerable, and rejection would be utterly intolerable. A triangle is then unconsciously created as a defence mechanism. If they are abandoned by one partner, they have always got the other. That is a characteristic defensive triangle.

Power triangles arise from the same root. The Betrayed is kept insecure through the knowledge that there is an Instrument of Betrayal waiting in the wings, which allows the Betrayer to feel more secure and powerful. Underneath, there may be enormous self-doubt and insecurity. These things are not usually consciously calculated, but fear of rejection may be a powerful motivating factor in many triangles.

I have also put "Triangles in pursuit of the unobtainable" in the diagram. These can overlap with family triangles, and may also have defensive or power components. But there is a special ingredient in the pursuit of the unobtainable, and often the motivating factor underneath is artistic or spiritual. Sometimes, when we seek unobtainable love, it actually has little to do with human beings. But we translate our creative or mystical longings into the pursuit of those we cannot have, those who are at a distance, or those who are in some way inaccessible. In this way we open up a dimension of the psyche which really has much more to do with creative potential than with relationship. This is the basis of the medieval ethos of courtly love, whose object was, ultimately, the creation of poetry.[5] If we don't understand this imaginative dimension of the triangle, we may wind up creating a

---

5 For an astrological analysis of courtly love, see *The Astrological Neptune and the Quest for Redemption*, Liz Greene, Samuel Weiser, Inc, York Beach, Maine, USA, 1996.

fantasy world around an unobtainable figure. This is a very special kind of triangle. As I said, there may be elements of early family dynamics, as well as defensive motives; but it needs to be looked from with a different perspective.

The last group – "Triangles which reflect unlived psychic life" – subsumes all the others. When we look at family triangles, we need to ask why we want so badly to be close to a particular parent. What does that parent mean to us? Why can we cope with relative indifference from one parent, yet require nothing less than absolute fusion with the other? In the end, inevitably, we will find bits of our own souls farmed out along all the points of the triangle – any triangle, whether motivated by family dynamics, power, defensiveness, pursuit of the unobtainable, or a combination of all of the above. I am sure there are exceptions, because there are always exceptions to any psychological pattern. But when a triangle enters our lives, regardless of the point we are on, there is usually some message in it about dimensions of ourselves which we have not recognised or lived. If a pattern of triangles keeps repeating, then it is a very strong message, and we need to listen to what it is trying to tell us. That is the bottom line, and it could offer us a way to cope with the less attractive emotional dimensions of triangles.

The family triangle

Oedipus and other tales

Freud developed the idea of the Oedipal triangle in a very specific context. In his view, we attach ourselves passionately to the parent of the opposite sex, and enter into a situation of rivalry with the parent of the same sex. Depending on how the Oedipal triangle is resolved in childhood – and this includes the parents' responses as well as one's own innate temperament – our later relationships will inevitably be affected. If we unequivocally "win" the exclusive love of the parent of the opposite sex – and the operative word is *unequivocally* – we suffer because we never learn to separate or share. We become puffed up with false infantile potency because we believe we have beaten the rival, and we don't realise that the beloved parent's motives may be rather murky. A parental marriage fraught with difficulty may lie behind a mother's or father's "favouring" of a child as a kind of replacement spouse. But the child, of course, does not know this, and feels all-powerful. This narcissistic identification with the parent may open the door to a later inability to cope with any kind of relationship disappointment. And one's relationships with one's own sex are also disturbed accordingly.

Audience: Disturbed in what way?

Liz: If a boy sees his mother and father in conflict, and "wins" the Oedipal battle by becoming his mother's surrogate husband, he may experience deep unconscious guilt toward his father. There is an instinctive sense of the illicit nature of the Oedipal bond, and if one succeeds, that is psychological if not physical incest. Also, he may lose respect for his father, whom he has pushed out of the way with great ease. At least, the boy imagines this, although it is more likely that the mother has done the pushing, or that the father has voluntarily extricated himself from the parental marriage, physically or emotionally, and found solace elsewhere. That is what I mean by "false potency". The boy's image of father may then be of someone weak, impotent, and easily beaten, and somewhere inside he will fear this in himself, because he, too, is male.

This boy may have to keep affirming his Oedipal victory later in life by turning every male friend into a rival, and relating exclusively to women. I think we all know men like this – one meets them at dinner parties, and they do not connect with other men, but only to the women who are attached to other men. His bond with his mother will have cost him his relationship with his father, which may mean he has no positive internal masculine image on which to draw, and no sense of support from the community of men around him. His sense of male confidence and male sexual identity must rely entirely on whether his women love him. That is a very insecure and painful place in which to live. There are many ramifications, but that gives you some idea of what we are dealing with. We could apply the same interpretation in the case of a woman and her father. Is it clear?

Audience: All too clear. Thank you.

Liz: If we unequivocally lose the Oedipal battle – and the operative word, once again, is *unequivocally* – we also suffer. Absolute Oedipal defeat is a humiliation which can severely undermine one's self-confidence. By "absolute", I mean that the child feels no emotional contact of any kind has been achieved with the beloved parent, and a profound feeling of failure ensues. The other parent is usually blamed, but it is not so simple as that; more often, the desired parent is quite incapable of offering any positive emotional response to his or her child. Unfortunately, it is usually impossible for the child to face this fact about an idealised love-object. And so the failure is accepted as one's own, and the rival is more powerful because one is clearly inadequate and unlovable.

Later in life, severe Oedipal defeat can generate a gnawing sense of sexual inferiority. It can contribute to many destructive relationship patterns, not least the kind of triangle where one is hopelessly in love with a person who is permanently attached elsewhere. One may play the unhappy Instrument of Betrayal, forever knocking at the closed door of a lover's marriage. Or one may play the Betrayed, helplessly repeating the Oedipal defeat in the role of the established partner who is humiliated by the greater power of the mother- or father-rival. With both unequivocal Oedipal victory and unequivocal Oedipal defeat, we are unable to establish a psychological separation from the beloved parent, and a part of us never really grows beyond childhood. We may become stuck in repetitive relationship dynamics where we keep trying to "fix" the original hurt through a triangle.

Freud thought that the healthiest resolution of the Oedipal conflict is a kind of mild defeat, where we get *enough* love from the beloved parent but are still forced to acknowledge that the parents' relationship is beyond our power to destroy. We may then learn to respect relationships between other people, and build confidence through establishing new bonds beyond the magic parental circle. One's extended family, peer group, and teachers may play an important role in helping the child to move beyond the parental triangle. We are here in the realm of what Winnicott called "good enough" – a good enough parental marriage, a good enough relationship with both parents, and sufficient love and kindness for the Oedipal defeat to be accompanied by a reasonable sense of security within the family.

In this most basic of triangles, it is important that we do not fear punishment from the parent-rival. Sadly, many parents, themselves emotionally starved and resentful in an unhappy marriage, do punish their children for "stealing" the partner's love. Someone must be blamed for the failure of the marriage, and often it is the child. We need to recognise that we cannot supplant one parent in order to have the other, but we also need to know that we will be loved by the parent we have tried to overthrow. Naturally this is an ideal which few families can achieve. A great many people suffer from one degree or another of excessive Oedipal victory or excessive Oedipal defeat. What really matters is what we do with it, and how much consciousness we have of it. And nothing is quite so potent an activator of consciousness as an adult relationship triangle.

There is a lot of value in Freud's psychological model, and there are many situations where absolute Oedipal defeat or absolute Oedipal victory is linked with a repetitive tendency to become involved in triangles later in life. But there are several areas where I part ways with Freud. I don't believe the parent to whom we attach ourselves is necessarily the parent of the opposite sex. The parent may be one's own sex. Oedipal feelings are not, after all, "sexual" in an adult sense, but have more to do with emotional fusion. So do many of our apparently purely sexual feelings in adulthood; sexuality carries many complex levels which are not always conscious. An Oedipal defeat or victory involving the parent of one's own sex may have equally painful repercussions, and be equally conducive to later relationship triangles. We may need to broaden our understanding of the Oedipal dynamic, because it doesn't always involve a "classic" heterosexual attachment. A boy may adore his father, and yet be unable to get near him because mother is always in the way. She may be determined to have her son entirely to herself, and may resent a relationship between the boy and the husband who has rejected her. That boy may grow up feeling that his father doesn't value him, because children are not usually able to recognise the machinations going on in the parents' marriage – although they invariably sense them. If one is rejected, it must be because one is deficient.

That can do many different things to a child's psyche. One may feel dislocated from one's own sexuality, because the beloved parent is a model for that sexuality and the bond is too weak or negative to allow a positive model to be internalised. It can also mean that a man will forever try to win his father's love by proving how manly he is. He may then unconsciously set up triangles which are not really about the women with whom he becomes involved, but are actually about impressing other men – or punishing them for his father's rejection. A woman may try to win her mother's love and admiration in the same way, or punish other women for her mother's failure to love her. The rival in an adult triangle may be secretly far more important to the individual than the apparent object of desire. We need only listen to the obsessive preoccupation the Betrayed and the Instrument of Betrayal have with each other to recognise that the situation may be far more complex than it seems.

Helpful Oedipal hints: Venus in the parental houses

Now, we know that the chart can tell us a lot about our images of our parents and our perception of the experiences we have encountered through them. We can save the fraught discussion of whether these images are objective or subjective until later. When we look at a chart, what hints about Oedipal difficulties would we expect to find?

Audience: Pluto aspecting the Sun.

Liz: Perhaps. But let's take it one step at a time. One thing we often find, with a pattern of adult relationship triangles, is that the parental significators show up very powerfully, and in such a way as to involve one's emotional needs and one's image of oneself as a man or woman. We might find planets in the 10th or 4th house, for example, which immediately suggests the parent is an embodiment of something mythic and archetypal. Having no planets in the parental houses does not mean there are no conflicts with the parents, or no subjective image which we project on them. But it is easier to perceive the parent as another human, however flawed. When planets occupy these houses, the planetary gods appear with the parent's face, wearing the parent's clothes. A piece of our own destiny, our own "soul journey", if you like, comes to meet us in early life, disguised as mother or father and passed down through the family inheritance. While this is not "bad" or "negative", it does imply something powerful, fascinating, and compulsive about the parental relationship which requires a greater degree of consciousness and a greater effort at integration. As Thomas Fuller once wrote, "Parents are Patterns."

It does seem that a pattern of triangles in adult life is frequently linked with planets in the parental houses. Very often we will see Venus in the 10th or 4th. It should be obvious why. Venus describes what we perceive as beautiful and of value, and therefore what we love, both in ourselves and in others. If a parent appears in the birth chart as Venus, that parent is going to be a symbol of what we recognise as most beautiful, most valuable, and most worthwhile. That in itself is not negative. But it may mean that we project our own beauty and worth on the parent, and a lot then depends on how the parent handles such a projection. We see deeply lovable, worthwhile qualities or attributes in the parent and we fall in love with the parent because we are in love with the attributes.

Hopefully, as we mature, we integrate these projections and recognise that the valued qualities belong to us as well as to mother or father. This process can help to create a lasting, loving bond between parent and child – a mutual valuing of the other for qualities which are shared. But not all parents are free of hidden agendas regarding their children, and often, if the parent is too hungry for love and admiration, he or she will unconsciously work to keep hold of the projection and remain Venus forever in the child's eyes. In other words, the Oedipal contest is prolonged beyond its appropriate time because the parent has an investment in remaining the best-loved and fairest of them all.

Venus, as most of you are aware, is not known in myth for her emotional generosity. She is a vain goddess and is repeatedly implicated in love triangles. If we leave the Venusian image projected on the parent, we may never recognise it in ourselves. Then we will keep looking for parental surrogates on whom we can place this image of all that is worthwhile and desirable in life, and we will keep finding Venusian love-objects who seem worth so much more than we do ourselves. Or we may try to reclaim Venus by playing her ourselves, pitting one lover against another in order to convince ourselves that we are really of value after all.

Audience: I am having a problem with all this. I have Venus in the 4th house, and I just can't see how this describes my father. I don't find much beautiful or worthwhile in him. He made my mother pretty miserable, and left us when I was four. I have barely any contact with him now. I do admit that I have had my share of triangles in my love-life. But I can't see the connection.

Liz: I understand that you are having a problem with it. But it might help if you could remember that the person who is speaking now, telling me you don't find much beautiful or worthwhile in your father, is the "adult" you. You have "adult" reasons, perhaps justified, why you feel anger and resentment toward him. These reasons have developed over time and have been emphasised by your perception of your mother's unhappiness. Your father's departure when you were only four must have hurt a great deal. But the perception of the parent described by a 4th or 10th house planet is the perception of a young child – and the closer the planet is to the cusp, the younger the child. Before your father left, he may well have been Venus for you, and that may be why it hurt so much when you lost him. How many degrees is Venus away from the IC?

Audience: My IC is 16° Scorpio. Venus is in 20° Scorpio.

Liz: They are 4° apart. If you progress the IC by secondary progressed motion, which means 1° per year, you will see that it made the exact conjunction to Venus when you were four years old – the time your father left. Your experience of him as Venus was actually at its height, its maximum power, at the very moment he abandoned you. I am not suggesting that what you say you feel about him is "false". But sometimes we can feel many things about the same person. Some of those feelings may be unconscious because they are so ambivalent. To love and hate someone simultaneously is very difficult for the ego to carry. How can you love someone who treated you and your mother so badly? That would make you a "bad" person, and it would be a betrayal of your mother. And it might open you up to more hurt, whereas if you feel nothing but contempt or resentment toward him, he can't hurt you ever again.

Try to think about these things later, after the seminar, and see whether the emotional situation might be more complicated than you have thought. You see, I have an idea your attraction to triangles may have something to do with feelings for your father which are deeply buried because they are very painful and unacceptable to the conscious adult you have become. I did say at the beginning of the day that this was hot terrain, and I am reluctant to probe you further about your personal life in a group situation like this. But do try to think about it. It is possible that you don't yet know everything there is to know about your early feelings for your father. Where Venus is, we love.

Audience: Could a rejecting parent then be represented by Venus? Would that mean it could be harder to take the projection back?

Liz: Sometimes, yes. If the Venus parent is rejecting, cold, or unavailable, we may find it very difficult to "take back" Venus because the parent is not reflecting our own worth back to us. But we always come back to the issue of subjectivity. A Venus parent's rejection is felt as particularly painful because of the value we attribute to that parent. Someone we love, and by whom we long to be loved, denies the thing we want the most. That can "fix" the fascination for the parent. Sometimes it is the opposite. If the parent behaves like a lover rather than like a mother or father, we may be equally unable to introject Venus. Parents are really bridges by which the archetypal realm is translated into human terms. All parents play this role for us, well or badly, regardless of whether or not the parental houses are tenanted. But when a planet appears in a parental house, it is particularly important, because the parent is a vessel or embodiment of something very specific involving our own inner pattern of development.

Venusian rivalry

If Venus is in the house of the parent of one's own sex, what kind of dynamic might ensue?

Audience: Mirror, mirror on the wall, who's the fairest of them all?

Liz: Yes, that is one scenario. Rivalry is one of the most characteristic patterns when Venus is a same-sex parental significator. This may even apply when it is an opposite-sex parental significator. One may feel like Snow White a good deal of the time. If Venus is in the 10th in a woman's chart, there may be deep and painful rivalry between mother and daughter. From the daughter's point of view, the mother may appear to be very jealous, although the jealousy may be expressed covertly as incessant criticism or subtle undermining of the daughter's feminine confidence. Sadly, the jealous or competitive mother is often an objective reality. But it is one's own Venus in the 10th, and one must, sooner or later, acknowledge one's own propensity to generate rivalry. The archetypal love-goddess, who must be the fairest and best-loved of all, is an archetypal image which has passed down through generations of the maternal line. Rivalry and envy are closely related, and when Venus is a parental significator, we may see beautiful, enviable qualities in the parent and wish we had them ourselves. Then we begin to compete in order to prove that we are Venus too – a bigger and better and more beautiful Venus.

Audience: I have Venus conjunct the IC, but it's on the 3rd house side. Would that also count?

Liz: Yes, it would "count", even if it is on the 9th or 3rd house side. Then, rather than progressing the IC or MC, we could progress Venus to see when it made an exact conjunction to the angle. This can give us some idea of when the experience of the parent as Venus was at its height. Would you be willing to comment on this chart placement in the context of your own experience?

Audience: Recently my father told me, "You are really the daughter of my dreams, but I can deal better with your sister." There are some things he envies in me. For example, he says I was brave in a special way when I was occupying an illegal flat – something he would never try to do. He loves writing poetry, but he never finishes his poems, and he really likes my poems.

Liz: And the sister that he says he can deal with more easily – did you feel you had to fight with her for his love? You said that Venus is in the 3rd as well as conjuncting the IC, so it also has some bearing on your perception of your sister. The 3rd is the house of siblings.

Audience: Yes, I think she was always fighting me for the love of both my parents. She was quite a demanding child. She was sick with bronchitis throughout her childhood, so they always had to look after her a lot.

Liz: You have just described a situation where your father has feelings of envy and admiration toward you, and your sister was jealous and demanding and fought to get your parents' attention. But you have said nothing of your own feelings toward both of them.

Audience: Ah.

Liz: I'll let you off the hook if you like.

Audience: No, I may as well jump right in. I really liked my father. I had very bad feelings about myself when I came into puberty. I felt he didn't want to touch me any more. Later I wondered whether he was afraid. But at the time I didn't feel valued as a woman. As soon as I became a female, I wasn't worth anything any more.

Liz: Now we are getting into the difficult stuff. This kind of experience is not uncommon when Venus is implicated as a parental significator. The moment you reached puberty, you were no longer acceptable to your father. Can you understand why not?

Audience: Because I became sexually threatening.

Liz: Yes. When you were younger, he was Venus for you, but when you arrived at puberty, you began to become Venus yourself. That is potentially a rather tricky situation, because Venusian qualities are shared between both of you, so you would both be deeply aware of each other as sexual beings. I hope the implications of this are clear to all of you. Mutuality of erotic feelings between parent and child does *not* imply any "abnormality", nor does it constitute an excuse for child sexual abuse. But children can be very seductive in a childlike way, with or without a Venus parental significator. They are "trying on" their sexuality. They neither want nor expect an adult sexual response, but they need to discover their sexual identity through expressing it to the parent – especially if that parent is personified by Venus. Those of you who are parents will know this. How many of you have children who are at the age when they start trying to get into bed between you and your partner, or are clearly playing one of you off against the other? I see there are lots of hands up.

These things are part of family life. They are human and intrinsically healthy. The erotic awareness that is part of any person's development process in childhood will be expressed in the family because that is the appropriate place for the child to express it. It is also important that the parent can respond positively, affirming the child's sexual identity – although it is, of course, not appropriate for this to be translated into a sexual approach. Some children carry more of an energy pack than others, or are more precocious in their erotic development. This may be reflected by certain factors in the child's birth chart. Or there may be a special affectional bond with one of the parents, which is the case when Venus is a parental significator. Equally, some parents may be more disturbed than others by the interchange, and this may be connected with synastry aspects between parent and child as well as the nature of the parent's sexuality and the state of the parental marriage. These things are human variables which cannot be forced into an artificial structure of so-called "normal" responses.

It isn't easy for parents to contain this natural process without falling into a family triangle. Probably few, if any, parents can; the important issue is how intense the triangle becomes, rather than whether there is one. A little girl with Venus in the 4th house is likely to feel strong rivalry with both mother and sisters, because father is the beloved, with whom she shares some very lovely and pleasurable feelings. If the parental marriage is insecure and the mother unconsciously begins to behave in a hostile or competitive way, or if the father cannot cope with his own responses to his daughter's incipient womanhood and rejects her in too brutal a fashion, the seeds are sown for triangles in adult life.

Audience: In my case, I didn't feel jealous of my mother, because I have the Moon conjunct the Ascendant and trine Venus. I really identified with my mother.

Liz: Identification and jealousy are not mutually exclusive. In the happiest and most emotionally stable of families, one may feel both deep love for and intense rivalry with the parent. One may find, for example, Venus in the 4th and Moon in the 10th, or, as in your case, Moon trine Venus. There may be a strong identification with the rival. If this is so, what do you think is going to happen?

Audience: It is a split in the soul of the child.

Liz: Yes, to a greater or lesser extent. The child may wind up being the Betrayer as well as the Instrument of Betrayal. That is not conducive to feeling good about oneself, so something is likely to be suppressed. The young ego simply cannot cope with such ambivalence. If one expresses Venus in the 4th, with all its adoration of the father, one will hurt and betray the mother. And if the Moon is trine Venus or in the 10th, how can one do this to someone whose feelings one is so identified with? Then Venus may get suppressed, and later in life one may wind up in a triangle without understanding the early pattern which is fuelling it. Or the feelings for the mother may be suppressed. One may become a "marriage wrecker", as they used to call it in the days when there were still marriages. A "marriage wrecker", psychologically speaking, is a person who moves in on an established relationship, not only because of genuine affection and desire for the love object, but also because there is a compulsive need to take on the role of – to literally become – the rival with whom one is secretly identified.

It is not easy acknowledging such a pattern in oneself. If we find ourselves as the Instrument of Betrayal, we prefer to believe that we have truly fallen in love with someone, and the fact that they are already in an established relationship is just bad luck. They made a mistake and married the wrong person, or they married unwillingly because there was a child on the way. Whatever rationalisations we give ourselves, we may justify our role as Instrument of Betrayal by devaluing the importance of the already existing bond. This may sometimes prove extremely naive, and lead to a great deal of disillusionment and hurt when one discovers that the "unwanted" spouse means far more to the beloved than one has been able to acknowledge. One may also discover, to one's horror, that one begins to behave exactly like the despised rival whom one had relegated to the "he/she only stays with her/him because of the children" bin. When Oedipal issues are unresolved, the urge to unseat a couple may be extremely powerful – especially if the rival is also one's close friend, which facilitates recreating the feelings of the original family triangle. Now, what about a man with Venus in the 10th? Are there any men here with that chart placement? No? What a pity. Direct feedback is always so interesting.

Audience: Mother is the beloved.

Liz: And what might that mean in terms of adult life?

Audience: He suppresses his feelings, and then later he falls in love with an older married woman.

Liz: Sometimes. Usually it's less obvious. The woman may be much younger, but her chart often resembles the mother's. However, I think you are right about suppression. Few young men are able to acknowledge erotic feelings toward the mother. The Emperor Nero did, but look at how history remembers him. There is also the threat of punishment from the father-rival. And there may be, as with Venus in the 4th in a woman's chart, the sense that one is the Instrument of Betrayal, acting against a parent for whom one may feel considerable love and attachment.

"Split anima" and "split animus"

The power of the ancient incest taboo, and the sense of betrayal of the father, may mean that Venusian feelings for the mother are entirely suppressed. A man may also see things in the mother which are not so lovely. Let's say that he has Venus in the 10th but also has a Moon-Pluto square or a Moon-Saturn opposition, or Venus is in the 10th conjunct Saturn or Chiron. Two very different images of mother are expressed by such combinations, one of which is beloved and beautiful, the other of which is threatening or hurtful. How can this man reconcile both of these images in one person?

Audience: He will move towards one and reject the other.

Liz: Yes, that is a characteristic pattern. The two attributes tend to manifest in later life as two people – the Betrayed and the Instrument of Betrayal. This is what Jung called a "split anima", or the female equivalent, a "split animus". Jung was quite preoccupied with the psychological dynamics of this pattern because he suffered from it himself. Although his definitions may be somewhat rigid and in need of greater flexibility in interpretation, they are useful in helping us to understand why we need triangles, and why the three points are secretly interchangeable. All three people are likely to suffer from the same unresolved parental dynamic. The inner split is particularly conducive to triangles when apparently irreconcilable opposites appear in the same beloved parent.

There are parents whose opposite sides are not very opposite. There are also parents whose opposites are very extreme. Such people are fascinating and often exercise great charisma because they are so unfathomable. The parent is beautiful and beloved, but also hurtful, cruel, unfeeling, devouring, or otherwise indigestible. It is very hard for a child's psyche to accept extreme opposites in one package. In adulthood, one may need two people through whom one can experience the ambivalent feelings. One person – usually the "illicit" lover – will get to play Venus, and the other – usually the established partner – will get to play Pluto or Saturn or Chiron or Mars or Uranus. But these roles are, of course, interchangeable.

Parental images which convey extreme opposites do contribute to a propensity for triangles. One gets involved with someone, and over time that person begins to take on the image of one side of the parent – usually the negative side. After a few years of living together, we begin to say to ourselves and our friends, "My partner's so possessive, I just have to have some breathing space." There is the voice of Venus in the 10th or the 4th, with the Moon square Pluto. Or we say, "My partner is so restrictive and conventional, I just have to be allowed to be myself." There is the voice of Venus in the 10th or 4th, with the Moon opposition Saturn. We discover that we aren't enjoying the beautiful, erotic, amusing relationship we hoped we would find. We then justify the lover who plays the role of Venus. The split is acted out, but it reflects two opposite qualities that we have not come to terms with in the beloved parent.

I cannot over-emphasise that such splits connected with the parents are, at the deepest level, concerned with opposites that haven't been resolved within oneself. As I said at the beginning, I believe that all triangles, including those arising from the family background, are ultimately concerned with our own unlived psychic life. If we were able to reconcile our own opposites, we could allow our parents to be contradictory as well. There is nothing extraordinary about a parent having both a lovable Venusian side and a withdrawn Saturnian side, or a demanding Plutonian side. Human beings are multifaceted, and they both love us and hurt us. We may also find these contradictions in our parents intolerable if the parents themselves cannot cope with their contradictions. Then we get no help in learning to integrate *our* contradictions. And some of these, in astrological terms, are simply too extreme to deal with in early life, even when the parents are trying hard. By this I mean configurations which link Venus or the Moon to Saturn or Chiron – these require a wisdom only time and experience can make available – or aspects involving Venus or the Moon and the outer planets, which are quite impossible for a young child to integrate on a personal level.

Split families

Triangles may develop within the family through the parents splitting up. Often this is portrayed in the birth chart by oppositions from the 4th to the 10th. Of course such natal aspects do not indicate categorically that the parents have separated; they reflect the child's perception of conflicts at work within the parental marriage. One *experiences* the parents in opposition, and when this happens, one usually takes sides; it is too painful to do otherwise. Sometimes one parent – and often both – cannot refrain from trying to elicit the child's loyalty as a weapon against the other parent. In this situation the bottom line, as ever, involves a contradiction within the individual, experienced first through the parents, reflected by opposing planets in the chart, and ultimately needing to be dealt with on an inner level. Unconscious manipulation on the part of the parents can make this a longer and harder process.

How many of you have parents who separated or divorced before you reached puberty? Quite a few of you have your hands up. Did any of you have the great good fortune of *not* feeling you had to take sides? Now I see no hands up at all. That isn't surprising. Even if we are subjected to no parental pressure at all, it is unlikely that we could cope with divided loyalties at such a young age. And in such circumstances, only incredibly wise and conscious parents could refrain from placing at least some emotional pressure on their child. Usually, if the parents are so unhappy that they are separating, they are not in the mood to be cooperative. Separations release primal emotions in us, and these may involve considerable vindictiveness – especially if the separation is triggered by a triangle.

Often the child winds up feeling like a football in the World Cup Final. There are certain scripts which appear to be read by lots of people. For example: "Your father was a cold, unfeeling man. He was incapable of loving. He didn't love any of us. Otherwise he wouldn't have gone off with that woman." The message to a male child might be: "I hope you don't grow up to be like him." The message to a female child might be: "I hope you don't grow up to marry somebody like him." Such messages do not have to be spoken. They may be communicated through martyrdom and ongoing misery. The Betrayed, when parents split up, will usually have great power over the child's psyche because of the compassion he or she can elicit from the child. Children are not equipped to step out of the fray and look objectively at the breakup. It must be someone's fault, either their own or one of the parents. And children also dare not reject those messages, because they are terrified of angering the parent who is now the sole caretaker.

In our society, when parents split up, the mother usually gets the child – even if this is not psychologically the best solution for that particular child. There are many instances where the father might be emotionally better equipped to raise the child, but the courts of law do not see it that way. The mother must be quite floridly appalling to have her child taken away from her. Almost invariably, unless the separation is amicable, the mother will get sole custody. If the parents are not actually married, the father's rights may be nonexistent in terms of access. Fathers' rights are presently a hot topic; perhaps some of you have been following the various articles in the papers. One might well question whether a father really merits having his child torn away and turned against him solely because he has betrayed his wife. But triangles have a way of generating very unpleasant emotional consequences which carry on down the generations and breed more triangles.

Divided loyalties

Divorcing or separating parents – or even those who remain living together but are emotionally alienated – will generally demand that the child choose between them. The love for the other parent must be denied, suppressed, silenced. This is terribly human. If we are hurt by someone, we find it hard to bear if someone else we love shows affection to the person who has hurt us. If there are oppositions between the 4th and the 10th in the child's chart, then the child's own inner division colludes with the parents' division. I have seen many clients over the years who have clearly felt great love for a parent, yet the love has had to be denied. When Venus, Moon, Neptune, Sun, or Jupiter is in a parental house, there is usually a powerful positive bond with the parent, even if very difficult significators are also shown, and even if the parent is absent. If any of these planets are in the 4th, they are likely to describe quite idealised feelings for the father. The Sun conjunct Venus or trine Jupiter or Neptune makes a similar statement. If there is alienation between the parents, it may prove impossible for the person to keep such feelings in consciousness. The ambivalence and sense of disloyalty to the mother may be too painful.

Perhaps the father has left because of another relationship. Perhaps he marries again, and has other children. Then the problem is compounded, because the child's own jealousy allies with the jealousy of the mother, making it impossible for the emotional bond with the father to be recognised. The relationship is destroyed, and the child, who is now grown up, says, "Oh, I haven't seen my father much since the divorce. I have very little to do with him. We don't have much of a relationship." All the positive, loving feelings have been pushed underground, because we don't cope well with divided loyalties. We suppress them because we have to survive psychologically. And we have to live with mother.

If there are planets in the 4th which suggest love and idealisation, and the parents split up, something of our own soul remains deeply unconscious and unintegrated. Then the suppressed feelings for the father may provide fodder for later triangles, because we are still seeking someone who can embody the planetary archetype for us. This can apply to both sexes. It should not be surprising if a woman coming from this kind of family background, with this kind of chart configuration, winds up playing the Instrument of Betrayal and hurls herself at a married man. Equally, she may find herself as the Betrayed, married to someone just like the father she adored and lost. Or she may become the Betrayer as a defence, because she is determined not to wind up like her mother.

A man with this background and chart configuration may wind up unconsciously choosing a woman like his mother and then, to his horror, finds himself in his father's shoes – and feels empathy toward this father for the first time. You can see why a triangle might be likely. The more unconscious the feelings are toward the beloved missing parent, the more certain they will be to emerge later in an adult relationship. And perhaps it is sometimes right and necessary that we work it through in this way. How else can we even begin to know we have lost something, let alone find it within?

These unconscious feelings may also cross sexes. They are not necessarily going to limit themselves to women who seek the missing father in other men, or men who find themselves in the same situation as their fathers. A man who has lost his father, and who has Venus, Sun, Neptune, or the Moon in the 4th, may seek the qualities of the father in women. Or if he is gay, he may seek them in another man. We need to think of these triangular dynamics, not from a perspective of rigid sexual demarcations, but as a way of attempting to heal a wound and find a lost piece of soul. They reflect our efforts to contact archetypal qualities in our adult relationships which we glimpsed first in the parent and which we ultimately need to find in ourselves. Because we carry something unresolved, we may faithfully recreate our parents' marriage. Then we may find ourselves in the same triangle, on any of the three points, with either or both sexes.

These underlying dynamics are actually very obvious. The difficulty lies in remembering them when we are in the middle of a triangle. It is very easy if we are the astrologer or psychotherapist, or even the friend with a certain amount of psychological knowledge. We may clearly see the familial roots of many adult triangles if we are observers, but it is extremely difficult to see them when we are involved in the triangle. And the more unconscious we are of our parental dynamics, the more emotionally compulsive the triangle is likely to be, and the harder it is to see clearly.

Audience: Even if you *do* see it, that doesn't mean you can get out of it!

Liz: True – we may still be bound, because we have to live something through. We do not heal anything through the exercise of reason alone. But the emotional pattern which the triangle brings to the surface may change, and the outcome may be very different, internally if not externally. The sad thing about triangles is that, if no insight is gained, everybody loses. On one level or another, all three people wind up hurt. Even if the Instrument of Betrayal succeeds in "getting" the parent-surrogate that he or she has been fighting for, it is a pyrrhic victory. The Betrayer has to choose in the end, so even if something is won, something is also lost. And the victory is no less pyrrhic for the Betrayed who succeeds in "getting back" the erring partner. We have exercised our Oedipal power and reversed the original Oedipal defeat that we suffered in childhood. But what have we really won?

Audience: Resentment.

Liz: Yes, resentment seems to come with the package, no matter which point of the triangle we favour. If we are the Instrument of Betrayal, we have led someone else into making a very painful choice, and there may be a lot of suffering, not only emotionally but also financially; and so there will be resentment. But more importantly, if we remain unconscious, we have done nothing to heal the inner split which lies behind the triangle. We have only achieved an external solution. Nothing has really changed.

Alienation from one's own sex

There is another potential consequence of family triangles which I have already touched on briefly – alienation from one's own sex. An unresolved Oedipal battle, if it takes place with the same-sex parent, may result in a loss of trust in one's sexuality. What effect might this have, in terms of our friendships and the way we interact with our own sex later? For a woman, what might it mean to have a mother who is an insurmountable rival, at whose hands one has suffered a humiliating childhood defeat?

Audience: All women become rivals.

Liz: Yes. Confidence in her femininity is undermined, and because she does not trust herself, she will not trust other women. They will all seem to have the power to "take away" those she loves. This mistrust of one's own sex can be very acute. A woman may have a wonderful friendship with another woman, and then she meets a really lovely man, and they get involved, and what does she do about introducing her friend to her partner? A chronic undercurrent of anxiety and suspicion may make life very difficult. Unconsciously she may even set herself up for betrayal. She may unconsciously select as friends those of her own sex who act out her unresolved conflict with her mother, because they have unresolved conflicts with *their* mothers. The same applies to men. If a man has felt humiliated and defeated by his father, then in any later relationship in which he becomes involved, the issue of rivalry may keep raising its head, because other men always seem to be potential threats. One must be on guard all the time. This is not possessiveness in the ordinary Pluto/Scorpio sense. Its roots are quite different.

Saturn, Chiron, and sexual insecurity

Configurations such as Venus aspecting Saturn or Chiron can contribute to this dynamic, not because they are in themselves Oedipal, but because they reflect certain insecurities which can be compounded by the family triangle. Mars aspecting Saturn or Chiron may also reflect anxieties which are heightened by family triangles and lead to feelings of defeat. These sets of aspects may compel a repetition of the failure later, or an attempt to heal the hurt by proving one's lovability and sexual potency through triangles.

There is no single astrological pattern which describes a propensity for triangles. Rather, there are many possible combinations which each describe different images of and responses to the parents, and different ways of reacting to the natural and inevitable Oedipal phase of childhood. Venus-Saturn and Venus-Chiron do not "cause" a person to be drawn into triangles. They describe an innate awareness of the limits of human love. In childhood, when there is no real comprehension of what this could offer in a positive sense, such awareness may lead the child into feeling inadequate, damaged, and powerless. The alienation of a beloved parent will then be attributed to one's own failings, and later in life one may feel one cannot "keep" a partner because a rival will always take him or her away.

Audience: Would Saturn in the 4th in a woman's chart, or Saturn in the 10th in a man's, mean the same thing?

Liz: There are likely to be feelings of rejection, which as a child one might take as an indication of one's own failure. But usually there will be additional significators of a more personal kind, like Saturn in hard aspect to Sun, Moon, or Venus. Or there might be an indication of an idealised parental image through aspects to the Sun or Moon from Venus, Jupiter, or Neptune. Then, if Saturn is also in the 4th or 10th, the rejection may be felt as sexual. Saturn alone as a parental significator may describe alienation, but not necessarily the complex emotional pattern of an Oedipal defeat.

Midlife Oedipal antics

Audience: Do Oedipal experiences tend to come out in midlife?

Liz: They often come out with a show of fireworks in midlife, because the planets making their cycles at that time – Saturn, Neptune, Uranus and, a bit later, Chiron – may trigger configurations which connect us to childhood issues. There is frequently a great deal of unlived life clamouring for expression under the midlife group of transits, and unresolved Oedipal issues that have managed to remain buried may finally break out because they are carrying unlived psychic life with them. But it depends on how powerful the Oedipal conflict is. It may come out much earlier. There are people who experience triangles from the very beginning of their relationship lives, including relationships formed at school during the teens.

Audience: I have been thinking about how many people break up their relationships at midlife, and I was wondering if this reflects the Oedipal issues coming up.

Liz: Not all triangles have Oedipal roots, and Oedipal roots themselves involve something deeper. If there is an Oedipal pattern which is unresolved, such as the Venusian issues we have been looking at, it is likely to erupt under the appropriate transits. That, for many people, may be the only way any kind of healing or resolution becomes possible. But behind the Oedipal issue is the archetypal issue. Why do we seek the love of that particular parent, and what does the parent symbolise for our own souls? This is invariably linked with what needs to be developed in oneself.

At midlife, if important bits of oneself have remained undeveloped, they may come bursting out, especially under Uranus opposing its own place. Often, the first place we meet these unknown bits of ourselves is in somebody else. It is the most characteristic way in which the unconscious psyche knocks on the door and demands integration. The need to become more of what one really is may begin with a sudden attraction. Unlived dimensions of ourselves may also appear in a rival, who may be more important psychologically than the person over whom one is fighting. But if there has been no pattern of triangles earlier, the eruption of one at midlife may not necessarily imply an Oedipal problem. And if it does, the problem needs to be seen in a larger context.

Toni Wolff, who was Jung's mistress for many years, once said that, if one's partner is involved in an affair with someone else, it is a good idea to ask the rival to tea and find out who they are. One might discover something about oneself. Especially in midlife, the rival may be the one who has the most to teach us about what we are not living of ourselves. An old, unresolved family wound may certainly be activated in midlife. But the activation could be fuelled by the emergence of psychic life which is trying to get integrated into consciousness. It has been split off and now appears outside as somebody else.

The unobtainable parent: astrological significators

An unobtainable parent implies an Oedipal defeat. But it may not be so simple. There are different kinds of unobtainability, and different responses to a sense of loss. Sometimes unobtainability is accompanied by feelings of great yearning, idealisation, and a kind of sweet, pain-ridden hopelessness. Even if unconscious, there is an image of the parent as both victim and redeemer, and this imbues him or her with a quality of divinity. Neptune in the 4th or 10th is usually descriptive of this kind of image. While the person may be quite unaware of this idealisation of the parent, it will usually emerge in later relationships.

Uranus in the 4th or 10th is also prone to idealisation. But Uranian unobtainability is not usually characterised by the poignant, bittersweet longing so typical of Neptune. With Uranus there is often a sense of loss, but it feels colder and may be accompanied by the conviction that one cannot meet the unobtainable parent's standards of perfection. We might also find planetary combinations like Moon-Neptune or Moon-Uranus when the unobtainable parent is the mother, and Sun-Neptune or Sun-Uranus when it is the father. With both these outer planets as parental significators, however, the very nature of the planet – collective rather than personal – suggests an image of a parent who is unreachable because he or she embodies a transpersonal quality. Uranus and Neptune as parental significators do not describe human characteristics, and any child who perceives the parent as a carrier for the larger life of the cosmos will probably carry a sense of loss – not necessarily because the parent has been a "bad" or rejecting parent, but because no human parent could possibly mediate this dimension of life.

Audience: What about a hard aspect between Venus and Saturn? That seems to me to describe unobtainable love.

Liz: This depends on how we define "unobtainable". Venus-Saturn describes a perception of *limited* love. Saturn feels different from the outer planets when it is involved as a parental significator or forms a hard aspect to Venus. Uranus and Neptune imply a sense that the parent is lost, far away on some other plane, beyond one's mortal grasp. It is a very special kind of alienation, which usually involves extreme idealisation. Saturnian parents may be perceived as hurtful and rejecting, but usually they are also perceived as human. When Venus is involved with Saturn, or when it is in the 4th or 10th and there are also Moon-Saturn or Sun-Saturn aspects, there may be a gnawing feeling that one is not worthy of love. The emotional limits which are experienced in childhood are felt to be one's own limits – as, indeed, they ultimately are, although their deeper meaning is not negative. Certainly Venus-Saturn configurations are regularly involved in triangles. But I would be more inclined to link these with what I have called defensive triangles.

Audience: How about Moon-Pluto?

Liz: Moon-Pluto does not usually describe an unobtainable parent. It may be quite the opposite. The parent often feels too close, too invasive and powerful. The mythic quality which all outer planets convey certainly applies to Pluto, and sometimes there is a profound experience of loss. But this is more likely to result in a deep mistrust of life. Idealisation is not something I would associate with a child's experience of a Plutonian parent. Chiron, on the other hand, may be involved when the parent feels unobtainable. We might see Venus-Chiron, Moon-Chiron, Sun-Chiron, or Chiron in one of the parental houses. The parent is unobtainable because he or she is wounded, a victim of life, someone too hurt to offer the love which is needed. The parent may also be the wounder who inflicts injury. But the child usually perceives this as something forgivable – even if the perception is forgotten in adulthood – because the parent has been wounded by forces in life much greater than himself or herself.

Audience: Almost any planet can be involved.

Liz: Almost any planet can be involved in a propensity for triangles. And there is a level on which all parents are unobtainable, because we cannot remain fused with them forever, and must eventually face our separateness. But the unobtainable, idealised parent, as an early experience which compels a person into triangles, is not usually represented by just any old planet. It is the outer planets – with the exception of Pluto – which seem to describe this special feeling. That is because the outer planets reflect collective energies rather than personal ones. Even if the parent carrying the image is at home all the time, he or she is mediating something much greater than one human being's feelings and behaviour. The outer planets can't really be mediated, except in a very limited sense. They seem huge and godlike, beyond mortal ken. That is why the parent carrying this projection seems unobtainable. A parent who hurts or rejects does not feel the same, and the emotional dynamics of the later triangle are different.

Audience: You haven't mentioned placements like Venus in Cancer or Venus in Capricorn – only the 4th and 10th houses.

Liz: I'm talking about parental significators, which I believe are represented by planets on the 4th/10th axis and by planets aspecting the Sun and Moon. Venus in Cancer by itself doesn't suggest a powerful parental issue which might fuel a later triangle. The Venus sign suggests particular qualities that one loves, values, and finds beautiful. But this may not necessarily be attached to the parents. Venus in Cancer or Capricorn may find beauty in one's home, one's land, one's roots, or the place of one's birth. But signs are not the same as houses. They describe qualities rather than situations. And they are not the same as aspects, which have movement and intent. The Venus sign doesn't have the energetic dynamic of a house placement or an aspect. It might tell us about what is loved in the parent because this is what is loved in life itself.

Oppositions between 4th and 10th

Audience: You talked earlier about oppositions between planets in the 10th and 4th. What about the rulers of the 10th and 4th in opposition?

Liz: The more indirect the significator, the more diluted it becomes. The experience of a planet in a house is direct and powerful. It is an encounter with a god in a particular sphere of life. When that sphere is parental, we meet the archetypal patterns of our fate embodied in our parents. Other factors, such as the 4th and 10th house rulers, will certainly tell us something about how we experience our parents. So will the signs on the MC and IC. But they don't describe the primal impact of a planet in the 4th or the 10th. I am looking at these because it is often the inability to process planets in parental houses which impels us, later in life, to enter triangles in order to work something through.

Audience: What about the ruler of the 10th or 4th in the 7th?

Liz: Then one may be looking for a partner who possesses qualities that belong to the parent. But that alone may not describe a family triangle. There may be qualities in the parent that are well worth finding in a partner. It doesn't necessarily reflect a difficult dynamic. It links the parent with one's image of the "other", but says nothing about whether there is a conflict or sense of Oedipal defeat.

Audience: Do you mean any kind of opposition between the 10th and 4th?

Liz: Some oppositions are more opposite than others. Mercury opposite Jupiter hurts less than Saturn opposite Neptune, because there is always some dialogue possible between the king of the gods and his messenger. They are not archetypal enemies. Other planets are. Then the parents may seem irreconcilably divided, and one feels one must give up the bond with one of them entirely.

Not all divorces end in the child feeling one of the parents is utterly unobtainable. Sometimes there is enduring anger or fear of further rejection. The child, now adult, may choose to repudiate the hurtful parent as an act of revenge. But some children experience a sense of hopeless, irredeemable loss. This often occurs when an outer planet occupies one of the parental houses and opposes a planet in the other parental house. In the end, it is one's own opposition, and therefore the split between planetary gods lies within one's own soul. The parents are perceived through that lens. An unobtainable parent leaves us with the feeling that something we love and need has been irrevocably lost. Hurt generally accompanies any experience of separation or irreconcilable conflict between the parents, but the special feeling of unobtainability leaves us with an unfulfilled and often compulsive need to find what we feel we have lost. When an outer planet is involved, what has been lost is not only a beloved person, but a sense of oneness with the larger cosmos. We must obtain what was unobtainable so that we can feel we are part of a larger life.

The rulers of the parental houses in the 7th, or the ruler of the 7th in the 10th or 4th, do link one's image of the partner with the parent. One's father might have loved reading and taught one how to read early; this parent may have fostered a love of books and an appreciation of people who themselves love books. One may, in such a case, have the ruler of the 4th placed in the 7th in Gemini, or Mercury ruling the 7th and placed in the 4th. So? That is not necessarily a family triangle, and the book-loving father may not be unobtainable. Not every link between our adult loves and our parental relationships is Oedipal or full of conflict. These chart links may describe qualities that we see and love and value in the parent. Then we see and love and value those things in someone else later in life. If we are at all lucky, there will be something in both parents that we can love and admire. But when the parental planetary picture in the natal chart suggests great love *and* great loss, the sense of unobtainability may shape one's later relationships.

The pursuit of the unobtainable parent, especially if outer planets are involved, can be expressed through non-human elements, such as a compulsive quest for perfect spiritual enlightenment, or a relentless determination to produce the perfect work of art. These things are by their nature beyond our reach, and they may serve as the Instrument of Betrayal which sabotages an existing relationship. The pursuit of the perfect love may also be another name for the pursuit of the unobtainable parent. While this compulsive pursuit may involve the Betrayer in a whole series of affairs, behind the myriad discarded lovers lies the flickering, half-glimpsed image of the vanished parent. Behind the parent lies something vast and ineffable.

Pursuit of the unobtainable is often the affliction of the Betrayer and the Instrument of Betrayal. But it may equally require us to play the Betrayed. The unobtainable may be one's partner; "unobtainable" does not always mean "married to someone else". The beloved may be unobtainable for many reasons. Being involved with a partner who is a drug addict presents us with a painful experience of unobtainability. We can't ever relate fully to the person, because he or she is married to the drug. The same could be said of an alcoholic partner. Falling in love with a priest committed to celibacy is another instance of unobtainability, because the third point of the triangle is Mother Church, or God. Here we can see very clearly the archetypal image standing behind the vanished parent, whose absence has been infused with the *mana* of divinity.

Audience: Could you say more about Saturn conjunct Venus? I am interested in what you are calling "defensive triangles".

Liz: I will talk in more detail about these later. Briefly, defensive triangles spring from strong feelings of inadequacy or unlovability. Such feelings are typical of Venus-Saturn aspects. We looked at this earlier. Venus-Saturn has an acute sense of the limitations of love, and will experience love as limited from very early in life. Often there is a kind of conditional love offered within the family – love which seems dependent on one looking or performing the right way, being the right kind of child, doing the right thing. Love may be present, but it must be earned. I doubt that this is entirely imposed by the parents. The child with Venus-Saturn is inherently deeply sensitive to Saturnian expectations, and reacts accordingly. In the end, it is one's own Saturn which imposes those exacting standards. Unconditional love is a wonderful ideal, but few human beings can maintain it all the time. Tired or stressed parents may be perceived as limiting because they cannot respond in just the right way, just when the child wants it. Emotional inhibitions in the parent may not block love, but may block the overt expression of it; the Venus-Saturn child sees only what is lacking.

With Venus-Saturn, one is painfully aware of one's own limitations, and feels one must work to earn the right to be loved. Feelings of inadequacy are the usual response to such a perception of life. With maturity and consciousness, Venus-Saturn may change its negative stance, and develop acceptance of and compassion for human limits. The sense that love must be earned may then operate as a deep sense of responsibility in relationships. One no longer assumes one is a failure because one cannot always love unconditionally; nor does one expect such love from others. However, without consciousness, the feelings of inadequacy may be extremely painful, and may drive the person into believing that he or she will inevitably lose the beloved to someone else. This can create enormous defences against commitment. On the surface, there may be a hard, unforgiving sense of being disappointed in others. Underneath, there is the gnawing feeling that one is a disappointment oneself. Triangles motivated by such unconscious feelings are a protection against being too vulnerable. Dividing one's affections between two people ensures that neither person can ever have the power to totally destroy one's life. Falling in love with a succession of unavailable partners may also be an unconscious means of avoiding deep commitment.

Triangles and society

Audience: There was something you said earlier that really struck me. You said that very often, the complex nature of triangles is at odds with what we have been taught about relationships. We are taught that we can only love one person exclusively. Would the inner split involve, not only a conflict between different qualities or parental images, but the very huge split between what one feels and the kind of taboos that our society imposes? I wonder whether one of the main elements in the difficulties we have in dealing with triangles is the guilt involved in what we are doing.

Liz: Collectively generated guilt undoubtedly makes matters worse – it is much harder to find and affirm one's individual values and feelings. The furious noise generated by what "they" say can easily stifle that quiet inner voice. And in matters of the heart, we are imbued with many social ideas and ideals which are utterly out of touch with human nature. We might even say that the split lies in the larger body of the collective. The medieval Christian world-view – that the flesh is evil and only the spirit counts – reflects a psychic split in the collective that still, even in our so-called enlightened times, causes a great deal of misery. That can make an inner split worse, and our perceptions and behaviour may deteriorate accordingly. But there are usually also indications in the individual chart of a deep dichotomy between one's inner values and one's perception of what the world requires. Otherwise, one would not be so identified with prevailing collective attitudes.

For example, a 10th house Saturn, or an emphasis in Capricorn, may suggest that worldly opinion matters a great deal to the person. Then a triangle may be especially painful because one is judging oneself and others with a kind of built-in Freudian superego. This makes it hard to deal with an inner split compassionately and constructively. Or the person may be extremely idealistic in matters of love, with configurations such as Venus conjunct Neptune in Libra. Venus-Neptune suggests there is intense romantic idealism and a belief in perfect, unconditional love.

The Saturn-Neptune conjunction in Libra has produced an entire generation of incurable idealists. Venus-Uranus and Uranus in the 7th can sometimes be extremely idealistic in terms of believing in the possibility of perfect relationship. The Moon in Libra or Aquarius can also reflect this kind of idealism. The person may hold a belief that love should be a certain way, either because the Great They say so or because one's own ideals demand it. Then our inner dichotomies seem unbridgeable and unforgivable. I do agree – the collective makes it hard for us to deal with triangles creatively. But the extreme susceptibility some people exhibit toward the collective reflects something in the individual.

Sexual exclusivity

Audience: When you quoted Toni Wolff saying one should invite one's rival for tea, it suddenly sounded as though it could be so easy to work things out. You could save so much trouble. But it is so difficult to invite them for tea without having a knife in your pocket, just in case things get really tough.

Audience: Or you could put something in the tea.

Liz: You may also have to be careful about your partner putting something in *your* tea, if he finds out you have been getting chummy with his lover. Many people have an investment in keeping their splits properly split. If the Betrayed and the Instrument of Betrayal become friends, it may remove one of the main purposes of the triangle, which is to act out the inner conflict rather than looking within. If the triangle is defensive or based on power motives, the Betrayer may need to play one end off against the other.

When we attempt to understand triangles, we look through our own lenses. If we are Uranian, we may say, "We should all be friends." This may be absolutely right in principle, but human emotions do not necessarily flow in accord with principles. We can also perceive a triangle from a Plutonian point of view. Then it is a life-threat. Someone is trying take away something that is ours, and we will die if we lose it; therefore we must fight, and the end justifies the means. We can look at triangles as a Neptunian, and see them as karmic, or a chance to have a really good self-sacrificial binge. Or, if we are Jupiterian, we can view them as an AFOG – Another F*****g Opportunity for Growth.[6]

Our birth charts will describe our attitudes toward triangles, both our own and other people's. Uranus will often try to apply logic. It "should" be possible to detach and sit down with the rival and discuss life. After all, the two of you love the same person; you have a great deal in common because you value the same things. Mind you, I don't think Toni Wolff spoke from Uranian logic. She spoke from bitter, hard-won wisdom born out of years of painful experience. But what is it that makes detachment so difficult?

---

6 This wonderful phrase was passed on to me by Anne Whitaker.

We must then ask the question: Why are we so insistent on having exclusive rights to someone? The area where we usually seek to claim exclusivity is in our sexual relationships. We can often bear a triangle if we have not been sexually betrayed. We may be capable of allowing our loved ones to move elsewhere intellectually, spiritually, and even emotionally. But to share someone sexually seems to be extremely difficult – perhaps not for all people, but for a great many people, even the Uranians who claim they do not or should not mind. Why does sex make us so incredibly vulnerable? We manage to live with some triangles, albeit grudgingly. But the moment the sexual element is involved, it seems most of us cannot bear to share.

Audience: I think it's fear. But I'm not sure what of.

Audience: We stake our claims through sex.

Liz: Yes, it seems we do. But why?

Audience: It is a mystery. I'm not sure there is an answer.

Audience: If there are any answers, they probably go beyond psychology. Maybe there is something biological behind it which is very powerful. The survival of the genes of one's own line is very basic and animal. It's part of the human dimension of relationship.

Audience: What about if you're gay?

Liz: If one is gay, triangles can be just as painful and difficult, and they spring from the same sources. The range of feelings and motivations is no different. This suggests that the "preserve the genes" element in sexual exclusivity is not all that relevant.

Audience: I think it is because we are really instinctual creatures, and it is a threat to have someone else invade your territory and take what you feel is yours. There are also a lot of fears around being of no value. If another person comes between me and my partner, it is a threat to who I am. What am I worth if someone else is valued the same as me? If my partner can share the same things with someone else, I'm not special any more.

Liz: I believe there is some truth in everything that all of you have said. But we aren't really any closer to understanding why intellectual and creative sharing don't make us feel as threatened as sexual sharing. There are people who are intensely possessive of their partners' inner lives, and resent any little thought-pocket which the partner keeps private. But sexual betrayal, for many people, is the worst hurt that can be inflicted by someone one loves. As one of you has already suggested, there may not be any answer. There is a mystery here. Sexual energy moves us into areas where we become extremely vulnerable, in a way that we do not experience in other spheres. It is worth thinking about the astrological 8th house, which is concerned with the experience of letting go, not only in the sexual act, but also in death. The operative phrase is "letting go". In sexual exchange, we are less in control than in any other area of relationship, and betrayal reflects back to us the reality of forces in life and in ourselves which we will never be able to master.

Audience: For some time I lived in a spiritual community, and we weren't supposed to feel any jealousy or try to make partners exclusive. So everyone had a turn at someone different. We all had relationships with different people. It was almost like a rota.

Liz: It's Tuesday, it must be George. How boring. But you have touched on something very interesting. There are, of course, no triangles in such a setup. The transformative potential evoked by the pain of a triangle cannot find a way in. We seem to need triangles. Much as we scream and whinge, we require them.

Audience: In this spiritual community, it's true that the spark went out of sex – all the lovely feelings of something magical happening. It just became a bodily release. Triangles resolve something. We are looking for that feeling of something being resolved, whatever it is.

Liz: Perhaps we are made aware of something unresolved. It has always been there, but we can't recognise it until it materialises in our outer lives. It is like having a subterranean itch which, when it finally surfaces on the skin, can at last be scratched. A general sexual free-for-all doesn't do this. Triangles reach the parts that other relationship dynamics cannot reach. We need triangles for our souls, however much they cost us. They open us up and potentially reveal things to us about our deepest inner natures. This may be one of the reasons why contrived attempts at sexual "liberation" so often become dreary and boring. There is no tension and no conflict, and the interest goes out of it. The inner world is no longer invoked.

Polygamy, Neptunian communes, and other amusements

Audience: Could you say something about polygamous societies and harems? Does the same emotional mess play itself out? Or is it my Neptune in the 4th that makes me believe equal relationships between three people are possible if one is open and honest?

Liz: I don't have an answer to either question. As far as your Neptunian vision goes, many things might be possible if we could live up to Neptune's ideals, which always require a sacrifice of some kind. Aspirations of this kind are worth honouring and striving for. But the gap between possibility and the actuality of human nature also needs to be respected. And more basic human emotions – those connected with the Moon, Mars, and Pluto – likewise need to be honoured. They may not be "higher", but they may be equally valuable and necessary to life, and sometimes they are more honest. Neptune's ideals may be noble and beautiful, but they can hide a multitude of infantile fusion-fantasies and unresolved separation anxieties. An inability to live up to Neptunian ideals and remain self-sacrificing in the emotional cross-currents of a triangle isn't necessarily a sign of psychological or spiritual weakness. It may be a sign of strength.

Regarding your question about harems and polygamous societies, I have never lived in such a society, nor had clients who have made this their way of life, so I can't tell you from any direct experience whether there are rivalries and jealousies. From what I have read in both literature and individual biographies, there are, and they can be murderous. History is littered with florid examples. Alexander the Great had two wives, the first a princess called Roxanne from Sogdiana, the second called Stateira, the daughter of the Persian King. Both appeared to accept their status, which was the social norm of the time. But when Alexander died, the very first thing Roxanne did was to poison her rival.

Under prevailing social customs, one may be entitled to several wives, or a wife and a concubine. The women appear to accept this because they cannot buck the system and might suffer severe punishment if they try. But there are often deep hatreds and hurts which cannot be voiced. In modern Western society we can divorce the erring partner for adultery. This may do nothing to reveal the underlying meaning of the triangle, but it gives us the feeling that we have some control over our lives. In polygamous societies no such option is permitted, so one has to make the best of it. In Britain in Victorian times, adultery was not considered grounds for divorce. A woman who left her husband because of his infidelity – however florid, and even if he infected her with syphilis – stood to lose her children, her home, her reputation, and any property and wealth she might have brought into the marriage. That was the norm of the time. Those women, too, had to make the best of their triangles.

We cannot really know how these individuals feel unless they tell us, and they may not tell the truth. Perhaps they don't know the truth. The belief that it is possible to have non-monogamous, open relationships is as old as the triangle. So is the argument about human nature being naturally polygamous. As with the animal kingdom, perhaps some humans are more polygamous than others. Geese mate for life; so do some humans. Cats are utterly promiscuous; so are some humans. We are back once again to individual character, whether that individual lives in modern London or ancient Sogdiana. Sexually "free" communes have existed since ancient times, always pursuing the ideal of freedom from the jealousy, rage, and humiliation that afflict so many people when the magic *temenos* of sexual exclusivity is broken. The longevity of the ideal suggests that it is an archetypal image. But the longevity of the ideal of monogamy suggests that it, too, is archetypal.

Jung's triangle required enormous sacrifice and suffering on the part of both women. It may well be possible to achieve a loving, harmonious triangle. But the price is very high. When people claim they have managed it, there is often a serious dissociation from the feelings. Sometimes the claim is made by the Betrayer, who has an investment in ignoring the emotional price others are paying. I have heard this claim a lot in New Age circles. There is often an odour about it which is not quite clean. And one can grow very cynical after one hears it enough from the mouths of group leaders and gurus whose philosophy justifies sexual exploitation of vulnerable disciples. I really have no answers. I am aware that our collective cultural and religious ethos does affect how we experience sexual exclusivity. Where we once sought our experience of mystical union in religion, we now seek it in human love. This places tremendous pressure on relationships. We want something from other human beings which may be possible only through spiritual commitment or involvement in creative work. We will look at this issue more closely when we look at triangles involving the quest for the unobtainable.

Triangles and sexual abuse

Audience: I would like to hear something about the triangle and sexual abuse of children within the family.

Liz: I can see this is going to be a hot day. Sexual abuse may reflect a destructive family triangle. But triangular or not, it usually involves a complex family dynamic. It is always easy to blame the abuser, but usually hidden family conflicts, particularly in the parents' marriage, are at work behind the scenes. The pathology of the abuser may be exhaustively examined, but this alone will not reveal the whole picture. This is understood very well in analytic approaches to family therapy. I have found in my analytic work that when there has been abuse, the individual's rage and feelings of betrayal are as great, if not greater, toward the parent who failed to offer protection as toward the one who perpetrated the abuse. This is a painful and difficult issue, but the question must be asked: Where was mother (or, less commonly, father), and why didn't she (he) notice what was happening? And what if she (he) did notice, and said and did nothing? Sometimes abusing a child springs from the wish to hurt, degrade, or take revenge on the partner. The child, forced into playing the role of the Instrument of Betrayal, becomes a means of injuring the one toward whom the rage is really felt.

Every case of abuse has its own individual backdrop, and when one comes to know the family history, no one comes away with clean hands except the child. I don't believe any child invites abuse. Children may express erotic feelings, but they are not courting adult sexual activity when they are flirtatious. However, they do get flirtatious. If the family dynamic is already a powder keg, and enough rage and destructiveness have built up, the child may be the unwilling recipient of the explosion. The lit match that ignites the powder keg may be the child's Oedipal inclinations. More often, it is the parent's consumption of alcohol. There may be many factors involved. A religious background which imposes impossible sexual repressions on family members may also be a factor, and this has little to do with triangles. There have been some particularly repulsive examples of this in the press recently, involving orphaned children looked after by abusive caretakers, both male and female, in religious orders.

The abuser, as we know from statistics, has probably himself or herself been abused as a child, so power issues resulting in the desire to inflict cruelty are often involved. The core of a specific case of child abuse may not be a triangle in the sense we are discussing today. It may be the backlash of something that is going on between the parents, or a scapegoat pattern embedded in the family psyche. But I don't believe the suffering of the victim ceases, nor is there real forgiveness of self and others, unless there is a deep understanding of the entire family dynamic. It is too easy to simply point the finger and blame the abuser. That does not stop the pain. Perhaps some of you who have been through this kind of experience have worked with it therapeutically. You will probably know that the sense of being betrayed, not only by the abuser but by the other parent, is often the hidden thing one dare not face. It needs to be faced. Yet even where there is unconscious or quasi-conscious collusion between the parents, there is usually a much longer family history. Blame placed on one individual is no ultimate solution. Child abuse is a bottomless pit in which the social services flounder, devoid of real understanding. I believe that healing depends on understanding the whole family setup, rather than just heaping blame on the abuser. The family triangle may be only part of the picture, if it plays any part at all. Naturally, some of you are just bursting to ask me if child abuse can be "seen" in a chart.

Audience: Well, yes, I was just going to ask that question.

Liz: I believe it is impossible to distinguish, in a chart, between psychological and physical events in childhood. Equally, it is impossible to tell from a chart what degree of consciousness parents bring to the patterns they embody for their child. The planets describe the archetypal core of a pattern, not whether or in what way it has been concretised. Even if we feel that some kind of abuse has occurred, it may be in a much subtler form. The violation of a child's psychic boundaries may be entirely unconscious and go unnoticed because no "event" has taken place. Some astrologers insist that such-and-such a configuration indicates child abuse. I am not convinced of this.

One may experience the parent as powerful, controlling, and invasive. Then we may expect to find a difficult Pluto involved. One may experience the parent as aggressive or violent, on one level or another. Then we may expect to find an unhappy Mars. Difficult Mars-Pluto and Mars-Chiron configurations involving parental significators may suggest feelings of being overpowered, humiliated, or manipulated. Mars-Neptune may suggest feelings of victimisation. Sometimes physical abuse is the form through which these experiences come, but most of the time it isn't. Mars-Pluto in the 4th may describe a father who is decent and caring, but who is a managerial type, used to dictating to those around him. A parent may be described by these planetary combinations and is experienced as expressing the archetypal pattern positively. Then the parent mediates the power and energy of Pluto and Mars, or the creative imagination of Mars and Neptune, or the restraint and tenacity of Mars and Chiron, in a constructive way which helps the child to identify with the best qualities of these aspects.

The 8th house can describe powerful encounters with the forces of the unconscious, and Chiron, Mars, Pluto, and sometimes Uranus, in configurations involving this house, may describe a psychic inheritance which is explosive and erupts in one form or another during childhood. But the eruption may be emotional and not physical, and it may not necessarily involve an experience or feeling of abuse. Often an emphasis in the 8th reflects the early death of one of the parents, or a separation between the parents which has been hard to bear, or other disturbing events within the family – the illness of a sibling, the psychotic breakdown of a family member, a drug or alcohol problem in one of the parents. Such experiences expose the child to the realm of the unconscious at a very young age, and teach a profound lesson about the limits of individual ego-control.

A child's Oedipal fantasies, healthy though they may be, can colour the perceptions of the parent's behaviour as well as the parent's character. Venus-Pluto in the 4th describes a strong emotional attachment to the father. But we cannot know from the chart alone whether this father responded, or on what level, or whether a sexual encounter, recalled many years later, is his daughter's or son's fantasy. There has been a lot of media publicity lately about the fraught issue of "remembering" abuse many years afterward. How many of these cases are real? How many are fantasies? How many are "true" on an unconscious psychic level, but "untrue" on a physical one? How many are the product of an angry adult retaliating against childhood feelings of rejection with the biggest, nastiest weapon he or she can find? How many are imagined memories reflecting a child's unrequited love? We cannot know unless we work with each case individually, and even then, we may never know the whole truth. This issue is currently open to a great deal of manipulation by therapists and the social services, and even more by solicitors. We may well wonder, at times, who is the real abuser.

Mars and triangles

Audience: I was thinking that Mars must be involved, not only in child abuse, but in family triangles in general.

Liz: Mars is often linked with parental significators when abuse, on one level or another, has occurred. We know this with hindsight. But Mars will not in itself describe a case of abuse, any more than any other planet does. The X-factor is the consciousness or unconsciousness of the parents, and how they have dealt with Mars in their own natures. That is not portrayed in one's birth chart. Only the archetypal nature of Mars is represented as an inheritance, and it may be embodied very positively by the parent. Mars by itself in the 4th or 10th, or aspecting the Sun or Moon, does not necessarily imply a parental triangle. Later on, when we look at the issue of triangles reflecting unlived psychic life, we will see that Mars may figure in many triangles. But so can any other planet. This has to do with what we are unable or unwilling to live of ourselves, rather than something inherently triangle-inclined in the nature of the planet. However, Mars and its signs – particularly Aries, but to some extent, Scorpio – are by nature competitive. They need to feel they can win, and if there is nowhere for them to win though personal excellence, winning over a rival in relationship may provide a good substitute. Here it is beating the rival which matters, not the love-object over whom the person is apparently fighting.

Sometimes there is competitiveness between parent and child if Mars is in the 4th or 10th. But competitiveness need not involve rivalry for a third person's love. Parent and child may fight over who is stronger or cleverer, without engaging in a battle over the other parent. We need to see Venus, the Moon, or Neptune also involved as parental significators if we are looking for a propensity for triangles, because Mars doesn't attach emotionally. Aries may seem a bit Oedipal, in that it likes a good contest and affirms its aliveness by winning. An Aries child may seek regular demonstrations that he or she is the best-loved, and other family members may become arch-rivals. But Aries' real need is to affirm the potency of the self. When there is a lot of Aries in the family charts, but little opportunity to express an independent, crusading spirit, this kind of rivalry may be a constant feature of family life. A creatively frustrated Aries adult may become involved in a triangle in order to gain a feeling of potency. Childhood Oedipal defeat can drive such an individual into a pattern of compensating through "taking" a series of love-objects away from other people. In this sense Mars may incline to triangles.

Power triangles

Pluto and power

I think we have looked at family triangles long enough. I have left out a great deal, but you will have to do your own thinking from this point on. Although they seem to provide the "cause" for later emotional difficulties, family triangles are not what lies at the deepest core of an adult propensity for triangles. But I think you are already getting the sense of this. I would like now to look at other types of triangles, and then at some charts, to see whether and how these astrological patterns apply in specific cases.

Triangles that arise from defensiveness or the urge to power may overlap with or be part of family dynamics, but they are also linked with essential character qualities. Family triangles, too, arise from essential character qualities, and the causal perspective is only one – and perhaps not the most important – lens through which to look at human development. But with family triangles there is usually an "outside" situation which mirrors the inner dynamic to a greater or lesser extent. This may need to be explored and understood if any emotional release and movement are to be achieved. However, the chart picture may not reflect a powerful family triangle. Defensive and power triangles have more to do with the individual's requirements for psychic survival, which may generate certain compulsive patterns when that survival appears to be threatened through emotional vulnerability.

A propensity for power triangles may be connected with a powerful Pluto emphasis in the chart. Venus-Pluto alone may have a predisposition for this, even if there is no link with parental significators. This does not mean that every person with a strong Pluto will become involved in triangles. But when one does, the reasons should be apparent to any of you who understand Pluto's nature. Being in control of one's life, for the Plutonian, is essential for survival. If one is under threat of abandonment or humiliation, one is no longer in control and could be destroyed. For Pluto, everything is a life-or-death matter. Life is not about having fun; it is about survival. One of the means by which the Plutonian may try to retain control is to divide his or her affections. This ensures that one's eggs are not all in one basket; they will therefore not all be broken if the relationship ends. The Plutonian will often play the role of the Betrayer, because this role in a power triangle provides the illusion of control.

Venus-Pluto: loving too much

Venus-Pluto aspects are not emotionally shallow or fickle. By nature, the individual attaches deeply and intensely, is extremely loyal, and does not let go easily. The beloved is essential for survival. Thus the individual may feel, unconsciously if not consciously, that it is just too risky to unleash that kind of intensity at one individual. Usually, when this happens, one loved a parent with great intensity and devotion, and felt humiliated or abandoned because the parent would not or could not reciprocate with the same intensity. If Venus-Pluto is found in a chart, the individual doesn't suddenly start feeling intense passion as an adult. The essential nature is that way to begin with, and it is likely that, however loving the parents are, it will not be enough. Siblings, and often the other parent, may be seen as a threat to the emotional exclusiveness which Venus-Pluto seeks.

Venus-Pluto will usually attach itself a family member – sometimes a sibling, if not a parent – with enormous passion. If one experiences rejection, or loses the loved one through death or separation, or experiences a humiliating Oedipal defeat, Venus-Pluto does not forget. There is an inner mechanism which says, "Never again will I be this vulnerable." Later in life, the Venus-Pluto Betrayer may ensure there are at least two people in his or her life, because if one of *them* proves to be a Betrayer, the other will still be there. A frightened Venus-Pluto may also unconsciously try to keep the partner feeling insecure through the threat or actuality of a rival, because this too can provide the illusion of emotional control. Pluto is not averse to some serious psychological game-playing in order to maintain control, and it is the Plutonian more than any other temperament who will somehow make sure that the partner finds out about the rival.

Pluto also needs drama to feel alive, and there is nothing quite as dramatic as the collision of passions we experience in a triangle. The Plutonian may need a triangle, not only because it offers a position of power in a relationship, but also because it makes one feel one is on the cutting edge of life. Every sensory perception is awake, every emotion alive, even if it is painful and threatening. The experience of intensity and drama which Venus-Pluto craves may, however, be unconscious. Often one's partner, setting the quiet family life alight through an act of sexual betrayal, is acting out what one would like to do oneself. If the Venus-Pluto individual's passions are blocked for any reason, they may be lived out through a partner who hurls himself or herself into the passionate, illicit encounter one secretly longs for but does not dare to pursue oneself.

In itself, Venus-Pluto does not speak of unresolved parental issues as the "cause" of later triangles. Unhappy early experiences might breed mistrust and exaggerate the need for control. But Venus-Pluto describes an inner quality, a *response* to the early environment, which can impel a child to turn ordinary family dynamics into a war zone where someone must maintain absolute power and someone must submit to humiliating defeat. This hints at why one child might work through the "family romance" in a relatively scar-free way, while another clings to the memory of Oedipal defeat in such a way as to affect the whole of adult emotional and sexual life. Venus-Pluto does not "make" triangles, but reflects enormous emotional intensity and a tendency to identify love with survival. Venus-Pluto's intensity and passion are fundamental to the individual's character. We are now in the zone of "character equals destiny", and we may begin to glimpse the inner necessity which makes us remember and process our childhood experiences in selective and highly individual ways.

Venus-Pluto may also be the Betrayed, who finds a partner to act out the betrayal. This may serve many purposes on an unconscious level. There may be a relentless need to recreate a childhood experience of humiliation in order to redeem the original hurt. One dreams of someone who will accept and value one's intensity and devotion. But the mistrust and possessiveness of the Venus-Pluto Betrayed may, sadly, ensure that the hoped-for redemption never happens. The partner may feel suffocated and withdraws, and one creates the thing one fears the most. It is a hard lesson, and many people never learn it. When one seeks to use a partner as a means to right a childhood wrong, the partner may feel used – perhaps justifiably so – and may rebel against the role in which he or she is cast.

The role of the Betrayed confers its own form of control. Those in a position to inflict guilt can wield great power. Being the devoted and betrayed partner can be an effective means of claiming the moral high ground, which Pluto may unashamedly use as a means of binding the loved one. If someone has done something unforgivable to us, we can remind them of it all the time. We can undermine their confidence, curtail their freedom, and let it be known in a thousand ways that they "owe" us something in recompense: "You have made me miserable. You have injured me beyond bearing. I will not forgive or forget until you make it up to me." Pluto may sometimes have a secret investment in martyrdom, although it is of a very different kind from the Neptunian variety.

The Plutonian Betrayed may have a secret investment in a partner who is uncommitted. I have often seen this when Venus-Pluto is accompanied in a birth chart by a radically different configuration such as Venus-Uranus or Moon-Uranus. This suggests an inner conflict between a side of oneself which needs space and freedom and a side which is inclined to attach deeply and permanently to one love-object. Sometimes two people, both with this combination of aspects, form a relationship, and the roles of the Betrayer and the Betrayed are truly interchangeable. Each one acts out the other's unconscious side. Or we may see Venus aspecting Pluto as well as Saturn or Chiron, and one chooses a partner whom one knows, deep down, cannot offer real commitment. There is often an intractable assumption that, in a more rewarding relationship, one will be left eventually anyway, and it is better to expect nothing from the outset than to risk having what one wants and then losing it.

An eye for an eye

The Plutonian may also be the Instrument of Betrayal. The power issues here are clear enough. "Taking" someone away from an existing relationship confers emotional and sexual power, and may also be an unconscious act of vengeance against those who inflicted hurt in childhood. We do need to remember that this harsher side of Plutonian love does not imply something intrinsically malignant or "bad" about Venus-Pluto. But thwarted Plutonian feelings are, for the individual experiencing them, tantamount to annihilation of the self. If there is too little consciousness and conscience, nothing less than global retaliation may be sufficient to right the wrong and restore a sense of potency and confidence.

Vengeance is frowned upon in Christian doctrine, although if we take our cue from the Old Testament, we are justified in claiming an eye for an eye and a tooth for a tooth. In this respect Pluto does not make a good Christian. Rejection is experienced as humiliation and a life-threat, and retaliation may be felt necessary for the survival of the soul. It is hard for those who are not strongly Plutonian to comprehend how compulsive this drive can be to return injury for injury. I doubt that any of us is in a position to pass moral judgement. There are times when some kind of revenge is psychologically necessary and also healing. But when we are embroiled in a triangle, we may sometimes fail to understand why we behave as we do, if we have a Plutonian nature and remain unconscious of the great emotional intensity, and the consequences of it, that this planet reflects.

Audience: Can Venus in Scorpio have some of these propensities? And what about Venus in the 8th?

Liz: Venus in Scorpio may share the propensities of Venus-Pluto, provided other factors in the chart, such as Moon-Pluto, support it. The person with Venus in the 8th may also find his or her way into a triangle.

But this is connected less with emotional intensity than with the need to develop a more profound and inclusive understanding of love through the transformative fire of crisis. Any planet placed in the 8th must learn to let go, through facing what cannot be altered. The ego's strength is challenged by the 8th, which reflects our necessity as part of the larger life of nature. The personal will is confronted by that which we cannot control, and this changes us. The houses are the arenas of life where we experience the "gods" who represent the essential patterns of our inner development. In the 8th, Venus, even in a peaceable sign like Taurus or Libra, may have to face those inexplicable life experiences which feel like fate and make us aware, usually unwillingly, that something other than the ego is running the show. Venus is cauterised by the experiences of the 8th, and emerges wiser, humbler, and deeper. Triangles are an optimum gateway to this cauterising fire. But there are other experiences, such as the loss of loved ones, which may embody the process to which Venus is subjected in the 8th.

Fear of intensity

Audience: I would like to understand more about why a person would fear emotional intensity. Maybe I am having trouble understanding this because I am a Pisces. It is the thing I find most rewarding in life. I also have Venus in Aries, trine Pluto. I can't imagine giving up that intense meeting with people, even if I get hurt.

Liz: Spoken like a true water sign! Feeling is the fundament in your life on which everything else is built, and, quite rightly, you have declared allegiance to it. But not everyone is born under water. Even if they are, there may be other factors in the chart which create conflict. From what you say, you are not afraid of your Venus-Pluto. That may give your life great richness, because you honour it and are prepared to pay its price. Not everyone can, however, and not necessarily because of "pathological" reasons. If emotional intensity is suppressed through fear, it may be acted out in power triangles. For a Plutonian scarred by childhood, the risk of further humiliation may not seem worth taking. We are not in a position to tell such people that it *is* worth taking, because we cannot always know where someone's limits lie. The water signs have great emotional strength, perhaps because they are better at giving themselves permission to fall apart. Airy people may have strengths in different areas, and do not have the same resilience in an emotional crisis. It takes them much longer to get over an emotional disaster, although they tend to be more restrained in their responses and make less of a fuss. They may suppress their feelings altogether for a very long time.

Airy people often carry highly structured ethical codes which make it impossible to unleash the sort of dramatic emotions which Venus-Pluto loves so much. These ethical codes may not preclude becoming a Betrayer. They are concerned more with experiencing and displaying emotions which are deemed "right". One cannot say these people "should not" have such ethical codes. They are as inherent in air as the need for intense closeness is in water. Venus-Pluto, embedded in an airy chart, may require gentler, subtler outlets such as artistic expression, because the raw stuff of intense emotional encounter may be too much to cope with. Finding alternative outlets is not the same as suppressing feelings. The fear of being destroyed because one wants something too much is always present with a strong Pluto, even if one is watery. It is endemic to the planet, and I doubt that it can be "cured". If we want something badly, and we get it, we may lose it and suffer far more than if we never had it. Have any of you seen the film, *Shadowlands*? Experience may teach us that one survives anyway, and that it is, as the saying goes, better to have loved and lost than not to have loved at all. But experience may also teach us mistrust, or stark realism about our inability to rebound from grief and loss.

Audience: That is true. I have had a lot of painful, dramatic emotional encounters, and I know now that I will always survive, and that I would not be without them. But when I was younger, I suppose I was very afraid. And if I did not have my spiritual convictions, maybe I would have become more cynical.

Liz: If Venus-Pluto is present in a chart, but there is also a great fear of the price one will have to pay for living it, the conflict may set certain psychological mechanisms in motion. These mechanisms can include triangles. Venus-Pluto, if it has no other outlet, may find itself in a triangle because that is the only way it can be expressed. There is no other avenue. What other avenues might the person find? The taste for drama, for that life-and-death cutting edge, needs to be satisfied. Venus-

Pluto may need a viable triangle where the third point is something non-human to which one can passionately commit oneself. If one is living a boring, superficial life, one is asking for trouble with Venus-Pluto, especially the hard aspects. It will, sooner or later, burst its bonds. Either the Venus-Pluto person will do the bursting, or the partner will.

I cannot stress enough that, if we have something unresolved in ourselves, we may not always be the ones to act it out. We may unconsciously choose someone who fits the role precisely from the outset. Or we may work on them until they fit the role. Of course, there needs to be a nugget of the same substance in the other person. Otherwise there is nothing to work on. But many nuggets would remain quietly sleeping if our inner necessity did not demand that we have a certain kind of experience. We should never underestimate the power that our projections have on someone with whom we live or are involved over a long period of time. We can, without realising it, turn a relatively easy-going, peaceable person into a jealous, suspicious, possessive partner. It is really very easy. All we have to do is undermine them on a regular basis. Never give them the feeling that they are truly wanted. Never give them the compliment that they need at a critical moment. Always hold back passion. Always keep them on the edge by intimating that there is someone else waiting in the wings. Given time and Plutonian persistence, we can turn a silk purse into a sow's ear.

Defensive triangles

Saturn and the repetition of rejection

Let's look more carefully at the ways we encourage the people close to us to act out a part that secretly belongs to our own inner drama. Take the example of a rejecting mother. One may have Moon-Saturn or Saturn in the 10th in the birth chart, and the mother that one needed seemed to be cold, unresponsive, or critical. One has come away with a wound. One's inner attitude toward oneself is cold, unresponsive, and critical, but recognising this takes time and consciousness. For a long time, it may seem that the wound is entirely inflicted from outside. This propels one into trying to heal the injury outside, by hurling oneself at other people who seem equally cold and unresponsive. There is a persistent hope that somebody will, by providing the right amount of warmth and affection, make the pain better. In other words, someone else will provide what mother did not provide, so that one can finally learn to love and appreciate oneself. Sadly, it doesn't usually work out like that. If one has a partner who *is* responsive, then within six months, with such a complex at work, one will begin to ensure that they become unresponsive. This is achieved entirely unconsciously. If we need to subject ourselves to a repetitive experience of rejection, how do we get other people to do the rejecting?

Audience: By being demanding.

Liz: Yes, that is one way – by demanding too much. What is "too much"? It is a lack of respect for the other individual's boundaries. Those vary, of course, according to the individual involved. But we do know instinctively where others' limits lie, even if we choose not to acknowledge this consciously. One can demand things which lie beyond the other person's limits, which require a sacrifice of their essential identity. Then one can become angry and feel rejected when one's needs are not met. One can invade their space all the time, and show disrespect for their psychological and physical privacy. One can, in short, display the psychic identification of a baby with its mother, which precludes separateness and seeks fusion rather than relationship.

As astrologers, we can watch this dynamic at work in certain clients. Analytically trained psychotherapists recognise when it is occurring, but sometimes astrologers do not. A client may arrive who is carrying a "rejecting parent" image inside, and he or she wants far more from us than we are capable of giving. Whatever we offer, it is not good enough. As "helpers", we are left feeling inadequate and vaguely guilty because we have not fulfilled our responsibilities. The client starts ringing up at funny hours of the night, or arrives forty minutes early and is reluctant to go when the session is finished. We are made aware that we have charged too much and have failed to give the required insights and answers. We start feeling resentful, and after a while we get really fed up and say, "Please go away and leave me alone. I cannot give you what you want." And then the person has got the rejection he or she unconsciously wanted, because rejection is the inner script through which that individual relates.

One can also work on a partner this way. He or she is driven into forcefully affirming Saturnian boundaries because one keeps trying to break the boundaries down. The partner may then act out the cold, unfeeling parent – who is really an embodiment of the demand for self-sufficiency imposed by one's own Saturn on one's own Moon – and may look elsewhere. The element of collusion in triangles arising from this kind of dynamic is probably 100%. That may make some of you really angry. But if you are feeling angry and you also have Sun-Saturn, Moon-Saturn, Venus-Saturn, or Saturn in the 4th or 10th in your chart, please try to look beyond the anger and think about it.

Defensive triangles may not be initiated by the person with these planetary significators. Moon-Saturn, Sun-Saturn, Saturn in the 10th, Saturn in the 4th, and Venus-Saturn, as well as similar configurations involving Chiron, may equally play the Betrayer, the Betrayed, or the Instrument of Betrayal. The Betrayer with such aspects usually has a handy justification for involvement with a third party: the partner is perceived as cold, rejecting, and critical. The Betrayed with such aspects will usually make the same accusation about the Betrayer. If we find ourselves playing either of these roles in a defensive triangle, we need to find the courage to recognise our own rejecting propensities – our own Saturnian defences against vulnerability, secretly projected and experienced vicariously. What else are we doing but rejecting, when we refuse to recognise the independent individuality of loved ones, invade their psyches with the wounded, childlike part of ourselves, and demand that they heal something in us which is not and never was their responsibility?

One may also be the Instrument of Betrayal with the same configurations, recreating the rejection pattern through involvement with someone who is committed elsewhere. This may involve spending a lot of time waiting by the phone, hoping the beloved will find a moment to slip away from the family and ring up for a couple of minutes. The Instrument of Betrayal may spend many hours feeling lonely and rejected, just as the Betrayed does, and just as the Betrayer does in a loveless relationship.

The psychic "payoff" of rejection

We may well ask what possible psychic "payoff" is involved here. All three people may feel hurt, lonely, and rejected. All three blame one or two of the others for their pain. This is not simply an issue of "repetition compulsion", which is Freud's term for the persistent recreation of the original hurtful situation in order to find some way of healing it. There is also an element of avoidance in such triangles, because each person has a justification for failing to be emotionally open. Defensive triangles protect us against the real vulnerability of deep emotional engagement with another, although our acknowledged hurt and unhappiness may mask this deeper fear. We may also ask what positive dimension lies in Saturnian inclinations. If Saturn is "just" defensive, then Saturn aspects are "nothing but" destructive and we may as well sign off and hope for a better incarnation next time. That, of course, is not what the planet is really about. What are we refusing to learn by involving ourselves in defensive triangles?

Audience: I suppose we don't want to be separate. But I am a bit confused by what you are saying. You said that these rejection patterns protect us from experiencing deep commitment. But if we are supposed to be learning separateness, then how can we do both? It seems to me to be a "Catch 22" situation.

Liz: Yes, I suppose it does sound like that. But by "deep commitment" I don't mean emotional fusion. I believe we cannot really make an emotional commitment unless we feel like independent entities and make this choice from consciousness of who we are and what we have to give as individuals. The urgent need to fuse, to be one with the other, is not commitment. It is hunger. It is human and it is not "wrong", but it is not something one chooses. It is something by which one is compelled, often from fear and feelings of personal inadequacy and helplessness. Saturn's exaltation in Libra suggests to me that relationship, as an interaction between two independent beings, involves mutual respect and genuine dialogue. It depends on those two beings experiencing themselves first as separate, and second as a partnership.

All of us here understand, at least intellectually, that one of the demands of Saturn is separateness and self-sufficiency. Any planet that

Saturn aspects has this demand placed on it. We have to develop autonomy and self-containment in this sphere of our lives. That doesn't mean closing off emotionally. We have to recognise limits – our own and others' – and learn to live within them, yet with open hearts. That is not an easy task. It is easier for Saturn-Mercury or Saturn-Mars, but more difficult for Saturn-Moon and Saturn-Venus, because the Moon and Venus are by nature propelled into involvement with others. There is a natural antipathy between Saturn and the Moon, and also between Saturn and Venus, even though Saturn is exalted in Venus' sign. Airy and earthy Venus placements perhaps find it easier to make friends with Saturn. Watery and fiery Venus placements find it much harder.

With these aspects, the inner *daimon* demands that we stop demanding divine love and start accepting human love. A person with Moon-Saturn or Venus-Saturn may feel that childhood was spoiled by rejection, emotional coldness, loneliness, excessive responsibility, or conditional love. The limits are felt from the beginning. This cold environment may be objectively "real" to some extent. But the intensity of the hurt, and the later emotional repercussions, are particular to the individual with these configurations. We cannot blame our childhoods for our Saturns. Moon-Saturn and Venus-Saturn have a task from birth, a *dharma,* which involves learning to love and be loved as real people. This requires self-sufficiency. Early rejection is not the "cause" of Saturnian defensive triangles. *It is the trigger.* The deeper issue lies in the individual's resistance to recognising what is required by the soul, or Self, or "acorn", as James Hillman calls it[7], or whatever name you wish to give that which lies at the centre of our being. The resistance is probably inevitable, because youth does not appreciate Saturn. Time and experience can work wonders with these aspects, and make it possible for them to display their most creative dimensions. But often there is a painful triangle along the way.

Chiron's defences

Audience: Would you include Chiron in these configurations? Does Chiron-Venus incline to defensive triangles?

---

7 James Hillman, *The Soul's Code*, Bantam Books, London, 1997.

Liz: Chiron can incline to defensive triangles in much the same way Saturn can. Fear of being injured or disappointed may impel the person to seek self-protection in a triangle. With Venus-Chiron, Moon-Chiron, and sometimes Sun-Chiron, love is often equated with pain. It is difficult to envisage relationship without wounding of some kind. That is not necessarily a "wrong" perception, because the reality of life seems to be that we do wind up hurting others and ourselves when we love, however great our efforts to avoid it.

Chiron can make us more tolerant of human limits. The youthful enchantment of being "in love" with an idealised image may change to a more inclusive love which embraces compassion and a willingness to accept a flawed human partner. Along the way toward that more inclusive kind of love, defences may be mobilised, because the process involves facing one's incurable hurts and flaws. Some people get stuck in these defences, and unconsciously utilise triangles for reasons similar to those of Venus-Saturn or Moon-Saturn.

Some individuals are born with aspects that predispose toward a profound recognition of the importance of what they are being denied and what they must learn. This makes them hypersensitive, and they may not recognise the language of love being offered. Moon-Chiron, Moon-Saturn, Venus-Chiron, Venus-Saturn, Sun-Chiron, Sun-Saturn, and Saturn or Chiron in the parental houses all make a statement about how one perceived the parents in childhood. We have all heard, if not experienced, stories of real, devastating cruelty and coldness in childhood. But for most people with these aspects, the root of the matter is not as simple as an unloving parent. Saturn and Chiron are the "special needs children" of the planetary pantheon. They require something which is impossible to find in another person. It can only be found within, with some consciousness and experience of life; and it cannot ever be found in its entirety, and we must learn to compromise.

The convoluted psyche

Triangles are one of the commonest defences against rejection. These situations are created unconsciously. We don't sit down and work out a defensive triangle on paper. The Betrayed and the Instrument of Betrayal in a defensive triangle may both have chosen someone who is fundamentally uncommitted. This gives an excellent justification for emotionally withdrawing while managing to avoid facing one's own fear of commitment. The individual caught in this pattern may unerringly select partners who, sooner or later, will prove to be a disappointment, because the real fear is of a relationship that works.

Deep mistrust is characteristic of both Saturn and Chiron. We may choose those toward whom we secretly feel superior, or whom we do not truly respect, because they seem "safer" and less likely to leave us. Then we can justify playing the Betrayer because we feel so disappointed. Or the expectation of injury can make us ensure that we are always in relationships which, sooner or later, let us down. The other person betrays us, and then we can say, "I knew you were going to do it. All men/women are like that." We can cut off emotionally and feel totally vindicated. Behind this is a deep reluctance to fully engage with another person. If we do, the vulnerability is intolerable. You think this is convoluted? It is. But it is often how the psyche works.

Audience: It really does. I had an experience of this sort with somebody. This man has Saturn in the 5th, trine Venus and square Uranus in the 12th, and the Moon square Saturn. When I was with him, I found myself turning into a real Plutonian. And I don't have a strong Pluto. It isn't on an angle, and it doesn't aspect my Moon or Venus. He always seemed to be testing me, setting me up to see whether I would lie to him. I became very secretive, deliberately, sometimes about really silly things, because I felt pressured all the time. I couldn't help it. I didn't want to share things with him any more, because I always felt I was being set up. When I tried to explain this to him, he didn't understand what I was talking about. He was just hurt because I wouldn't be open with him any more.

Liz: What you are describing is a sad illustration of the way in which mistrust creates its own fate. If we are at the receiving end of mistrust, it is sometimes hard to avoid doing the very thing toward which the mistrustful person is pushing us. No matter what we do, our partner or lover refuses to believe that we care for them. They will test and test, and sooner or later one gets very fed up and looks for a relationship where one is trusted and one's love is believed.

Audience: Or you wind up proving they are right because you are so angry.

Liz: Yes, this is the "I may as well be hung for a sheep as a lamb" response. Being the recipient of extreme suspicion can drive us into feeling, "If that's what you think of me, that's what you will get." Extreme insecurity and possessiveness may create the very thing the person has the greatest fear of. It is very sad, because there is no deliberate attempt to create such a situation. It is unconscious. Yet extreme mistrust is a form of rejection. One is saying, "I know that you are really a treacherous and untrustworthy person. No matter what you say or do, I know that your declarations of love are false." This can be extremely hurtful and demeaning, although the mistrustful individual is so caught up in his or her expectation of hurt that this obvious emotional truth is overlooked.

There is no situation as clearly linked with parental issues as the defensive triangle formed because of insecurity. But although the childhood factors may be obvious, we are still faced with the dilemma of selective memory and the highly subjective ways in which children react to "imperfect" parenting. A causal approach to defensive triangles is really insufficient and will not help us to understand the teleology, although it may alleviate feelings of self-blame and help us to gain more trust in ourselves.

The child with difficult configurations of Saturn or Chiron is predisposed to experience the limitations of parental love. The rejections are always remembered, and the expressions of parental affection are usually forgotten. It is not so much the actuality of childhood as the way we experience and remember childhood that is described by these astrological configurations. We need to look more deeply at what the planetary signature is really telling us about ourselves. There is an element of unlived life acting itself out through a defensive triangle, and it may be connected with the need for self-sufficiency and the necessity of accepting human limits.

The pursuit of the unobtainable

Neptune's triangles

Now I want to talk about triangles which involve the unobtainable – but not, this time, in a parental context. Here we will usually find Neptune configurations. Neptune does not necessarily imply Oedipal unobtainability. Parental involvement may be suggested if Neptune appears in the parental houses or aspects the Sun or Moon. The idealised parent who is always just beyond one's emotional reach may appear later as the idealised lover or partner who is equally out of reach. But the quest for unobtainable love is not merely a quest for one's mother or father. As well as Neptune aspecting the Luminaries, Venus-Neptune – or even an angular Neptune with many aspects – describes an intuitive perception of a greater unity behind life. This perception can prove very destructive to one's personal life if that unity is sought exclusively in human relationships.

Neptune always has one foot in another dimension. There is a fantasy, or a memory – depending on one's philosophical or spiritual framework – of an "other place" to which one longs to return, a place of peace and oneness and bliss. Here there is no death, no separateness, no loneliness, and no pain. The "return to the womb" element is obvious, but this life-source is not really one's personal mother or father. It is an image of a vast archetypal *fons et origo* which is projected on the idealised parent but points to something far beyond. Not wanting to leave the womb is one level of Neptune's longing, and the pursuit of unobtainable love may be seen reductively as a quest for a state of fusion that existed before birth and can never be found in any flesh-and-blood human relationship. This may need to be faced if one has a strong Neptune and finds oneself in a painful triangle. But it is not the only level. There is a genuine openness to subtler dimensions of reality which makes ordinary human relationships seem like sad, pale copies of the "real" thing. This is fundamental to the individual's nature, rather than caused by parental wounds. But it will often be mixed up with an early family triangle, and the two in combination are peculiarly prone to engage in compulsive triangle-making.

The quest for perfect love

A powerful Neptune may keep searching for the perfect love, hoping to find that moment of ecstasy, that soul-mate with whom one can merge entirely. No human relationship can match up to Neptune's vision of love except, perhaps, in its initial, magical, "in love" stage. The tendency to search for love outside an established relationship may therefore prove irresistible. Neptune is not known for its emotional directness, and the individual may find it quite impossible to end one relationship before the next, more promising one begins. In this area Neptune can certainly display what is euphemistically called "deception", which I would define as an inability to cope with confrontation. One hopes, in Neptune's characteristically muddled way, that it will somehow all come right without having to speak the truth. Usually it all comes wrong.

Even if one has worked very hard on the issue of parental triangles and parental separation, one cannot "cure" Neptune. It needs imaginal outlets through which the vision of oneness and the longing to be "taken out of oneself" can be expressed. Venus-Neptune and Moon-Neptune may easily end up in a love triangle if the Neptunian side of one's nature is too ruthlessly stifled. This may be because the chart is too earthy or airy, too Saturnian or too Uranian, too controlled or too rational, and there is a reluctance to let go on the imaginal level that Neptune requires. The family background may also predispose the individual to rejecting Neptune's otherworld domain. We have only to look at Prince Charles, with his Venus-Neptune conjunction in Libra, to understand how a marriage based on Saturnian expediency could lead only to disaster.

Venus-Neptune itself, regardless of parental issues, can incline to triangles. Moon-Neptune and Sun-Neptune can also incline to triangles, although in the case of these latter two aspects, the family background is usually implicated in some way. They can all be difficult aspects in terms of relationship, because of their exceedingly high expectations. If one doesn't want a human triangle in one's life, one will need to create a non-human triangle involving music, theatre, poetry, literature, a spiritual path, healing, humanitarian work, or any other Neptunian channel one favours. It may be meditation, astrology, or dream-work. But something of Neptune's world needs to be the third point of the triangle, where one becomes the Betrayer by losing oneself, from time to time, in the ecstasy of merging with something greater than oneself.

Audience: The third point can also be alcohol or drugs.

Liz: Yes, it can be, and often is.

Audience: Does Neptune in the 5th give a propensity for triangles?

Liz: Yes, for all the reasons I have just described. Neptune has affinity with the archetype of the victim-redeemer, and the Neptunian may be as gifted at playing the role of the Betrayed as the role of the Betrayer seeking a perfect love. Here there is often a kind of long-suffering attitude toward the unfaithful partner, which may be comprised partly of compassion – or pity – and partly of a belief that one must suffer in love in order to "save the sinner". I don't want to spend too much time on the psychology of this today, because you can all go and read what I have written about it. But the Betrayer, the Betrayed, and the Instrument of Betrayal may all be caught in Neptune's web.

Uranian triangles

Uranus may also be implicated in triangles in pursuit of the unobtainable. It is an outer planet and reflects something greater than the individual and what might be found in an individual human partner. Venus-Uranus contacts, and Uranus in the 5th, 7th, and 8th, may be inclined to triangles because one is seeking an ideal of perfection which is impossible in human relationship. There is a glimpse of a brighter, cleaner reality, a perfectly functioning system where the darker, more barbaric human emotions are no longer capable of disrupting the orderly beauty of the cosmos. If one seeks fulfillment of this vision in an established relationship, it is not surprising if – following on the heels of disappointment in an all-too-human partner overly preoccupied with whether the shirts have been ironed or the pension fund is sufficient – one looks for it elsewhere. Uranus has difficulty with the reality of the physical body, and this, too, can lead to the pursuit of perfection when one's partner – or oneself – begins to grow older. If the chart balance is too weighted in air and fire, then

Venus-Uranus may feel repelled even by a young, beautiful partner, because familiarity reveals the ordinary clay of which the beloved is made.[8]

Uranus withdraws from intense emotional experience, particularly if possessiveness and dependency are part of it. Such feelings may repel the Uranian, whether they are one's own or one's partner's. A new lover may seem to allow the possibility of a relationship without suffocation. After a time, the new lover, too, may seem emotionally suffocating, because the real problem lies with the Uranian nature rather than with the apparent emotional excesses of the partner. Moon-Uranus and Venus-Uranus are not easy bedfellows for a partner with Moon-Pluto, Venus-Pluto, Moon-Neptune, or Venus-Neptune. This is even more the case when one has both types of configuration in one's own chart. Then it is likely that, sooner or later, one of these aspects will appear in the established partner, while the other beckons toward greener pastures or manifests as the rival.

Like Neptune, Uranus does not need Oedipal backup to generate difficulties in relationship – although too claustrophobic an emotional atmosphere in childhood may turn relatively balanced Uranian needs into a knee-jerk reactive rejection of all human emotional demands. Uranus ultimately needs outlets other than the merely human if one wishes to preserve one's established relationships without the complications of triangles. If one has not come to terms with the Uranian elements in one's own nature, then a triangle may be the form through which the unlived life is experienced. Especially with hard aspects to Venus, Moon, or Sun, it will often be the partner who acts out Uranus. If one can recognise one's own Uranian propensities, this may not make it easier, but it may be possible to consciously create channels through which one can pursue one's ideals without expecting an ordinary human partner to encapsulate the divine plan single-handed.

The frequently voiced Uranian demand for equality, openness, and non-possessiveness in relationship is not usually a viable alternative, since the Uranian's belief in such openness will probably not be shared by the partner – and not necessarily because the partner has a "problem". Demanding that one's partner be willing to accept one's other lovers – "Why can't we all be friends?" – is often a disguised

---

8 For a more detailed exploration of Uranian issues in relationship, see *The Art of Stealing Fire*, Liz Greene, CPA Press, London, 1996.

demand that the partner panders to one's inability to cope with the emotional consequences of one's actions. Unless the partner is truly in accord – which *can* sometimes be the case, although I have found this to be the exception rather than the rule – it is a form of psychic bullying which hardly lives up to the "democratic" ideal to which the Uranian person aspires. Moreover, the shoe is not usually welcome on the other foot.

Audience: What do you mean? What shoe?
Liz: The left one. Uranian ideals of freedom have a tendency to break down when the partner rather than the Uranian becomes involved in a triangle. It is what we euphemistically call a "double standard". There is an inherent split between Uranian idealism and the nature of human emotions – including the human emotions of the Uranian. Uranus' need for a sense of cosmic connectedness may be satisfied by a non-human third point of the triangle: friendships and the sharing of intellectual, spiritual, or social ideals outside one's established partnership. But if one lives with a partner who has strong Uranian needs in relationship – Moon-Uranus, Venus-Uranus, or Uranus in the 5th, 7th, or 8th – then it may be wise to avoid demanding a constant level of physical and emotional intimacy which is intolerable to the Uranian nature, however conscious the person might be.

Triangles which involve unlived life

Connie: the Betrayed

I believe there is always an element of unlived life in every triangle, and it seems we are sometimes unable to discover that unlived life except through the extreme emotional stress which triangles cause. Perhaps the best way to begin exploring this is to look at a chart which someone in the group has given me. I always think people are very brave offering their charts for group inspection.

Audience: Or foolhardy.

Audience: Or they have never done it before.

Liz: Yes, it is probably a state of blissful ignorance, which is about to be rudely shattered. Connie, are you happy to talk about your circumstances?

Connie: Yes.

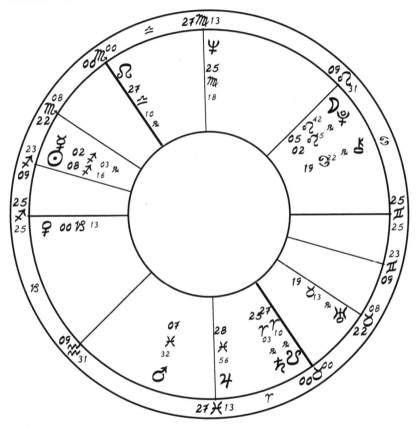

Connie
[data withheld for purposes of confidentiality]

Liz: Which is your favoured point on the triangle? The Betrayer, the Betrayed, or the Instrument of Betrayal?

Connie: I am the Betrayed. I have had a thirty-year marriage in which the love just disappeared. My husband left me for a younger woman, who also happened to be one of my closest friends.

Liz: This is an extremely painful experience which is, in effect, a double betrayal. Perhaps we could look first at the family patterns in your chart, to see if that gives us any insight. We may not find anything relevant, but we can start there. Let's look at the 4th and 10th houses. You can all see that Uranus is in the 4th.

Connie: I must say that I am a total novice. Isn't Uranus on the edge of the 5th house?

Liz: Uranus is in 19° Taurus. The cusp of the 5th is 22° Taurus, so Uranus is in the 4th. It is not really "on the edge", although we could say it has some relevance to the 5th. I tend to give house cusps, excepting the angles, a narrow orb – perhaps only 1° – in terms of reading a planet as "in" the next house. An orb of 3° in this case would suggest to me that Uranian issues mainly apply to the 4th. With the angles, I am inclined to allow a much wider orb – up to 10° either side for a conjunction of a planet to an angle – because the angles are powerful receiving points and symbolise the archetypal "cross of incarnation" which forms the essential structure of the horoscope. The angles are the same with all house systems (except equal house), whereas the succedent and cadent house cusps will vary according to whether one uses Placidus, Koch, Campanus, Regiomontanus, or Arthur's New Millennial Quadrant System.

Audience: What?

Liz: Never mind. The IC is 1° Taurus, and Saturn is in 25° Aries, so Saturn is conjunct the IC from the 3rd house. Here is another significator which relates to the father. We should also look at the Sun, which is in 8° 16' Sagittarius in the 11th. But the Sun *is* "on the edge" – it is just over 1° from the 12th house cusp in 9° 23' Sagittarius. The Sun is square Mars and trine a Moon-Pluto conjunction. That conjunction may tell us quite a lot about the mother-image. But let's look at father first. Uranus in the 4th and Saturn in the 3rd but conjunct the cusp of the 4th – any thoughts?

Audience: Are you asking us for an interpretation?

Liz: Why, yes. You needn't look so frightened. What is your immediate impression when you look at those two planets?

Audience: With Uranus in the 4ᵗʰ, I think of a father who is unreliable – somebody who is fixed on certain ideas, or wants to change the world, or lives through his business, or travels a lot. He is unreliable. Maybe it's not his fault, but he's not always there. He can be there one day, and then, the next day, snap! he is off.

Connie: In my formative years, he certainly wasn't there. He was in the army. After the war, he was well established in the world, and he was a dominating father.

Liz: Did you experience your father as a negative figure?

Connie: An unwelcome visitor.

Liz: When did he go off to the war?

Connie: I was a baby.

Liz: I would begin by raising a question about your conscious attitude towards your father. The early separation and the sense of him being a visitor in the family seem to be described by Uranus, and the perception of him as "dominating" and "unwelcome" seems to be described by both Uranus and Saturn. But there may be something more as well.

Connie: He wasn't a well-liked man. Many people found him difficult.

Liz: No doubt. But it is *your* feelings for him that are relevant here, not other people's. The way you have portrayed him suggests that you want nothing to do with him.

Connie: That is true.

Liz: That is what I am wondering about. The reason I am wondering is because of the Sun and its aspects.

Audience: Venus is the dispositor of the IC.

Liz: Yes. There is also a Sun-Pluto trine. And Jupiter is at the end of Pisces, just in trine to and dispositor of the 12ᵗʰ house Sun in Sagittarius.

These aspects suggest a good deal of fascination and admiration for this father. But it would have been very difficult to acknowledge, because Saturn and Uranus give a different message. You seem to feel he abandoned you.

Connie: Yes.

Liz: As an adult, you know that he went off to fight. But children don't really understand things like World Wars. All they know is that father has gone off and may never come back. The sense of being abandoned by someone who seems to have exercised great fascination and charisma could be very difficult to carry. That is why I am wondering about the feelings you have described. Also, I keep looking at Moon-Pluto, and wondering about that, too. Your mother was presumably left alone during the war years, to look after the children. Do you have brothers and sisters?

Connie: No.

Liz: Saturn is in the 3rd, often the signature of an "only" child. So you and she were alone.

Connie: My grandmother was also with us.

Liz: It is possible that your mother needed absolute loyalty from you because you were all she had. Moon-Pluto is a statement about your mother-image, and it is a very intense, demanding image. If you did feel love and affection for your father, you couldn't show it, could you? The crisis in your marriage undoubtedly has deeper roots, and I am pretty sure that parental issues make up at least some of those roots, because of the emphasis in the 4th house. It is worth thinking about what must have happened when your father came home. You had your mother all to yourself. Suddenly you didn't any more. In fact, she betrayed you by "going off" with your father. It makes me wonder, too, about this friend of yours who went off with your husband, and what the link is between her and the mother with whom you were so close but who was suddenly not yours any more. Something of this early dynamic may be echoed in your marriage dynamic. Does this make any sense to you?

Connie: It is something I haven't really thought about.

Liz: Transiting Pluto in 8° Sagittarius is on your Sun at the moment. The Venus-Mars-Pluto configuration which kicked off our seminar is triggering your Sun precisely. Maybe it will stimulate you to think about things which previously you might not have thought about. Uranus and Saturn are both father significators in the chart. Neither is comfortable. In contrast, the Sun is in Sagittarius, disposed of by the Ascendant ruler, Jupiter, which is in dignity in Pisces. Jupiter is trine the Sun. The Sun is also trine Pluto in Leo, the Sun's natural sign. Venus, as one of you has pointed out, rules the IC and is in the 1st, conjunct the Ascendant. It is in an out-of-sign square to Neptune.

There are two fathers portrayed here. One is rejecting, unstable, and untrustworthy – that is Saturn and Uranus. The other is glamorous, powerful, beautiful, and unobtainable – that is the Sun-Jupiter-Pluto and Venus-Neptune linkup. You seem to have acknowledged one but not the other. This is what Jung called a split animus. Perhaps your husband also has two sides, and you have seen one but not the other, until now. It might be useful for you to look at his chart in context of your father-image, because your image of your father is not only Saturn and Uranus, but also Sun-Jupiter-Pluto and Venus-Neptune.

Audience: I want to ask a question. The marriage has lasted thirty years, so now it is having a Saturn return. Is that relevant?

Liz: It is, indeed, the marriage's Saturn return, and it is certainly relevant in terms of the phase the marriage has reached. A cycle has come to completion and a new one is beginning. That won't tell us about specific events, but it does tell us that the marriage as an entity has matured – Childhood's End, as it were.

Uranian eruptions

Connie: I have my husband's chart here. I'd like to talk about that first, and try to understand him. But I'm not entirely comfortable about having it put up. He isn't here to answer.

Liz: Perhaps I could mention some points which seem relevant, rather than displaying the entire chart on the overhead projector.

Connie: Yes, that seems a good compromise.

Liz: Like you, he has a Sagittarius Ascendant. His Sun is in Aquarius. The Sun squares Uranus, which is the ruler of Aquarius. Maybe this is a side of your husband which you have not acknowledged. Perhaps you wanted someone who seemed opposite to your father – someone who would be there for you all the time. Maybe he appeared to fulfill that role. But it is interesting that the two rulers of Aquarius – Saturn and Uranus – appear in your birth chart as father-significators, and your husband is an Aquarian with Sun square Uranus.

Connie: I actually thought he was my mother, not my father.

Liz: Maybe he appeared to behave more like her. It is possible that he has not lived his Uranian side during the years of the marriage. There's also a Moon-Uranus conjunction in his chart. This man is not heavy-duty domestic material. He may have been suppressing this side of himself, but nevertheless, that is what the chart portrays. There is a freedom-loving, adventurous Sagittarian Ascendant. Both Sun and Moon aspect Uranus. He needs a lot of space. It may be that both of you have played roles based on past insecurities, and these roles may not be entirely in accord with your basic characters. Now he is displaying something that you experienced through your father in childhood. You are suddenly confronted with a side of him you didn't know was there.

   Your husband has pitched you into painful feelings of abandonment and betrayal which must be triggering your memories of early abandonment. That Uranian shock-horror tendency has been enacted for a second time in your life – the man in your life is suddenly not there any more. There is some connection between him and your father, not only because of the Uranian link, but also because you have experienced the same thing through both of them, even though the circumstances are entirely different. There is something undomesticated and freedom-loving about your husband's nature which he may have been sitting on for thirty years. He has got the Sun right at the IC, and he may have been trying to compensate for a lack of stability in his own early background. He may have tried to be what his own father wasn't.

I am only speculating, of course. But if he was behaving in a traditional uxorious way all these years, trouble would have come, sooner or later.

Perhaps he is trying to find something of himself that he lost very early through trying to be overly responsible. Perhaps you are discovering something about him that, for your own reasons, you did not want to acknowledge either. None of this really has to do with another woman. It is connected with unlived Uranian and Jupiterian qualities. Triangles are always symbolic. They may hurt like hell, but they are also symbolic. Although it won't take your pain away, beginning to look at the symbolic level may get you a little nearer to understanding what this triangle means in your life. There is some connection here between your father going off and your husband going off, and some similarity between them which neither of you has known about. And there may be a great release in it for you, too.

Audience: He has Sagittarius rising. Connie's Sun is in 8° Sagittarius, with Pluto on it. Has it reached her husband's Ascendant?

Liz: No, the Ascendant is in a much later degree. Connie, when did everything blow up?

Connie: Six months ago.

Liz: You are both in the middle of the second Saturn return. Saturn has gone over your husband's natal Venus-Jupiter conjunction in Aries in the 5th house. Now it has returned to its own place, also in the 5th. I don't need to elaborate on the contradiction of Venus-Jupiter *and* Saturn in the 5th. He has had to face growing older, and this may have brought the *puer aeternus* in him alive, kicking, and desperate that time is running out. Transiting Jupiter has gone over his Sun, setting off his natal Sun square Uranus, Moon conjunct Uranus, and Sun square Moon.

Connie: So why wasn't it something like a long trip?

Liz: Perhaps it *is* a long trip. Transiting Saturn on Venus, and Saturn returning to its own place, are not aspects of "falling in love". They paint a different picture, a Saturn-Jupiter-Uranus picture – a struggle between the mature, responsible husband and the youthful *puer* who has never been fully lived. Before we look at your transits, it may be helpful for you to get a sense of this picture first.

Why did these aspects come out through a love affair rather than a journey? A love affair is one of the most potent and transformative ways in which we hurl ourselves into life. Once upon a time, travel was mysterious, dangerous, exciting, and nourishing to the soul. Travel can still be romantic, but few people will make the effort to stray outside the known routes, and the unknown routes are getting fewer all the time. Now one rings up one's travel agent, books a ticket on one's Visa card, leaves an airport, eats a tasteless lunch out of a plastic container, watches a dreadful film, goes to sleep, and arrives at another identical airport. One stays in a modern hotel which looks like every other modern hotel, burns oneself to a crisp on the beach, and then comes home. Even Everest has become a bore, with mobile phones and easy-access emergency services in case it gets a bit tough. And the dangers of travel are too well-known now. Being at the wrong end of a Kalashnikov in the hands of a terrorist cannot compete in mystery with the delicious dangers of illicit love. Love affairs have so many levels, all of which bring us alive in a very powerful way. This "illicit" love affair is a form of rebellion. It is a statement – not necessarily to you, but certainly to life – that he will not slide quietly and sedately into old age.

Your husband's natal Venus is now being trined by transiting Pluto, having just been bludgeoned by Saturn, so this 5th house Venus in Aries is coming awake. The Venus-Jupiter conjunction in Aries in the 5th could be part of a big package of unlived life that seems to have erupted into your husband's awareness six months ago. Saturn spent a long time stomping back and forth over the Venus-Jupiter conjunction before the affair started. When Saturn goes over an unlived part of the chart, we suddenly realise what we haven't got.

Connie: Is this my fault?

Liz: No, I don't believe it is. Your husband is responsible for what he lives or does not live of his own soul, just as you are responsible for what you live or do not live of yours. You did not "make" him behave in any particular way. Even if you tried, it has always been his choice whether or not to agree. He must have had his own agenda for trying to be a conventional husband. There may have been collusion in building a particular kind of marriage which stifled certain dimensions of both of you. But this is totally understandable – after all, it is what most people do – and it is not your "fault" if he suddenly felt life was escaping him. Because Saturn activated this conjunction as it approached its second return, he must said to himself, "My life is passing by. Where are all the challenges? Where is all the excitement?" Venus-Jupiter in Aries is an incurable romantic – not in the Neptunian way, where we long to lose ourselves, but in a grand, theatrical, self-mythologising way.

Audience: It craves excitement and the joy of the chase.

Liz: Yes, and one cannot chase what one already has. Venus-Jupiter, especially in fire, wants to break out on a regular basis and have an absolutely wonderful, exciting time. One can do this in ways which do not involve extramarital affairs. But that is not easy. Jupiter and Venus are the two most unfaithful gods in Greek myth; both are inveterate Betrayers. It is better to have a really wild youth, so that a committed relationship doesn't seem so confining later. One may feel frustrated, but the frustration is not exacerbated by a sense that one has lost out. But his generation mitigated against such a birth configuration being lived freely in youth. Both of you spent your childhoods in wartime Britain, and the times were not conducive to over-the-top Venus-Jupiter joyousness. If your husband had got some of that excess out of his system earlier, the Saturn transit might not have hit him quite so hard now. I believe he is trying to discover something within himself, albeit in a clumsy and hurtful way.

Fathers and lovers

Now, Connie, what are you trying to discover? Your husband is not here to speak for himself, but you are. Transiting Pluto is now on your Sun. This transit has many levels of meaning. Amongst them is a separation from the father and the birth of your own individuality as a result. I believe your real emotional experience of father is only now being dredged up from the unconscious, and you have to face it. Transiting Uranus is opposite your Moon-Pluto conjunction. That adds to the picture of a freeing process going on inside you. You are separating, not only from father, but from mother, too. A parental pattern is being broken up, and a family complex is being released.

Connie: It is extraordinary that you say that. I have to say that I have been struggling to understand what has happened, and I have gone back over and over everything, without much insight. But through all the rampaging and anger and distress, the first time I felt I had turned a corner was when I said aloud, "Pull yourself together, for heaven's sake. You're not his daughter."

Liz: Perhaps, on some level, you *were* his daughter. By recognising consciously that you are not his daughter, you have put distance between you and the painful emotions of your childhood, which have been mixed up with the equally painful emotions of the present. The difference is that, for a child, abandonment feels like the end of the world. One is a passive victim; one can do nothing except grieve and rage. As an adult, there are other options besides grief and rage. One is not passive in the same way a child is. You may not be able to control the situation, but you can choose to respond in different ways, and recognise that you have a future with or without your husband. For a small child, it feels as though there is no future without the parents.

Because of Uranus transiting opposite Moon-Pluto, this is not just an issue of repeating and potentially healing an experience of abandonment by your father. Just as your husband is discovering something about himself, I believe you are discovering something about yourself. I suspect you have been identified with a motherly role for many years, compensating for an early family life that was dreadfully disrupted by war, and holding on to a kind of desperate security which has not allowed your life to flow. There is something in this Uranus transit about separating from the mother and letting go of a certain kind of role that you have been playing at home. Although you are a double Sagittarian, I would guess that the Moon-Pluto conjunction has been very dominant, and perhaps much of the fire in your chart has been held back.

Connie: In outer life I have lived the fire. I was an actress by profession. But you are right – at home I have been someone quite different.

Liz: It is good to know you have had some outlets for this extremely fiery chart. I am sure that has helped a lot. But many people play a different part in their marriage from the one they play in the outer world. Domestic life is where the family complexes tend to take control.

Devotion to family life may have been your form of compensation for early instability, just as your husband may have compensated for his apparent lack of a father by being too fatherly, and not enough of the Uranus-Jupiter person he really is. Your life was shaped by a wartime childhood, with a father who might die at any minute and a mother who must have been fearful and depressed much of the time. I never underestimate the effects of this kind of collective disaster on individuals who are caught up in it.

Your Moon-Pluto conjunction speaks of sensitivity to an early atmosphere of darkness and depression. You, more than many children, would have been deeply aware of your mother's unhappiness and the proximity of death all around you. There is also a Saturn-Pluto square in your chart, which suggests a sense of constant threat and a determination to survive, whatever the odds. This square is generational. It coincides with the outbreak of the war, and describes a perception of something dangerous in the collective environment that mobilises the survival instincts. The need for stability may be overly powerful because of this background and temperament, even if the main configurations of the chart reflect a more volatile and adventurous nature. Now something is being freed inside you, through the agency of the triangle.

Connie: I do feel that something is shifting. I thought for a while I could not survive this. But now I am beginning to realise I am still here. The worst has happened, and I am still here.

Liz: Are you happy to continue with the discussion? I know this is difficult to talk about in front of the group.

Connie: Yes. I was hoping you could also comment on the third chart, in the same way you did with my husband's.

The Instrument of Betrayal

Liz: I will mention some relevant configurations. There is no birth time for this lady. You have given me a "flat" chart, so we have no Ascendant. But we know that the Sun is in Scorpio, exactly square Pluto. Her Moon is in Sagittarius. We don't know the precise degree because there is no birth time, but this Sagittarian side connects her strongly with you as a friend, and with your husband's Ascendant as well.

There is also a group of planets in Gemini – Mars, Saturn, and Uranus – and whatever degree it is in, the Moon is going to be opposing one or other of these, and possibly all three. Pluto may be transiting opposite the Moon, or it may not come to it until a bit later. But it is presently opposing her natal Uranus, which is exactly opposite your natal Sun. Now, what could we work with here, bearing in mind Toni Wolff's words? What is the Instrument of Betrayal carrying for Connie and her husband?

Audience: There is something that seems to be happening in all of the people I know who are having this transit of Pluto to natal Uranus. It seems to suddenly reveal something which has been hidden. From the beginning of this discussion, I got the feeling that what is happening is the very best thing that could happen at this point.

When there is a split in people, and their full characters are not being lived out, that perpetuates the split. But the moment the truth is revealed, the split has a chance to be resolved, and those aspects which have been underground can be brought into the light and be lived. All three of these people are so Sagittarian. I think that Sagittarians always live with a constant conflict between their desire for freedom and their strong attachment to conventionality. I think that is at the root of the split.

Audience: But the Instrument of Betrayal is a Scorpio, with the Sun square Pluto. That is a very different thing.

Liz: Indeed. She has Sun in Scorpio square Pluto, and Connie has Moon conjunct Pluto. It sounds as though Connie has lived her Moon-Pluto through her deep devotion to her family life, and now she is living it again through her emotional suffering. The Instrument of Betrayal...Shall we make up a name for her, Connie?
Connie: We could call her Phyllis.

Liz: Very well. Phyllis may be discovering her Plutonian side through her betrayal of her friend and the intensity with which she has attached herself to Connie's husband. It is rather like a hall of mirrors. You have the Sun and Ascendant in Sagittarius, Connie, but you don't seem to have lived it within your marriage. Your husband has Sagittarius rising as well, and he doesn't seem to have lived it either. Now the third party comes on stage, with the Moon in Sagittarius. Jupiterian energy is breaking loose all over the place, and it is transiting Pluto that is bringing it out. And Plutonian energy, too, may be breaking out, because I am pretty sure Phyllis also has an unlived life which is now making its appearance in this triangle. Is she married too, Connie?

Connie: No. She was married once, but divorced. She said she wanted to be free.

Liz: And now she is discovering the Pluto side of herself. Ah, well. It seems the gods will not be cheated.

The Scorpion and the Centaur

Audience: It seems to me that it is liberating everyone.

Liz: I agree. In both Connie and Phyllis there exists a Jupiter-Pluto combination of energies. This may be one of the reasons why they became friends. They are mirror images of each other. You don't have anything in Scorpio, Connie, but you have a Sun-Pluto trine and, more importantly, that powerful Moon-Pluto conjunction. On an emotional level you are very, very intense. There is something between you and Phyllis that I think you could learn a great deal from. The same energies are there. But Scorpio and Sagittarius have a natural antipathy. Although they share a love of drama, the basis for the drama is very different. Where Scorpio is dark, Sagittarius is bright. Scorpio's sense of the dramatic arises from the feeling that all emotional encounters are life-death struggles. Sagittarius' sense of the dramatic arises from the intuition of a larger-than-life realm, a place where the gods may be seen in their shining glory. On a bad day, Scorpio views Sagittarius as superficial, hypocritical, and false, while Sagittarius views Scorpio as negative, destructive, and manipulative. There is an archetypal dichotomy between them.

Myth tells us some interesting things about the relationship between these two signs. Herakles' battle with the Hydra is usually associated with Scorpio. He must fight this dreadful slimy thing with nine heads that lives in a dark cave and eats people. He can't get it to come out of hiding until he shoots flaming arrows into the cave and drives the creature out into the light. Then he can't kill it in the ordinary way, because every time he cuts off a head, it sprouts another nine. In the end, he can only destroy it by holding it up in the sunlight, which it can't bear. This myth is about bringing things up from the depths of the darkness into the light. It is a very Scorpionic image – the hunt for the destructive monster that lies within, and the transformation which is effected by exposure to the light of consciousness.

Having conquered the Hydra, Herakles then leaves the scene, but his arrows have the Hydra's blood on them, and this blood is a deadly poison. On the next stage of his journey he meets his friend, Chiron the centaur. But a battle breaks out between Herakles and some nasty, uncivilised centaurs, and Chiron gets in the way and is accidentally wounded by an arrow carrying the Hydra's poison. Although he is wise and good, Chiron is not immune to the aftermath of Herakles' battle with the Hydra, any more than we are immune to the backlash of eruptions of collective darkness such as war.

This psychological backlash may carry on down the generations, as any child or even grandchild of a Holocaust survivor can tell you. Beneath the characteristic Sagittarian *joie-de-vivre* and optimism, there is always a dark, *a priori* sense that life can inflict terrible, unfair wounds. That is why Sagittarius seeks meaning in life – we formulate a meaningful world-view in order to make sense of the darkness and suffering we see around us. That is one of the functions of religion as well as philosophy. Every sign remembers the previous sign, and seeks to move beyond it. The zodiac is a cycle. This is also the transition of the 8th house to the 9th. It is understandable that, remembering what lies behind, Sagittarius will turn its face to the light and focus on the universal picture. It is also understandable that Scorpio must attend to the ongoing battle, because courage and concentration must be constantly applied if the Hydra is to be destroyed. The two signs face different ways. This combination of energies is in your chart, Connie, and in your rival's chart. Each of you could change places at any moment and play the other one's role. At the moment your friend appears to be playing Jupiter – the irresponsible *puella* who has no respect for the institution of marriage and runs off with her best friend's man. But perhaps she is also playing Pluto. I would guess you see her as a Plutonian at the moment – predatory and treacherous.

Connie: Yes. And secretive.

Liz: But your Sun-Pluto and Moon-Pluto suggest that you can express Plutonian qualities as well. I wonder to what extent covert Plutonian dynamics have been a means by which you have tried to hold your husband's loyalty. That could be one of the most painful and also healing truths you might have to look at. In what ways have you tried to "keep" him, in order to avoid going through abandonment and hurt? This experience could liberate you, because it isn't only your husband who needs freeing. There is, as we have seen, a parental dimension to this triangle. But there is so much more.

Connie: If I am really honest with myself, I can see that I have done some manipulating in my marriage. I know that. I suppose it is a misuse of power.

Liz: "Misuse" implies that somewhere there is a rulebook which stipulates the "right" and "wrong" uses of power. I am not sure life is that simple. In intimate relationships, we all exercise a certain degree of emotional manipulation. Most of the time the motives, from an emotional perspective, are entirely legitimate, and spring from the simple desire to remain with the person one loves and needs. And the partner must be willing to *be* manipulated. It is a dance of two. Perhaps you have sometimes overdone it. But it would be astonishing if you had done otherwise, given your background. You were desperate to keep a stable marriage. You may have done this in ways that made it difficult for your husband to live out his Jupiter-Uranus side. But he colluded with you, probably for similar reasons. Now it is time for this old pattern to break apart.

Audience: You said earlier that Connie's husband has a 5th house Saturn. That might be one of the reasons why he has needed to keep everything stable and secure.

Liz: Yes, Saturn in the 5th suggests that he takes love very seriously. Some people with Saturn in the 5th avoid deep involvements, but this is usually a defence, because they fear the weight of a potential commitment. By nature, a 5th house Saturn is loyal and responsible in matters of love, although not always demonstrative. But the person described in this chart is an Aquarian with a Sagittarius Ascendant, a very strong Uranus, and Venus-Jupiter in Aries in the 5th. Saturn has had to work very hard to keep all that down.

Connie: His Aquarian side is really showing now. He wants us all to be friends.

Liz: Oh, dear. Well, in the famous words of Mandy Rice-Davies, he would say that, wouldn't he? However, it is worth trying for several reasons, not least because you would learn a lot about yourself from understanding your friend's behaviour. Also, it might help you see more clearly what your husband is really doing. It would be too easy to blame your friend for taking him away from you. It would be too easy to blame yourself for your own imagined failings. And it would be too easy to blame your husband for being callous and unfeeling. No doubt you have to feel all those things for a while, but there is something beyond the orgy of recrimination.

Your husband may be searching for a lost side of his own soul – a Jupiter-Uranus side – which he sees in his new love. He may be in for a shock. However, she is undoubtedly a good hook, with the Moon in Sagittarius and, probably, a Moon-Uranus opposition. You are also a good hook because you are a double Sagittarian, but you have not lived this side of yourself in the marriage, and he has not been able to experience it through you. He is looking for it elsewhere. Yet it belongs to him. What he is searching for is something you, too, might need to search for and live more fully. This might be more creative than sinking into the negative side of Moon-Pluto, which may be something your mother did a lot – feeling victimised and oppressed. "Life has treated me appallingly!" is a favourite Moon-Pluto script. What has happened to you *is* appalling, on one level. But on another level, it has nothing to do with you as a "failed" wife. It has to do with three people who have not lived their inner lives sufficiently, and now the unlived life is demanding an outlet.

Connie: Everything you say makes a good deal of sense to me. I need to think about it all. But I don't know what to do with the pain.

Liz: I don't have an antidote to give you for the pain. Interpreting a horoscope is not a cure for emotional suffering. Insight can help you to carry the pain, but it will not take it away. It is going to be there, however much you understand, and it should not be blocked or denied. You need to go through the process of grieving, because you are having to let go of something inner as well as something outer. Transiting Pluto usually demands that we relinquish something, and the thing we often lose first is our pride. What you have experienced is a betrayal, and betrayal is the fundamental core of all triangles. Betrayal shatters ideals and illusions, and plays hell with our pride. It also breaks parental identification. There is no more powerful instrument for cutting the umbilical cord than betrayal. Betrayal makes us grow up, whether we are the Betrayer, the Betrayed, or the Instrument of Betrayal.

It might be helpful to reflect on what you thought your marriage was about, and whom you thought you married. Then have a good, hard look at your parents' marriage. What kind of marriage was it? Do you know why they married? How did she feel about him? How did he feel about her? The more you look, the more you may see that you have been living in a kind of cocoon filled with your own ideas about your husband, yourself, and the nature of love. You are not unique in this. All human beings do it, to a greater or lesser extent. Sometimes what is outside the cocoon is in accord with what is within it, and sometimes not. Sometimes it changes over time, through no one's "fault". The more you see where your fantasies, expectations, and fears have obscured who you really are, the freer you will be. Something is breaking down that I suspect you badly need to get out of. I don't mean that you badly need to get out of the marriage; you don't yet know what the outcome of present events might be. It might sort itself out, or it might not. But even if it does, you will still have to deal with the sense of having been betrayed.

The archetypal nature of betrayal

There is a very provocative essay by James Hillman called "Betrayal", which can be found in a collection of his work called *Loose Ends*.[9] I would suggest that you read this essay, and pay particular

---

9 James Hillman, *Loose Ends*, Spring Publications, Zürich, 1975.

attention to the story about the father and son with which he begins. Hillman suggests that betrayal is an archetypal experience which is the chief instrument of individuation. There is something transformative in recognising how our fantasies of life and love prevent us from growing up and becoming full members of the human family. Betrayal is the means through which these fantasies are made conscious. We attempt to enclose ourselves and other people in our fantasy-world, which is usually meant to compensate for childhood pain. Since all childhoods have pain, the assumptions we carry are also archetypal, and reflect an alternative child-world that resembles Eden in its innocence and fusion-state with the divine parent. The serpent in the Garden is an image of this archetypal role of betrayal, which is inherent in the state of innocence and, sooner or later, rises up to destroy our fusion.

There is no formula to cope with the pain of betrayal. An archetypal perspective can help us to look at things differently, but the pain cannot be rationalised away. But there is a difference between blind pain and pain that is accompanied by understanding. If you play the role of the "failed" wife, Connie, it is a *cul de sac*. It goes nowhere and you will learn nothing. You will injure and demean yourself. Nor has your husband been "taken away" from you. It is very human to see one's partner as having been taken away. But the truth is that people get up and walk away. And if he is so passive and lifeless that someone can come and steal him out of his armchair, what are you doing married to him anyway? If you start thinking in a new way, something highly positive can come out of it. I have great faith in Pluto transits. When Pluto conjuncts the Sun, it is a real chance for us to emerge as individuals. Something must end in order for something new to begin. It is a birth, believe it or not.

Connie: I find it very hard to see it that way.

Liz: Of course. But you can try. Don't expect the pain to go away. Indulge in bouts of rage if you like. Think and write and say dreadful things. But also, start asking some questions.

Repetition compulsion

Audience: I have a question. I know a situation where a young man married his childhood girlfriend. They both worked for an insurance firm, and they had a young son. Now this man has left his wife for somebody else who works in the insurance firm, and they also have a young son. My question is this: I can understand why he felt the need to break away from his marriage. He was obviously very cocooned, and he wanted to get free. But why did he go for somebody exactly like the woman he left?

Liz: We don't know that the two women are exactly the same, only that they both work for the same insurance company. But it is possible they have certain things in common. This is usually the case. It underlines what I have been saying about the inner dynamics of triangles and the compulsion to express a piece of unlived life. When there is no consciousness, emotional situations do tend to repeat. The same dynamic draws the same kind of person. It is sometimes known as "out of the frying pan, into the fire". One feels one is in a dreadful, suffocating situation, and it seems all wrong. Then one thinks one has found redemption, but the redemption turns out to be another version of the thing one got out of, because one hasn't actually recognised the inner reality one is really looking for.

Many triangles repeat themselves – different costumes, same characters and script. Some triangles are truly transformative. They break apart an old parental pattern, and the new relationship is genuinely happier and more rewarding. Or the triangle serves the purpose of freeing energy and inner potentials. Even if the old relationship is re-established, or one winds up with neither party, everything has changed. But we are still ourselves, however much we try to rearrange our outer lives. If an inner issue has not been dealt with, the same patterns will arise in a new relationship. The compatibility may be greater with another partner, but one still has the same psyche. Perhaps your friend doesn't want to face the issue of why he got himself into the original situation in the first place. Perhaps he is trying to ensure that his view of reality remains the same. He wants his life to change without having to change himself.

Audience: When I heard that he had left his marriage, I thought, "I can understand why he left his wife." Then I felt terribly disappointed. I suppose I am being too critical. I wanted to see him go off with an exotic fan-dancer.

Liz: Perhaps he has. You don't know what they get up to at home. Anyway, there is no guarantee that we will learn anything from our experiences. I believe there is always a profound reason why triangles come into our lives, and when they do, we will always see the relevant transits – as we do in Connie's example, with Pluto going over the natal Sun. There will always be a powerful transit connected with the experience which can tell us about its deeper meaning. But there is no guarantee that the ego will learn anything from it. The transit indicates that the psyche is trying to push something into life, into conscious awareness. We can turn our backs on the opportunity. We have a choice. Unfortunately, a great many people learn little, or nothing at all. They are torn apart by conflicting emotions, and their lives are upheaved. They come out no more conscious than when they went in, except that they are older and more embittered.

Age may catch up with a pattern of repeating triangles. One becomes cynical and tired and can't be bothered to try again, because one knows it will be a repeat of the one before. One learns to put up with unhappiness, and then everyone thinks one has finally settled down. But resignation is not the same as conscious awareness, and bitterness is not the same as genuinely letting someone or something go. As I said, there is no guarantee that we will learn anything. Moreover, we can't always be brave and heroic. We all need some element of familiarity in our lives. Some people will always look close to home for their triangles. Others find somebody on the other side of the world. It depends very much on the nature of the individual chart. There may be truly mythic journeys made within the same insurance company. Whether or not your friend has learned anything from his experience remains conjecture. You could be underestimating him.

Audience: I have noticed, when a triangle is broken, that there is an enormous release of energy. It doesn't matter whether or not the people in the established relationship manage to be at peace with what has happened. There is a huge release of energy. It often happens without your needing to do anything about it. You start waking up in the morning with a different energy within yourself, especially with long-term relationships where one has developed a form of symbiosis. When that link is cut off, you can see people flourishing tremendously. The Sagittarius energy in Carol's chart says something about having hope and trust in the future. The outcome has something to do with growing up and understanding life better.

Integration and forgiving

Liz: A triangle can be like a grand trine in a chart. The energy circles around and around, and doesn't go anywhere. Within triangles, all three people tend to project elements of themselves on each other. The triangle holds these projections in place, and there may be enormous resistance to change. We might even say that the triangle forms *because* there is resistance to change, so whatever is seeking expression from within is experienced through projection. When such a triangle breaks up, the projections come back home again. Psychic energy is released, whether it is through death or the voluntary relinquishing of someone. The timing of this is not accidental. In one, two, or even all three parties, unconscious issues have finally reached a point where they can be integrated, even if this is expressed by simply letting go. The moment we are able to do that, the projections begin to become conscious.

Audience: James Hillman talks about the glory of forgiveness as an important spiritual experience, a kind of grace.

Liz: I don't believe real forgiving comes any other way. It *is* a kind of grace. It cannot be created by an act of will. It is very sad to hear the Betrayed saying, "I forgive you," not because it is truly heartfelt, but in order to get the straying partner back again. Underneath there may be no forgiveness at all – although this may not be entirely conscious – and then the punishment can go on and on. I think forgiveness can only come from recognition of one's collusion and the taking back of projections. Before that, forgiveness is not really possible. It seems to emerge out of something being genuinely integrated in oneself. The entire process is transformative. I don't know whether it is the forgiveness which transforms, or whether the forgiveness is a by-product of the transformation. I suspect it is the latter. We cannot manufacture forgiveness if we have been betrayed. We can only work to integrate what belongs to our own souls.

Audience: So the real issue is inside, not outside.

Liz: That is what I mean when I say that, at bottom, triangles involve our own unlived psychic life. Something changes in one's consciousness when one begins to recognise this. That is why Toni Wolff's little piece of advice, which sounds a bit snide on first hearing, needs to be taken very seriously. One begins to recognise oneself in the mirror of the rival. One may also begin to see that the partner is acting out something one isn't living oneself. Something is released when we understand these things.

Audience: She may not have meant it literally.

Liz: She did mean it literally, and she acted on it. But of course she meant it symbolically as well. The rival is within oneself. If we can understand the rival as an inner as well as an outer being, then having the rival to tea means, in effect, inviting our shadow to tea. It means making a relationship with that which is unlived in ourselves.

Audience: It doesn't sound very comfortable.

Liz: It isn't very comfortable, inwardly or outwardly. As has been pointed out, one wants to put something in the tea. And there are very good reasons why we do not live certain dimensions of ourselves. It is not that they are innately terrible. But to the ego, they *seem* terrible. Allowing these things into our lives, and acknowledging that they are our own, threatens all our most entrenched values. Inviting the rival to tea is tantamount to dismantling the image one has carried of oneself all one's life. I do believe that, in the end, psychic integration is the teleology of all triangles. Even when the outer planets are involved in parental triangles, the thing to which we are so deeply attached in the parent is something that belongs to our own souls. This "something" may involve stretching beyond personal boundaries and allowing a deeper, broader level of reality into our lives. Nevertheless, it is connected with our own life journey.

Close encounters of the Uranian kind

Uranus in the 4th may initially be projected onto, or experienced through, the father. In Connie's case, her father was there and then, suddenly, not there. Connie's 4th house Uranus was first experienced as an external event. Later, when her father returned, Uranus was perceived as a negative character quality belonging to her father. But in the end, it is her natal Uranus, and symbolises something within Connie. It is not a personal planet, but reflects a collective urge toward an ideal of perfection. As it is in Taurus, it portrays a generation group searching for new definitions of security and new values which are less bound to the material world.

Because this quest is collective, it is not easy to acknowledge personally, and many people of Connie's generation have felt "forced" to relinquish their material stability. The upheaval of World War Two reflected this on an outer level. If Connie wishes to befriend Uranus, she needs to be willing to expand her vision and see the universe differently. She has to recognise the larger evolutionary patterns at work, not only in her own life but in the life of the human family. Then the independence and detachment which she saw in a negative form in her father might become a positive force in her own life.

Uranus is hard for the ego to digest, and not only because it is a collective planet. It is indigestible because it requires distancing ourselves from our emotions and instincts. Uranus is the natural enemy of the Moon, and threatens our deepest and most primal security needs. Allowing Uranus into one's personal life means acknowledging that relationships can exist without the necessity of a reassuring physical and emotional presence. Uranian bonds are mental and spiritual, forged from shared ideals and the recognition that we are fellow travellers on a vast evolutionary journey that began at the dawn of time and whose ultimate goal cannot even be imagined. These bonds may be indestructible, but they cannot be seen, touched, or fixed to the dinner table or the bedroom. In this vast, impersonal context, the little hurts and disappointments of everyday life are banal and meaningless. This is very hard for the lunar side of us to countenance. Our feelings are no longer special, and neither are our loves and losses.

From the Moon's perspective, if my beloved is not here with me, there is no relationship. People who have been forcibly separated by distance sometimes learn that there is a connection that continues on subtler levels. It is easier to experience this invisible connection in a friendship. A friend may move far away, and one sees him or her only every few years. But each time there is contact, the relationship continues as though nothing at all has changed. The friendship is still alive and growing, although there has been no visible effort to make it so. There is a remarkable novel by the Australian novelist Patrick White, called *Voss*.[10] It deals, in part, with this theme of the invisible dimension of relationship that transcends time and space. For those of you who, like me, find novels sometimes more inspiring than didactic texts, I would highly recommend it.

Uranus, when it is concerned with relationship, challenges us to recognise bonds that are not dependent on material and emotional life. When it is in the 4th, this applies to the bonds we make with "home" and "family". Home, for a 4th house Uranus, may not be the land in which one was born or the bricks and mortar house in which one lives; and family may not be those bound by blood. Uranus in Connie's 4th is a description of something she experienced first through her father. He went away, but the bond continued. He was not physically or emotionally present, but he was present nevertheless, and the bond could not be destroyed even by Connie's negation of her feelings.

Had it been destroyed or irrelevant to her inner life, she would not have been drawn to the same Uranian qualities in a husband. The Uranian ability to see beyond emotions to the deeper intellectual and spiritual basis of relationship needs to be integrated into Connie's own consciousness. On the human level, she has been through an unfairly painful and humiliating experience. On a more profound level, probably no other means would have sufficed to put her in touch with this dimension of her life journey.

Parental significators as embodiments of unlived life

When astrological symbols are experienced first through the parents and then later through a triangle in which the same experience repeats itself, they describe something within us that needs to be lived. Planets in parental houses are not only descriptive of parental patterns. They are descriptive of unlived dimensions of ourselves, especially

---

10 Patrick White, *Voss*, Penguin, London, 1960.

when they don't agree with other factors in the chart – like a 4th house Uranus sitting side by side with a Moon-Pluto conjunction in the 7th. Moon-Pluto looks at Uranus and says, "That has nothing to do with me. *I'm* not like that. I'm loving and devoted. My father was the cold, unfeeling one who didn't care about his family. Now it's my husband. *He's* the one who ran off." We may have a 4th or 10th house Jupiter placed in a chart which is mainly earthy and watery, and we say: "My mother was selfish and demanding. *I'm* not like that. My father was the irresponsible playboy, not me." Yet it is one's own Jupiter. Unless it is owned and integrated, it may pop up as the unfaithful partner or the Instrument of Betrayal. Or if the parent did not live the archetype in any way, and it remained unconscious in the family psyche, one may find oneself becoming the Betrayer against one's will, driven by something over which one has no control.

Audience: Does this apply to any planet in the 10th or 4th?

Liz: Yes. Even if the parent embodied the planet in creative ways, it is still our planet and belongs to our own destiny. Obviously, it helps if we have a positive model.

Audience: It is much more difficult to get a grip on these planets if they are not exhibited by the parents. We don't know what we are looking at.

Liz: It *is* harder if the parent is vehemently denying that he or she is like that. Sometimes we get a fully lived but destructive or hurtful expression of the planet. That also makes things difficult. We may repudiate the planet because we cannot see any positive possibilities in it. The enactment of Connie's 4th house Uranus was quite overt – her father left. But it was a hurtful experience. When he returned, he behaved in a Uranian way, but exhibited the less attractive dimensions of the planet. This was also a hurtful experience. Partly because of this, and partly because of the conflict between Uranian attributes and other qualities in her chart, Connie grew up with a fear of Uranian energy, which she tried to block both within herself and within her marriage. Yet she married a Uranian man, with Sun in Aquarius and both Luminaries strongly aspecting Uranus. There is a certain archetypal inevitability about what has ensued.

Planets in the parental houses are not always overt. A 4th house Uranus may not reflect an obvious childhood separation, because the qualities and patterns Uranus describes may be ruthlessly stifled by the parent. The father may be deeply, desperately Uranian. But his generation and family responsibilities, as well as other factors in his chart, may have silenced whatever revolutionary, inspired qualities he had in his soul. His child senses, but does not understand, the strange, cold, abrupt, disconnected energy he radiates. Parental significators don't necessarily describe events, or even the outward behaviour of the parent. They describe archetypal patterns which we share with that parent. But the parent may spend a lifetime struggling against those patterns. Let's take the example of Jupiter in the 10th. In myth, Jupiter is king of the gods. He is brilliant and imperial, a showman and a shape-shifter. He seduces women and boys. He hurls his lightning bolt and the heavens are illuminated; he thunders and the earth shakes. We consider our poor, sad mother, who has exhausted herself looking after the children and has suffered ill health for years, and we think, "This can't be right. What a silly interpretation. The 10th house is clearly not the mother."

But we could stop reacting and start observing. We could watch her controlling the whole family from her bed, throwing vapours which dominate the atmosphere in the house, and we might realise that the entire domestic environment revolves around her. She is indeed the ruler. When she is unhappy, everyone hears about it, and they dare not be happy themselves. Even the dog is afraid to bark when she has one of her headaches. When she wants something, she gets it immediately, because no one can cope with their guilt otherwise. Her depression is so dramatic. Her misery is so theatrical. We realise that she should have been on the stage, or been the CEO of a large international company. We may then start recognising that she is truly, unmistakably Jupiterian. But it is a disguised Jupiter, an unconscious Jupiter, stifled for perhaps perfectly understandable reasons, and allowed only an indirect route to expression in life. And because it is *our* Jupiter in *our* 10th house, we need to find a more honest and productive way of living it.

Audience: How did you know I have Jupiter conjunct the MC?

Liz: I didn't. It was a lucky dip. A planet in the 4th or 10th may not be enacted obviously, but it will be part of what we experience through the parent. If the parent has not creatively lived the archetypal pattern symbolised by the planet, it is indeed much harder to understand what we are dealing with. We may not realise what we are meeting through a triangle which appears in our life later. The Saturnian parent who rejects, and then turns up in a triangle as a cold and rejecting partner, has something to do with our own need to acquire boundaries. If we view this fundamental Saturnian experience from a more detached perspective, what is rejection, in the end, if not someone else drawing boundaries which we find intolerable? It may be our own lack of boundaries that attracts us into a triangle where we are the Betrayed, rejected by a Saturnian partner who says, "I want to be separate." Or we may be the Betrayer, fleeing from a partner whose emotional needs seem stifling but who secretly mirrors our own inability to cope with loneliness. The hard and painful lessons that come from these kinds of experiences are lessons about what is undeveloped in ourselves.

We may have to discover our primal passions if Pluto is in the 10th or 4th. We might disown this at first, and say, "My mother was terribly manipulative," or, "My father was so controlling." Why do people become manipulative and controlling? If someone is expressing such Plutonian qualities, they are not doing it because it is fun. Relationships are equated with survival, and there is a desperate need to ensure that loved ones remain close. Pluto is mobilised when one feels under threat. People become manipulative because they are terrified of losing the object of their love. We are all capable of this, given the right level of attachment and the right level of threat. If we disown these attributes, Pluto may turn up in a triangle. Then we may have to discover how possessive *we* can be. We may acquire a deeply possessive partner, and get as far as saying, "I have chosen someone just like my mother/father." That is a useful piece of insight, but it is only the beginning. It is our own 4th or 10th house Pluto. Often we only realise we have a Pluto through the experience of betrayal. We discover that we feel passionately, that we need intensely, that desperation can make us treacherous and manipulative, and that control may seem the only way to survive. This process of self-discovery may be frightening and humbling, but it allows us to fully become what we are.

Weak or missing elements

We can look at many other things besides planets in the 10th and 4th to get a sense of what triangles may reveal about our unlived side. Sometimes unlived life is described by a lack of one of the astrological elements. Often the rival in a triangle embodies the element we cannot express. It may not be as obvious as a situation where we have no planets in earth, and our rival has six planets in Capricorn. We may have several planets in earth, but we may not be connected to them very well. They may be undeveloped, or the ego may fight against them. Our rival may have an earthy Ascendant or an angular Saturn that he or she is expressing very strongly.

The temptation, if one is cast in the role of the Betrayed or the Instrument of Betrayal, is often to demean oneself and idealise the rival. This is one way in which missing elements make their appearance. We look at others and feel inferior to them because they seem to have what we lack. But recognising that the rival carries something unlived in oneself does not imply that one is competing with someone "better" or "superior". Needing to develop something that another person expresses easily does not imply inferiority. If one is the Betrayed or the Instrument of Betrayal, it can stick in one's throat to look at the rival and admit, "Yes, this person has something I need to develop," because pride gets in the way. But we will not get very far in understanding a triangle if our pride is so great that we are not prepared to look more deeply. We will also not get very far if we are too busy performing the *mea culpa* ceremony and belittling ourselves.

We may turn a weak or missing element into an object of contempt. That is the opposite of idealisation, and it happens equally often when an element is unexpressed. It is a very common human defence against feelings of inadequacy. Wherever we are badly adapted or feel awkward and clumsy, we may attempt to cope with our discomfort by looking down on those who embody our undeveloped qualities. We may be weak in the element of air and despise intellectuals because they "live in their heads", "don't feel anything", and are always "talking about something rather than experiencing it". We may be weak in the element of earth and despise people who are preoccupied with the concrete world: they are "materialistic", "unimaginative", "rigid", and "boring". We may be weak in the element of water, and despise emotionally expressive people because they are "hysterical", "manipulative", or "incapable of rational thought". We may be weak in the element of fire and view more self-expressive natures as "narcissistic", "pushy", and "insensitive". It is common enough and human enough, when caught in a triangle, to use contempt rather like we use aspirin. It helps to take away the pain. But when we do this, we may miss something extremely important.

I once had an extraordinary conversation with someone in a seminar. The theme of the seminar was not about triangles, but the subject came up, as it often does. This particular woman had found herself in the role of the Betrayed. Her husband had become involved with a young woman from southeast Asia, and this provided the fuel for some scathing pronouncements on the inferiority of southeast Asians. I tried probing a bit to find out what this was all about, and then, at her request, we looked at the woman's chart. The sweeping statements she was making were in fact a description of some very difficult issues in her own chart. These were projected, not just on her rival, but onto an entire race. Personal hurts can link up with our most deeply rooted prejudices, and both are connected to profound unconscious feelings of inferiority. If we catch ourselves doing what this woman did, we need to think hard about what lies beneath.

If we are the Betrayer, we may project an undeveloped element on two people – the Betrayed and the Instrument of Betrayal. If water is weak in our chart, we may have a watery partner who is "manipulative" and "suffocating", and a watery lover who is "poetic", "imaginative", and "tender". If earth is unexpressed, we may have an earthy partner who is "unimaginative" and "boring", and an earthy lover who is "sensuous" and "well-grounded". If we lack fire, our fiery partner is "insensitive" and "domineering", but our fiery lover is "imaginative", "romantic", and "in touch with the cosmos". The Betrayer, unconscious of his or her own problem, cannot see that these are two sides of the same energy, and that they are both within him or her. The difficulty in integrating an unadapted element may itself generate a kind of split which pushes a person into a triangle. A missing or unexpressed element is not always found in a rival. As the Betrayer, we may experience it in the two people between whom we are divided.

Hard aspects

Hard aspects are another indication in the chart of qualities which may be difficult to integrate. They, too, may enact themselves in triangles. If we identify with one planet in the aspect and disown the other, the unacknowledged planet may make itself known by popping up in a triangle. We may experience this planet as coming at us from the outside, through the wiles of the Instrument of Betrayal, or in the treacherous actions of the Betrayer, or in the unrelenting grip of the Betrayed on the person we want to be with. I would like to refer again to Connie's chart, to see whether hard aspects might give us some insight into her very painful dilemma. What hard aspects in this chart do any of you think might be conducive to the kind of projection I am talking about?

Audience: There is a T-cross between Venus, Jupiter, and Neptune.

Liz: Yes, a T-cross can take a long time to integrate. There is an out-of-sign square between Venus and Neptune, and also between Venus and Jupiter, and an opposition between Jupiter and Neptune. Can you see what might be happening here? What doesn't get lived?

Audience: Jupiter.

Liz: I would be inclined to agree, despite the fact that Jupiter is the chart ruler and the dispositor of the Sun. Connie seems to have expressed Venus in Capricorn square Neptune in Virgo quite freely. It is self-sacrificing, loyal, devoted, and longs for constant intimacy. Venus-Neptune, especially in earth, tries to selflessly serve those it loves. But what about the Venus-Jupiter square?

Audience: That's "Me first!"

Liz: Yes, Venus-Jupiter is focused on its own pleasure. It can be extremely generous, but the generosity may vanish if too much sacrifice is required. This is the generosity of someone with a full larder, who can afford to distribute largesse. When the going gets tough, Venus-Jupiter is often on the next plane out. Venus-Jupiter says, "Love shouldn't require hardship. I want my fun. Otherwise I'll look elsewhere."

Connie, you probably lived this aspect on stage. But in personal life I suspect your Jupiter gets projected – especially since both your rival and your husband are Jupiterian.

Connie: I would say that is true. I have always felt he was more selfish. But now I am being forced to put myself first.

Liz: You are learning how to look after Number One and make sure you get some enjoyment in return for your emotional investments.

Connie: My father used that very expression – looking after Number One.

Liz: Yes, I suppose he would have. Funny how he keeps turning up.

Connie: Like the proverbial bad penny.

Liz: With a hard aspect, it is important to find a balance between both planets. With a T-cross, at least one planet is usually relegated to the unconscious. It isn't easy, with Venus square both Jupiter and Neptune, to know whether to sacrifice oneself or pursue one's own pleasure and fulfillment. We should not assume that, because Jupiter is in Pisces, it is innately self-sacrificing. We experience joy in the sphere of life reflected by our Jupiter sign. Contrary to popular opinion, Pisces does not always rush about serving others. Jupiter in Pisces can reflect tremendous joy in abandoning oneself to emotional and creative excess, which is why it is associated with artists, and with the theatre in particular. Actors are not usually known for their lack of ego, although extreme generosity may be spontaneously expressed in grand magnanimous gestures. Connie may not get the balance perfect between these three planets, but it is important to honour all of them as much as possible. Disowning and projecting any one of them can lead to a lot of trouble.

More charts from the group

I would like to put up another chart now, and continue exploring how unintegrated planets "materialise" in relationship triangles. This chart was given to me by Frances, who is here today, but the individual concerned, who is called Luis, is not. Frances assures me that the chart is offered with his consent. I will have to take that on trust. This chart has been hand-drawn on a transparency, not computer-generated, so it may not be very clear to those of you sitting in the back. Frances, I'm not sure what the thing in the 2nd house is.

Luis: mother-love

Frances: It's Chiron. Wounded.

Liz: Sorry, it looks like a squashed insect. We need some information about Luis before we carry on. You said he has given you permission to talk about the chart, and he wants to read your notes afterward. I assume there is a triangle in his life.

Frances: There are several triangles of different kinds. Luis' father was a very famous man. The father died when Luis' mother was pregnant, and the mother married another man, also someone famous, ten years later. So there was an early triangle, because Luis was ten when his mother remarried, and he had her to himself for ten years. He then married when he was quite young. Now he is involved with someone else, and this woman is also married. He works in the field of psychology, but has never been in therapy himself.

Liz: Does his relationship with a married woman cause him pain?

Frances: No.

Liz: He's happy to have these triangles in his life?

Frances: I think it's just the life he leads.

Liz: So he doesn't want an exclusive relationship. Some triangles like this seem to work reasonably well. People are apparently happy to stay in them, except that there is usually one person who doesn't know what is going on, and it wouldn't work for them if they ever found out – which they have a way of doing, sooner or later. In Luis' case, we don't know to what extent his wife, and his lover's husband, are privy to the situation.

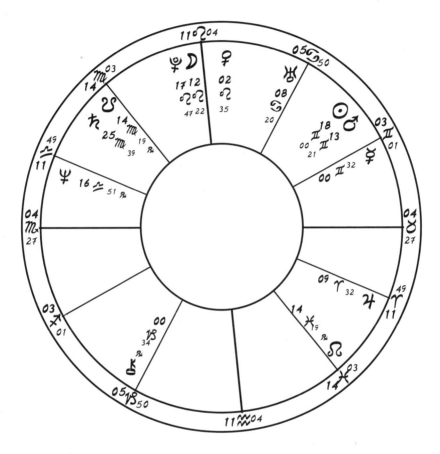

Luis
[Data withheld for purposes of confidentiality]

Frances: I don't know. But I think you are right. If his wife knew, it wouldn't work for her.

Liz: What is Luis living out through this double triangle? It's interesting that he has never known his father. This might be connected with his Sun in the 8th, trine Neptune and square Saturn. Saturn is one of the 4th house rulers. Uranus is the other 4th house ruler, and it is involved in the generational opposition to Chiron. Luis' father is a mystery; he has vanished into the unknown. He was, you say, a very famous man. That is a hard spirit to live up to. Then the mother married the second famous man. Looking in the ephemeris very quickly, to see what progressions and transits were operating when this second marriage took place, it seems that Luis' progressed Moon was conjunct natal and progressed Chiron at the time. His progressed Sun had moved past the exact square to natal Saturn, but not by that much, and the progressed MC was still within orb of a separating conjunction to natal Pluto. Transiting Neptune had been hovering over his Ascendant the year before. This collection of planetary movements makes me think his mother might have been involved with the second man for a year or so before the marriage, and this, rather than the formal marriage, constituted the real shock. How did Luis get on with his stepfather?

Frances: Ostensibly very well. He doesn't report much discord.

Liz: He doesn't report much discord about anything, does he? The power of his relationship with his mother is clearly described by the planets at the MC. Mother is everything. She is mother and lover, both at the same time, and his experience of her seems to be so powerful that his married lover may be a stand-in for her.

Audience: So he is repeating something with his triangle.

Liz: There is certainly the feeling of a recreation of the maternal relationship, although I think this is only part of it. Is this married lady unhappy in her marriage?

Frances: No, I wouldn't say particularly unhappy. She is bored.

Audience: There seems to be a lot of narcissism here.

Liz: Can you explain more clearly what you mean? Do you mean narcissism in the clinical sense?

Audience: No, I mean self-centredness, I suppose. There is a lot of Leo at the MC. He wants to be famous and glamorous like his father and stepfather.

Liz: Yes, the emphasis at the MC suggests that he needs other people to see him as very important. Other people's opinions matter a great deal. He wants to be special in the eyes of the world. But I think he is also carrying very high expectations from his mother. Why does a woman marry two famous men? One wonders what is at *her* MC that she has lived out through her husbands and expects from her son. Narcissism in the clinical sense is usually linked with the need to be the mother's divine child-redeemer. There is no sense of identity except in relation to the mother's image of her child's specialness. I think there is an element of that here. Luis was all his mother had of a man who died before his son's birth. The Moon at the MC suggests a powerful emotional bond, and Pluto there implies that he was deeply aware of her grief and loss, as well as her need to be special and surrounded by special people.

Audience: The experience of death seems to be linked with the mother.

Liz: Yes, that is what I mean. The image of mother is Moon-Pluto, so he sees her as tragic in some way. She is a gifted, special woman with a tragic fate, and he cannot abandon her.

Frances: I have wondered why he is not interested in a really passionate, exclusive relationship. He has Moon and Venus in Leo. Pluto is so exclusive. It is strange that he can live sharing a woman.

Liz: He seems to be preserving his bond with his mother by *not* entering a passionate, exclusive relationship with either his wife or his lover. It is a strangely static setup. It has a defensive feel. I do wonder what is going to happen when Pluto arrives in opposition to his Sun, because, as you say, the coolness with which he approaches his relationships does not ring right with this chart. The Moon-Pluto and the Scorpio Ascendant contradict the image he presents. He is not as detached as he appears.

Audience: He is not here today. He wants to benefit from what we see in his chart, but he doesn't want to be seen. I think he is very skilled at hiding and yet getting what he wants. If the mother is an overpowering, ambitious, domineering woman, and he has learned very early that his survival depends on hiding, then perhaps he is too afraid of her to commit himself to anyone else emotionally. Or maybe he can only experience love when he is hiding.

Liz: I agree. I believe he is afraid of his passions. It is not only his mother he fears, but the power of his own emotions. I don't think he has ever had a deep relationship with anyone other than his mother.

Frances: I don't think so either. His mother is too powerful.

A defensive triangle

Liz: He has not separated from her yet. This triangle protects him from relationship. He has not yet found himself; psychologically he hasn't come out of the birth canal. When transiting Pluto opposes the Sun, I expect he will.

Audience: There seems to be an issue with fame, which is more than just his mother's expectations. I think he needs it himself.

Liz: Yes, he needs it himself, because it is his Moon-Pluto at the MC, but he has to find it in his own way, and not in accord with his mother's dreams. Is he famous, Frances?

Frances: No. I think he could be, but he has backed away from it.

Audience: He wants to be famous himself, but he hides from life, and gets to feel important by obtaining another man's most cherished possession. That's a very Geminian way of obtaining power – by stealing something belonging to someone else.

Liz: That's a bit harsh on Gemini, but there may be something in what you say. I am thinking of the myth about Hermes, in which he steals Apollo's cattle. But this is more than Geminian light-fingeredness. The only way Luis can make contact with his dead father is to claim the object of the father's desire. A famous dead father is very hard to fight in an Oedipal contest. Although Luis' mother wants her son to be famous, that is really asking him to be a double of his father rather than acknowledging his own individuality. Apart from the Freudian implications, a boy needs to fight his father to test his developing masculinity and begin his separation from the mother. If the father is absent because of divorce, at least there is a father out there somewhere whom he can verbally abuse. He can go and meet this father and have some kind of dialogue with him. But if the father has died before the boy has even seen him, that father is a god. He has never been humanised. In Luis' case this is compounded by the father's fame. The father has vanished into the mythic realm. How can a boy test himself against the invisible?

You have made a good point – there is an element here of acquiring the father's power, his *mana*, by possessing the father's woman. She is represented by the married woman with whom Luis is involved. This woman's husband has a treasured possession which is being taken away from him, and there may be something about the husband which plugs into Luis' fantasies of his father. If we had all the charts here, we might be able to see the connection between the husband's chart and that of Luis' father. But more importantly, this double triangle seems to me to be primarily defensive. Luis is not yet fully formed as an individual, and that makes him vulnerable. His setup is an excellent defence against vulnerability.

Audience: He feeds off others.

Liz: Not really. I would say he is still in the birth canal. He doesn't have an independent psychological existence yet.

Audience: Transiting Uranus is coming up to the IC. I wonder whether that has to do with father issues.

Liz: I am sure it does. Transiting Uranus has already opposed Venus, and is presently at the IC and opposing the Moon. Then it will oppose Pluto. Luis' bond to his mother is breaking apart. Pluto opposite the Sun implies a separation from the father's overpowering image. The whole family complex is being shaken loose.

Audience: Maybe something is going to happen to the mother that will make him wake up.

Liz: There might be a concrete event. But it is just as likely that the separation described by these transits is psychological and will be enacted through the triangle. Is his mother still alive?

Frances: Yes.

Liz: Sometimes, with transits like this over the MC or IC, an actual event occurs involving the parents. There may be a confrontation, or one of the parents may get ill or even die. Equally often, nothing "happens" to or with the parents. Things "happen" in one's adult relationships, because the family issues have been displaced and projected. Because this triangle sounds like it is, at least partly, fuelled by a recreation of the original family dynamic, it may be through the triangle that freedom from the psychological baggage of the past starts to emerge. Why has Luis given you his chart today? What is happening in his life right now?

Frances: He wanted to come himself, but he couldn't make it.

Liz: I understand that. But why now? He must be aware, on some level, that things are moving inside. I started off wanting to look at the hard aspects, but this has turned out to be something quite different, which touches on issues we were talking about earlier. This triangle has an unreality about it which suggests that it is a means of remaining *in utero*. And the uterine waters are about to break.

Audience: This man obviously fears powerful women, and so he plays a game with a committed relationship. He pretends it's a committed relationship, but he could get out any time he wants. If the split is shared by everybody in the triangle, then wouldn't the woman with whom he is involved also want to avoid a committed relationship?

Liz: It's likely that she has a similar psychological dynamic. That is often the case with this kind of triangle. Like Luis, she may be unformed, and unable to enjoy a full relationship. Frances, you said that this lady is "bored" in her marriage. "Bored" is a word I worry about when one uses it to describe somebody that one lives with. If her husband is that boring, why doesn't she go? Why does she stay with such a boring partner?

Frances: I don't know.

Liz: There does seem to be a split in this lady which mirrors Luis' own split. The "boring" husband is a kind of maternal/paternal container which protects her from fully entering life. She gets the illusion of life through this triangle. Luis is doing the same. Neither of them is actually engaged. There is no conflict; neither of them is hurting; nothing is happening.

Audience: Just fun and pleasure.

Liz: Yes, just fun and pleasure. Although that is not to be sneered at, the psyche may not allow that kind of situation to go on, because it is static. The morality is not the issue. That is up to the individuals, and none of us are in a position to judge it. But nature doesn't like a vacuum. The psyche doesn't tolerate stagnation. This triangle may be perfectly right for the people involved from a moral point of view, but nothing moves or grows. The approaching transits, because they are going to open things up in Luis, may start shaking the whole structure. We don't know what this woman feels about Luis. We only know what he has said to you about his feelings for her. That is not likely to be very edifying, because he won't tell you the truth anyway. He doesn't know it himself.

Audience: Maybe he is just a curious Gemini.

Liz: I don't believe people offer their charts to be examined in a seminar just because they are curious. There is a timing to these things. One doesn't say, "Oh, Frances, why don't you take my chart along just for fun, and let me know what they say about it." There is a reason why people want to know something at a certain time. And a Scorpio Ascendant, with its inherent mistrust of others' motives, is the least likely of all Ascendants to offer such personal information without a very strong need to do so.

I suspect Luis can sense that things are happening inside because of the transits of Uranus, and also because Pluto is creeping within orb of opposition to the Sun. It is even closer to opposing Mars. He knows, deep down, that something is starting to shift, although he may not acknowledge or recognise what it is. This triangle is essentially defensive. It illustrates vividly the way in which some triangles are meant to keep real relationship out. This kind of triangle doesn't hurt. It doesn't go anywhere. There is no struggle, no yearning, no suffering. The triangle prevents life from moving. That may work for a period of time – even a very long time. But sooner or later, someone will get fed up; someone will find something out; someone will want something different; someone will kick the anthill. Does Luis' lover have children?

Frances: Yes.

Liz: He will be forty-seven this year. Does he regret not having children himself?

Frances: I think that he does, now. But for a long time he said he didn't want any.

Liz: Do you know how his wife feels about this? We haven't considered her role in all this.

Frances: No, I don't. I know she is a Virgo, and Luis' Saturn is conjunct her Sun.

Liz: His Saturn on her Sun suggests that his bond with his wife is much deeper than it might appear, although a sense of responsibility may play as large a part as affection. His affair might also be a means of ensuring that his wife cannot hurt him.

Frances: Liz, I am sure he would be grateful if you had anything to say to him personally.

Liz: I wish him the best of luck. I would not presume to judge his situation on a moral level. I hope he can get away with it for as long as possible. And when the time runs out, which seems likely very soon, then it might be worthwhile for him to have a good, hard look at some inner issues.

Interlude: archetypal planetary dichotomies

Now I would like to look at the issue of unlived life from a slightly different perspective. We have considered the parental images and the challenge of a weak or unexpressed element, and also the difficulty of integrating both ends of a hard aspect. Any of these factors can generate unconsciousness of important dimensions of oneself, which may then surface in a triangle. The list I am putting up on the screen now is a list of what I would call archetypal planetary dichotomies. It is not a complete list, and it is not meant to be fixed and unchanging. It is also not meant to provide a "spot the triangle" technique. It is meant to stimulate thinking. These pairs of planets symbolise archetypal opposites. They are planets that inherently do not like each other. They represent opposite ends of a psychic spectrum.

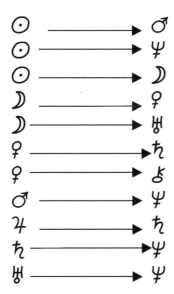

Implicit in this list are the signs and houses which the planets naturally rule. In other words, where I have put up Jupiter and Saturn, I also mean Sagittarius and Capricorn as well as the 9th and 10th houses. I am not suggesting that there must be an aspect between each pair of planets. For example, a strong, angular Mars in a chart, with a lot of planets in Pisces or the 12th house, implies an archetypal dichotomy between the Mars principle and the Neptune principle. Every chart has dichotomies. Some have a greater tension between opposites than others, simply because the planets and signs and house emphases line up along one of these archetypal battle lines. These conflicts are natural, inherent, and not in any way "bad" or "pathological". They can be enormously creative. But they suggest that integration may require a lot of inner work.

Audience: I don't understand why you have made the Sun and Mars archetypal opposites. They are both fiery.

Liz: Yes, they are both fiery, and in some birth charts, depending on signs and aspects, they can work beautifully together. But in myth, Apollo and Ares loathe each other, because they are distinctly different masculine images which govern antithetical levels of life. They represent the spiritual, reflective dimension of the masculine and the instinctual, physical one. When they are in hard aspect, or if the archetypal conflict is exacerbated by, for example, an angular Mars in Scorpio in a very airy, "civilised" chart, there may be a deep and difficult split. The Moon and Venus are similar. These planets represent two opposite poles of the feminine, and they are often at war.[11] If you are a mother, it is difficult to be an *hetaira*. This is not just social conditioning; it is an inherent problem. A commitment to child-bearing and child-raising makes the free, individualistic life of the *hetaira* virtually impossible to express. The instinctual dimension of the feminine is antithetical to the feminine as intellectual companion and playmate, whether in a man's or a woman's chart.

Likewise, if one is a solar male, one is Apollonian; one is civilised and reflective. Apollo was the gentleman of Olympus. It is very difficult for such a man to be self-assertive in an instinctual way, because his ideals are so high. I have met many men who suffer from this conflict, and don't know how to deal with anger or aggression or physical force, because they want to be conscious, considerate, and ethical. The same applies in a woman's chart. Tensions between the Sun-principle and the Mars-principle, or between the Moon-principle and the Venus-principle – whether these show up through aspects,

---

11 See Erich Neumann, *The Great Mother*, Princeton University Press, 1972, for a thought-provoking discussion on the polarity of the mother-archetype and the *hetaira*.

element balance, angularity, or house placement – point to an inherent dichotomy in the image and expression of what we experience as male or female within ourselves.

Audience: What about Venus and the Sun?

Liz: The Sun and Venus are not archetypal enemies. They are friends. Apollo is often shown in frescoes and sculptures accompanied by Venus as the Morning or Evening Star, because she is his "light-bearer" who rises or sets just before him. There is only one hard aspect they can make – a semisquare – because they are never more than 48° apart. Although on a basic character level the semisquare suggests some discord between one's sense of individual destiny and one's ideals in relationship, this aspect does not reflect a "split" in the deeper sense.

Audience: What about a conjunction?

Liz: As I said, these planets are not intrinsic enemies. Also, I want to emphasise once again that this list does not describe actual aspects. A square between the Sun at the end of Leo and Mars at the beginning of Sagittarius, in a chart with Aries rising, will not provoke as much inner conflict as a chart with the Sun at the end of Aries trine Neptune at the beginning of Virgo, in a chart with Pisces rising. It is a question of who is friends with whom, and which bits of the chart get relegated to the psychic ghetto.

Try to think of these planets as symbolic lines of energy. Chart configurations tend to group themselves along certain archetypal lines, which become obvious when we see a theme repeated two or three times. For example, a chart may have many planets in Sagittarius and the Sun in the 9th sextile Jupiter, but there may also be an angular Saturn in Capricorn. Jupiter and Saturn do not need to be in hard aspect for a conflict to be generated. In a very Jupiterian chart, Saturn will always be problematic, no matter how many nice aspects it makes, because the basic temperament is aligned on the opposite side. This is the archetypal *puer-senex* conflict, the eternal battle between potential and reality.

The Sun and Moon are also archetypal opposites. Solar energy, which is self-focused, pulls in the opposite direction from the lunar need to belong. The Sun is itself, separate and unique. It shines by its own light. A chart with the Sun in Leo and several planets in Cancer may reflect a deep inner conflict. These kinds of conflicts can only be understood by looking at the overall chart picture. They are not indicated by a specific aspect. This list of planetary dichotomies is meant to suggest conflicting principles, not particular aspects.

Audience: How about a Sun-Moon trine?

Liz: I think I just explained that a specific aspect, taken out of context, will not tell us much about the archetypal dichotomies in a chart. Perhaps I am not putting this clearly enough. Think of this list as gods or basic energy fields, each with its own nature. They are portrayed in a chart not only by the planets, but also by the signs and houses. If a chart is strongly Neptunian through the planet, its sign, or its natural house, and there is also an angular Mars or the Moon in Aries, then the Mars principle is like a sore thumb sticking out of the chart. Mars and Neptune themselves may not be in aspect. One of the ways in which these kinds of archetypal conflicts come out is through triangles.

Audience: Would the Sun and Pluto be in conflict as basic principles?

Liz: To some extent. The Sun struggles against Pluto because Pluto is a collective survival instinct which does not take account of the individual. The evolution of nature is ruthless in its progress and does not step aside to save one special dinosaur or dodo, however gifted that individual creature might be. The battle between Sun and Pluto is also imaged as the mythic dragon-fight – the battle between individual consciousness and the blind compulsions of the instincts. The Sun is concerned with meaning and individual destiny. But these principles are not always in conflict. They can sometimes speak to each other in a friendly fashion, provided the solar ego knows its place in the larger scheme of things. We can make peace with fate on a collective level if we have both a sense of individual purpose and a respect for those deeper forces which concern the survival and evolution of the life-force itself.

The archetypal combinations I have listed describe particular kinds of conflicts which seem to be predisposed to triangles. Saturn and Neptune are an obviously antagonistic pair. One may have the two planets in trine in one's birth chart, but their principles are eternally in conflict. The earthy kingdom of Saturn is inimical to Neptune's inchoate otherworld, and if both are strongly represented – in other words, if these two principles are the main themes in the chart through signs, houses, angularity, and aspects – it may be difficult and painful, although ultimately enormously creative, to reconcile the dichotomy. A triangle may be one of the means through which the individual attempts some kind of reconciliation.

Audience: You don't have Mars and Saturn on the list.

Liz: No. That is because I don't feel these two are inimical as archetypal principles. Mars and Saturn in hard aspect can reflect a lot of frustration, but we should remember that Mars is exalted in Saturn's sign. The ancient war-god is born parthenogenically, without a father. He is chthonic and earthy, and reflects the aggressive instinct in nature. He is not an alien in Saturn's domain. There is no deep, irreconcilable split between them. They can relate to each other if the individual is willing to earth his or her goals and accept the necessity of realism and self-discipline. Mars and Saturn in hard aspect do not seem to generate the sort of triangles that Moon and Venus in hard aspect do – they do not reflect a "split anima" or "split animus" problem. Perhaps it is also because neither planet is really concerned with relationship.

Venus-Chiron should be obvious as a polarity. Venus is in love with beauty and harmony, and Chiron reflects our awareness of everything in life that is distorted, wounded, and unhealable. If a chart is strongly Venusian and, at the same time, Chiron sits on an angle or makes strong aspects to the Sun, Moon, or Venus, there is likely to be a deep and painful dichotomy. Chiron's world is inimical to the beautiful landscape that Venus inhabits. There is no point of contact between them; each suffers by acknowledging the reality of the other. That is when triangles may provide an arena to work through the conflict. When the two principles can find no other way to create a dialogue within the individual, the triangle may become the means by which the dialogue is begun.

More charts from the group (continued)

Catherine: the invisible rival

Here is another chart from the group. Would you like to tell us what you wanted to talk about, Catherine?

Catherine: It is all right to put both charts up. My boyfriend wanted to come today, but he couldn't, and I promised to take notes. He is happy about having his chart discussed. I feel we are in a triangle. It is about very high ideals. I think it has something to do with what you call the pursuit of the unobtainable. ˙

Audience: Could you speak a bit louder? We can't hear.

Liz: Turn around and shout at them, Catherine. Unleash your aggression. Use your Mars in Aries.

Catherine: I think the triangle aspect of my relationship has to do with what you call the pursuit of the unobtainable. We both have very high ideals, and we both want to pick things over, just in case the ideal might happen with somebody else. It is a tremendously exciting and unusual relationship. But there is always a feeling of instability. There is no commitment.

Liz: You are saying you are in a relationship where both of you want to keep open doors, in case something better comes along.

Catherine: Right. It is not something that is emotional. It has to do with ideals.

Liz: So you have a provisional relationship.

Catherine: Yes, although he has an obsession with me. I have had many bad experiences with manipulation in other relationships, and I am trying to do things differently. Sometimes he is almost desperate to be with me all the time. So it's strange that we both seem to avoid commitment.

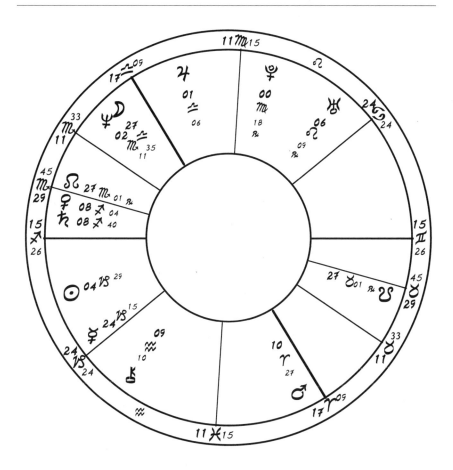

Catherine
[Data withheld for purposes of confidentiality]

Liz: But you are not really in a triangle – at least, not a physical one.

Catherine: I think he is unobtainable because he has a spiritual ideal of the perfect other. I suppose I am the same.

Liz: Go on.

Catherine: But perhaps I am wrong.

Liz: We need to look at what is portrayed in the charts. Can we give your partner a name?

Catherine: He is called William.

Liz: Let's look at your chart first. There are several things that my eye goes to, not least the exact conjunction of Venus and Saturn. Transiting Pluto is spot on that conjunction today. 8° Sagittarius seems to be coming up like mad at the moment. Another thing that might be relevant is the parental significators: the out-of-sign conjunction of the Moon and Neptune in the 10th, and Mars conjunct the IC, just on the 3rd house side. The Sun in Capricorn is in a T-cross, square Jupiter on one side and Mars on the other. It is also trine Pluto, which sits in the 8th along with Uranus. These placements suggest some deep dichotomies. Neptune and Chiron are in square. All these aspects may be relevant. Let's begin with the Moon-Neptune conjunction, which seems to reflect your idealism and longing for total fusion in relationship. The dream of Moon-Neptune is an emotional world where there is no conflict, loneliness, or separateness. This conjunction is in the house connected with the mother, which suggests that something of this quality of fusion existed very early in your life. Yet Venus conjunct Saturn is saying something else. What do you think is happening here?

Audience: Moon-Neptune longs for a total and complete bond with somebody, without any boundaries. Venus-Saturn is restricting and limiting, and actually needs boundaries. It's also very insecure.

Liz: Yes. Venus-Saturn and Moon-Neptune describe very different early experiences and very different perceptions of love. It might be hard to reconcile the opposing perceptions and needs. I would be interested in knowing more about your parents, Catherine, because the parental houses are emphasised.

Catherine: My father was a gambler, and also very strong and compassionate. As for my mother, her Sun is conjunct my Neptune, so I connect with her very well.

Liz: Your father seems to be appropriately described by the Sun square Jupiter and Mars, trine Pluto, and sextile Neptune. Your mother, with whom you seem to have a lot of empathy, appears in the chart as a sad or sacrificial figure, because of the double statement of Moon-Neptune and Neptune in the 10ᵗʰ. But the Moon is also square Uranus, so she, like you, may have carried a conflict between her longing for emotional closeness and her desire for independence. Did she need a great deal from you in your childhood?

Catherine: Yes. I think she lacked confidence. She was a very unhappy person.

Liz: It does sound as if you carry some quite deep insecurities, although in the end we cannot "blame" your mother for these. They are the inevitable product of the dichotomy of two such different sets of aspects as Moon-Neptune and Venus-Saturn. In a way, you had to mother your mother, and therefore you yourself did not get nourished. If a child has to play the role of the parent, the child gets no childhood. Capricorn children tend to take the role of caretaker very seriously when it is asked of them, because there is a basic need in Capricorn to be responsible and useful. If there is any looking after required in the family, Capricorn will say, "I'll do it." With Moon-Neptune in the 10ᵗʰ, and your mother's Sun right on the conjunction, you must have had a virtually psychic empathy with her pain. You may have willingly accepted the role of caretaker, at your own expense. If you felt loved *because* you were a caretaker, then you may have felt unlovable *except* as a caretaker. This is what is called "conditional" love – one feels lovable only when one is fulfilling the conditions. That is Venus-Saturn. You may have very little sense of your own worth unless you are helping someone. Yet Moon-Neptune longs for so much more. Perhaps you had more in the early months of life, before your awareness of your mother's unhappiness presented you with another experience of love.

Catherine: I have worked as a psychotherapist for several years. Now I have decided I don't want to do this work any more. I don't have enough time for myself. I feel as if I have been looking after people since I was born. I am beginning to feel angry about it.

Liz: Good. I think you began your training as a psychotherapist at about two days old. Now transiting Pluto has arrived on your Venus-

Saturn in Sagittarius, and you are starting to value yourself more. The old pattern is starting to break apart.

Catherine: I have a big battle in myself about this. I do have compassion for other people, but I feel very trapped.

Liz: I don't question the reality of your compassion. But helping others has also been your way of feeling worthwhile. You may have believed you were not worth anything unless you were fixing someone. This pattern will, of course, come into any relationship you get involved in, and you may find it hard to trust another person's love because you believe you have to keep working to earn it. The creation of this provisional life you spoke about, which acts as a brake on real commitment, has a very defensive element in it. It is, in part, the pursuit of an unobtainable parent who was too unhappy to provide real support and emotional nourishment. But it is also a way to avoid the pain of rejection.

Catherine: I keep thinking I should settle down, because that would help me to become more normal.

Liz: That sounds like the sort of thing your mother might have said.

Catherine: She *does* say that to me.

Liz: No doubt she believes it, which may be why she has felt so trapped and unhappy in her own life. It isn't a question of becoming "normal" by "settling down". It may be more important to understand why you need to have signs on all the doors that say, "Keep exit clear". You seem to have a very great fear of being either exploited or abandoned. I think you have experienced both in early life, on the emotional level. The urgency with which you try to ensure that no relationship will make you feel either used or cast out has probably been very necessary as a survival mechanism. It would be absurd to say, "You should stop doing that and settle down." But you may need to recognise why you are so compulsive about avoiding real emotional engagement. With Sagittarius rising and Venus also in Sagittarius, conventional "settling down" may not be your cup of tea even at the best of times. Also, Uranus is in the 8th, square the Moon and trine Venus, and you need a lot of breathing space in any relationship, however deeply committed you might be. Trying to make this independent side of your nature go away would probably not work any better than trying to hide from the intense need for commitment described by Venus conjunct Saturn, Venus square Pluto, and Pluto in the 8th.

Catherine: I suppose I don't really trust anyone.

Liz: That is not necessarily as terrible as it sounds. Venus-Saturn is a realist, and as Hillman points out in his essay, one *should* never trust anyone – at least, not in the childlike way of Moon-Neptune, which wants unlimited, unconditional love every moment of the day. In that sense, you certainly cannot trust anyone to be the mother you longed for in childhood. If you are looking for a Moon-Neptune kind of love, especially with the Moon in Libra, the likelihood is that, whomever you are with, sooner or later they will hurt you because they are human. Your challenge has something to do with the ability to accept separateness and the limits of human love. That may be a more constructive way of approaching your relationship than using a provisional ideal like a suit of armour.

Audience: Catherine will need freedom in any relationship. Uranus in the 8th will stay with her all her life. There is always the feeling, "I have to get out of here. Otherwise I will be suffocated."

Liz: Yes, there are a number of things in the chart that would make it very difficult for you to feel comfortable in a highly structured relationship. But structure and conventionality are not the same as commitment. The way you are dealing with things makes me uneasy, because of the artificial imposition of rules. "We are going to have an open relationship. We are never going to make any promises because something better might come along. We will not show possessiveness." There are too many intellectual constructs, and too much hiding of real feelings and needs. Neptune is the only planet in water in your chart, and it seems you are very frightened by your needs and passions.

Catherine: But I do know I need William.

Liz: Can you show that need to him?

Catherine: To a small degree. But I get uncomfortable when he is very intense, and I think he would feel the same if I became too emotional.

Liz: Why don't we look at the other half of this equation. Here is another 10th house Moon, this time in 26° Aries, and involved in a grand fire trine with Uranus, Mars, and Jupiter. The Sun conjuncts Saturn in Capricorn. Chiron is in the 8th, opposite Uranus. Venus is in Sagittarius, exactly square Pluto. As in your chart, Catherine, there is the suggestion of a strong dichotomy. On the one hand there is Venus square Pluto, which may describe the intensity you have mentioned.

On the other hand, there are a number of placements, like the grand trine in fire involving Uranus, which suggest a strong need for freedom. It isn't quite the same as your picture, but there is a similar kind of tension between needing a great deal of space and having very intense, possessive feelings. Your need to create a provisional relationship seems to involve profound insecurity as well as a conflict between freedom and closeness. William's issues may involve a similar sense of insecurity because of his Sun-Saturn conjunction, which echoes your Venus-Saturn conjunction. I wonder how the balance in the relationship will be tipped as you become more confident under the present Pluto transit.

Catherine: I would like to understand his insecurities better. He doesn't seem to have the same fears I do.

Liz: Don't count on it. I think there is insecurity, and his need for a provisional relationship may, like yours, have elements of defence in it. But it is not so specifically connected to his sense of worth in relationship. Saturn-Sun does not carry the same gnawing sense of being unlovable that Venus-Saturn does. The anxiety is more diffuse. It is linked with the father, who is also represented here by Neptune in Scorpio in the 4th house. This seems to suggest the lack of a stable or strong father-figure. As a Capricorn, William needed to have a father he could look up to as an embodiment of law and authority. Our Sun-sign tells us a lot about what we look for in a father, so that our own archetypal path can be experienced in human form. The Sun-sign describes the father we seek and might become ourselves, but not necessarily the one we find in childhood. William found a "weak" father, a father he couldn't rely on, and, to add insult to injury, a father who might have seemed disinterested in his child. William might take a long time to find Capricornian qualities in himself – to discover his own authority and sense of competence in the world. The involvement of Saturn with the Sun suggests that it may be part of his journey to do this alone in early life, without the help of a truly supportive father. This would make him unsure of himself for a long time, and he may fear commitment because he is afraid he will fail. But it is a different kind of insecurity from Venus-Saturn. Does he understand your Venus-Saturn anxieties and respond when you feel so fearful of rejection?

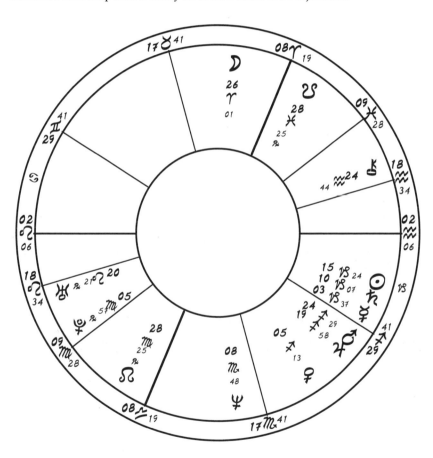

William
[Data withheld for purposes of confidentiality]

Catherine: He finds it strange, and also unexpected, because I don't usually show it. He has no problem being sympathetic and protective. But I don't think he really understands it.

Liz: It sounds as if the two of you are working very hard to be sensitive to each other's vulnerability. There is a difference in the kind of anxiety which makes you both try to live a provisional relationship. As long as you understand the reasons for each other's defensiveness, I think you can avoid hurting each other too much. But if he cannot empathise with the gnawing loss of confidence you sometimes feel about yourself as a woman, he may inadvertently hurt you in his efforts to avoid his own emotional needs. It will require a great deal of understanding on your part, because he can make you feel very insecure without consciously meaning to.

His Venus-Pluto square is an example of a hard aspect which constellates a split. He enjoys the free-spirited Venus in Sagittarius, but doesn't welcome the powerful needs of Pluto. He may pretend he doesn't have a Pluto, and he may sometimes seem very cold. Or he will start talking about the perfect woman he may meet some day. In other words, he projects his Pluto onto you, and reminds you that you cannot possess him. If you react blindly with typical Venus-Saturn feelings of rejection, you will activate a very uncomfortable synastry configuration – your Venus-Saturn lining up on his Venus-Pluto. You may then reject him in order to assuage your own hurt, and a power battle could ensue where both of you try to prove how little you really need each other. A great deal depends on how conscious you both are of these mechanisms. The provisional quality in the relationship is being used as the third point in the triangle. The rival is not a real person, but an imaginary person whom each of you might meet one day in the future.

Catherine: Yes.

Liz: This is a fantasy triangle created in an effort to protect yourself in case there is a real triangle. It is a means of trying to prevent a repetition of childhood hurts.

Catherine: I understand that. But I want to love and be loved without being wounded. I think that's my struggle. I want to experience how love should be.

Liz: "*Should* be"? If you have a rule book, I'd love to see it. But I suspect the author is Neptune, which means it has been written in invisible ink.

Audience: Liz, there is a phrase I keep remembering which Catherine used earlier: "Until we find something better." This seems to say quite a lot about how they see themselves in their mutual insecurity. With Sun-Saturn in the 6th, William is very self-critical. He can be very reliable and hard-working, but he doesn't feel very confident in himself. Both of them are Capricorns, and they could really count on each other for a long-term relationship, but in the process they would have to give up the illusion of somebody "better". Maybe this "something better" is really a fantasy of what each of them wishes they could be. I am getting lost. Help!

Liz: You aren't lost at all. What you are saying is very important – the fantasy of the "better" partner is really the fantasy of the perfect being each of them would like to become in order to merit love. This fantasy arises from painful feelings of inadequacy. I would be interested in hearing about what the "something better" is meant to be or do.

Catherine: It isn't somebody better in the sense of being more beautiful, or more intelligent, or richer. It is very hard to describe. My idea of "something better" is someone who totally understands me, whom I wouldn't have to fight with or explain myself to. I believe I could have a spiritual union with someone which makes those kinds of problems unnecessary.

Liz: Oh, dear. Do you remember the awful line from that awful film, *Love Story?* "Love is never having to say you're sorry." I believe it is quite the opposite. It seems to me that love involves mutual respect, and that includes being capable of recognising when one has blown it, and being able to swallow pride and apologise. Catherine, you are describing the ideal Moon-Neptune mother, who loves unconditionally and has a profound psychic understanding of her child's needs. No explanations are necessary, and no sense of disappointment or limitation intrudes on the bond because there is no separation between mother and infant. You are also describing someone who is watery in temperament, and who can empathise and respond without having to engage in open confrontation. It is interesting that neither you nor

William has much in water in the chart – only Neptune in both cases. Perhaps both of you are hoping that a perfect person with eleven planets in water will arrive one day, offering the warm, healing flow of feeling that both of you find so difficult to express.

Both of you are using the image of the perfect partner in order to keep hurt at bay. Each of you seems frightened of different things. William is afraid that he will be vulnerable, dependent, weak, and a failure like his father. You are frightened of being humiliated, rejected, and trapped like your mother. Neither of you has much confidence in your own worth. The fantasy of the perfect soul-mate helps you to avoid a relationship in which you would need to accept each other's limits. That really means accepting your own limits, which requires recognising that no one "outside" is going to give you perfect, unconditional love. Both of you are really saying: "We are waiting for someone to come along who will heal our wounds and give us the love we didn't get in childhood. Then we will be able to love ourselves. We will keep our distance until that magic person comes." This seems preferable to loving a real person, because you would have to relinquish the parental fantasy and be the people you actually are – mortal, imperfect, and, like other human beings, fundamentally separate.

Your ideals are neither irrelevant nor unimportant. But I have some misgivings about the real motives behind their use as the third point of a triangle. In a way, you degrade each other by implying that somewhere, one day, there will be something better. You are hurting each other and yourselves by living this kind of provisional life. I am not entirely convinced by the ideal spiritual union which you think might be around the corner, Catherine. If it is, you will find out soon enough. But to keep real involvement on ice by means of a fantasy is, to put it bluntly, a cheat. William's rival is your fantasy of perfection, and your rival is his fantasy of perfection. You can't help each other that way. Perhaps transiting Pluto on your Venus-Saturn will help you to recognise what lies at the root of this.

Your parents, I fear, were not very good models. You have an inner image of a suffering Neptunian mother and a self-absorbed Mars-Jupiter father who appears to have taken very little notice of the feelings of anyone around him. Your image of what happens to a woman when she loves is not a very nice picture. The woman who loves is hurt and abandoned – that's the script you seem to have inherited. Your mother appears to you as one of life's victims, and you don't want to be one.

Fair enough. But I think there may be a better way through than the one you have chosen. At any rate, the relationship sounds like it is worth working at more honestly. There is something not quite straight about this creation of a fantasy triangle which keeps you both insecure. I am also thinking about the Capricornian need for stability and bonds which endure over time. After all, you are both Capricorns.

Audience: But both of them have Venus in Sagittarius, too. They both need freedom.

Liz: Yes, that is true. But the two are not mutually exclusive. They often seem that way, because Jupiter and Saturn, and their signs, symbolise one of the archetypal dichotomies I was talking about earlier. Also, freedom has many different expressions. Travelling, having independent working lives and separate friends and interests – all these things can please Venus in Sagittarius without destroying a solid relationship. And Venus in Sagittarius does not necessarily require freedom from the partner. It requires a partner who is himself or herself free – who can laugh at life and share a sense of adventure.

Audience: People with Venus in Sagittarius love best at a distance.

Liz: Absence makes the heart grow fonder? I'm not sure about that. Perhaps you speak from experience, but I think you may be maligning Sagittarius. This sign is not averse to passion, and it is certainly capable of lifelong commitment. But the spirit in which feelings are offered matters a great deal. It is the inspirational potential of love which fires Sagittarius. Saturnian routine is anathema because it crushes the spirit, and a relationship which is static or takes commitment for granted will inevitably invoke the universal Jupiterian cry of outrage: "Is this all there is?" If Sagittarius has a travelling companion who can share the great adventure of life and is open to new possibilities, then intimacy and intense emotion can be very welcome, and so can a long-term bond. However, a partner whose mind is focused entirely on shopping at Tesco every Saturday morning will naturally give Sagittarius itchy feet. Venus in Sagittarius recoils from the threat that there are no future possibilities to explore within the relationship. Equally distasteful is the same sexual position on the same two nights of the week at the same time after watching the same television programme. I don't think commitment is the problem. Boredom is. Catherine, thank you for being so open and for letting us work with the charts. Now we seem to have come to the end of the seminar. One more question?

Audience: Working as a professional astrologer, when you get situations where people come with issues about triangles, is there anything that you personally would recommend an astrologer not to lose sight of?

Liz: There are so many different kinds of triangles, and so many different reasons for them. In my own experience, it is rare to find a person who callously and unfeelingly sets out to betray. More often, people are driven by emotional forces they do not understand, and they suffer accordingly. As astrologers, I feel we need to keep our personal moral judgements out of a chart reading as much as possible. We all have a background of experience with triangles – from our childhood, from our parents' marriage, and from our own encounters. Those experiences will have shaped certain moral and ethical attitudes which may be totally appropriate on the personal level. But they may not be appropriate for the client.

When confronted with a client involved in a triangle, declaring that his or her behaviour is "moral" or "immoral", or that they "should" or "should not" do what they are doing, is totally pointless and may do great harm. We need to refrain from taking sides and exacerbating the splits which are already at work. There may be triangles which are completely valid. There may be others that are very destructive, although not necessarily for conventional moral reasons. We cannot truly know why people do things unless we are standing in their shoes. And the psyche has its own morality, which is concerned with being on the side of life. Something may be immoral socially but very much on the side of life. Something may be moral socially and yet be utterly anti-life.

Triangles push all our buttons, especially if we have been in one and been hurt. It is important to be conscious of our own issues about them, and then see what the chart turns up. As astrologers, it is one of the most sensitive areas we can work with. Our own conflicts and our own past come to meet us with every relationship question we get from a client. We only have our own experience to draw on. We need to value and utilise that experience. But we cannot assume our personal moral stance is going to be helpful to the people we counsel.

That's all for now. Thank you all for coming.

Bibliography

Greene, Liz, *The Astrological Neptune and the Quest for Redemption*, Samuel Weiser, Inc, York Beach, ME, 1996.

Hillman, James, *The Soul's Code*, Bantam Books, London, 1997.

Hillman, James, *Loose Ends*, Spring Publications, Zürich, 1975.

Neumann, Erich, *The Great Mother*, Princeton University Press, 1972.

White, Patrick, *Voss*, Penguin, London, 1960.

About the Centre for Psychological Astrology

Director: Liz Greene, Ph. D., D. F. Astrol. S., Dip. Analyt. Psych.

The Centre for Psychological Astrology provides a unique workshop and professional training programme, designed to foster the cross fertilisation of the fields of astrology and depth, humanistic, and transpersonal psychology. The main aims and objectives of the CPA professional training course are:

- To provide students with a solid and broad base of knowledge within the realms of both traditional astrological symbolism and psychological theory and technique, so that the astrological chart can be sensitively understood and interpreted in the light of modern psychological thought.
- To make available to students psychologically qualified case supervision, along with background seminars in counselling skills and techniques which would raise the standard and effectiveness of astrological consultation. It should be noted that no formal training as a counsellor or therapist is provided by the course.
- To encourage investigation and research into the links between astrology, psychological models, and therapeutic techniques, thereby contributing to and advancing the existing body of astrological and psychological knowledge.

History

The CPA began unofficially in 1980 as a sporadic series of courses and seminars offered by Liz Greene and Howard Sasportas, covering all aspects of astrology from beginners' courses to more advanced one-day seminars. In 1981 additional courses and seminars by other tutors were interspersed with those of Liz and Howard to increase the variety of material offered to students, and Juliet Sharman-Burke and Warren Kenton began contributing their expertise in Tarot and Kabbalah. It then seemed appropriate to take what was previously a random collection of astrology courses and put them under a single umbrella, so in 1982 the "prototype" of the CPA – the Centre for Transpersonal Astrology – was born.

In 1983 the name was changed to the Centre for Psychological Astrology, because a wide variety of psychological approaches was incorporated into the seminars, ranging from transpersonal psychology to the work of Jung, Freud and Klein. In response to repeated requests from students, the Diploma Course was eventually created, with additional tutors joining the staff. The CPA continued to develop and consolidate its programme despite the unfortunate death of Howard in 1992, when Charles Harvey became co-director with Liz Greene. In February 2000, Charles tragically died of cancer, leaving Liz Greene as sole director. In the new Millennium, with Juliet Sharman-Burke capably handling the administration, the CPA continues to develop along both familiar and innovative lines, always maintaining the high standards reflected in the fine work of its former co-directors.

Qualifications

Fulfilment of the seminar and supervision requirements of the In-Depth Professional Training Course entitles the student to a Certificate in Psychological Astrology. Upon successfully presenting a reading-in paper, the student is entitled to the CPA's Diploma in Psychological Astrology, with permission to use the letters, D. Psych. Astrol. The successful graduate will be able to apply the principles and techniques learned during the course to his or her professional activities, either as a consultant astrologer or as a useful adjunct to other forms of counselling or healing. Career prospects are good, as there is an ever-increasing demand for the services of capable psychologically orientated astrologers.

The CPA's Diploma is not offered as a replacement for the Diploma of the Faculty of Astrological Studies or any other basic astrological training course. Students are encouraged to learn their basic astrology as thoroughly as possible, through the Faculty or some other reputable source, before undertaking the In-Depth Professional Training Course. The CPA offers introductory and intermediate courses in psychological astrology, which run on weekday evenings.

THE CPA DIPLOMA DOES NOT CONSTITUTE A FORMAL COUNSELLING OR PSYCHOTHERAPEUTIC TRAINING. Students wishing to work as counsellors or therapists should complete a further training course focusing on these skills. There are many excellent courses and schools of various persuasions available in the United Kingdom and abroad.

Individual Therapy

In order to complete the In-Depth Professional Training, the CPA asks that all students, for a minimum of one year of study, be involved in a recognised form of depth psychotherapy with a qualified therapist or analyst of his or her choice. The fee for the CPA training does not include the cost of this therapy, which must be borne by the student himself or herself. The basis for this requirement is that we believe no responsible counsellor of any persuasion can hope to deal sensitively and wisely with another person's psyche, without some experience of his or her own. Although it is the student's responsibility to arrange for this therapy, the CPA can refer students to various psychotherapeutic organisations if required.

Criteria for Admission

The following guidelines for admission to the In-Depth Professional Training Programme are applied:

- A sound basic knowledge of the meaning of the signs, planets, houses, aspects, transits and progressions, equal to Certificate Level of the Faculty of Astrological Studies Course. The CPA's own introductory and intermediate courses will also take the student to the required level of knowledge.
- Being able and willing to work on one's own individual development, as reflected by the requirement of individual therapy during the programme. Although a minimum of one year is required, it is hoped that the student will fully recognise the purpose and value of such inner work, and choose to continue for a longer period.
- Adequate educational background and communication skills will be looked for in applicants, as well as empathy, integrity, and a sense of responsibility.

Enrolment Procedure

Please write to the Centre for Psychological Astrology, BCM Box 1815, London WC1N 3XX, for fees, further information, and an application form. Please include an SAE and International Postage Coupon if writing from abroad. The CPA may also be contacted on Tel/Fax +44 20 8749 2330, or at www.cpalondon.com.

PLEASE NOTE:
- The CPA does not offer a correspondence course.
- The course does not qualify overseas students for a student visa.
- The course is for EU and Swiss residents only, although exceptions may sometimes be made.

About the CPA Press

The seminars in this volume are two of a series of seminars transcribed and edited for publication by the CPA Press. Although some material has been altered, for purposes of clarity or the protection of the privacy of students who offered personal information during the seminars, the transcriptions are meant to faithfully reproduce not only the astrological and psychological material discussed at the seminars, but also the atmosphere of the group setting.

Since the CPA's inception, many people, including astrology students living abroad, have repeatedly requested transcriptions of the seminars. In the autumn of 1995, Liz Greene, Charles Harvey and Juliet Sharma-Burke decided to launch the CPA Press, in order to make available to the astrological community material which would otherwise be limited solely to seminar participants, and might never be included by the individual tutors in their own future written works. Because of the structure of the CPA programme, most seminars are "one-off" presentations which are not likely to be repeated, and much careful research and important astrological investigation would otherwise be lost. The volumes in the CPA Seminar Series are meant for serious astrological students who wish to develop a greater knowledge of the links between astrology and psychology, in order to understand both the horoscope and the human being at a deeper and more insightful level.

The hardback volumes in the series are not available in most bookshops, but can be ordered directly from the CPA or purchased from Midheaven Bookshop, 396 Caledonian Road, London N1, Tel. +44 20 7607 4133, Fax +44 20 7700 6717, www.midheavenbooks.com. Paperback volumes may be ordered from Midheaven Bookshop or from The Wessex Astrologer, PO Box 2751, Bournemouth BH6 3ZJ, Tel/Fax +44 1202 424695, www.wessexastrologer.com.

Hardback volumes available in the CPA Seminar Series:

The Astrologer, the Counsellor and the Priest by Liz Greene and Juliet Sharman-Burke

The Family Inheritance by Juliet Sharman-Burke

Venus and Jupiter: Bridging the Ideal and the Real by Erin Sullivan

Water and Fire by Darby Costello

Where In the World? Astro*Carto*Graphy and Relocation Charts by Erin Sullivan

Planetary Threads: Patterns of Relating Among Family and Friends by Lynn Bell

Earth and Air by Darby Costello

Astrology, History and Apocalypse by Nicholas Campion

Paperback volumes available in the CPA Seminar Series:

The Horoscope in Manifestation: Psychology and Prediction by Liz Greene

Apollo's Chariot: The Meaning of the Astrological Sun by Liz Greene

The Mars Quartet: Four Seminars on the Astrology of the Red Planet by Lynn Bell, Darby Costello, Liz Greene and Melanie Reinhart

Saturn, Chiron and the Centaurs: To the Edge and Beyond by Melanie Reinhart

Anima Mundi: The Astrology of the Individual and the Collective by Charles Harvey

Barriers and Boundaries: The Horoscope and the Defences of the Personality by Liz Greene

Direction and Destiny in the Horoscope by Howard Sasportas

The Astrological Moon by Darby Costello

The Dark of the Soul: Psychopathology in the Horoscope by Liz Greene

Incarnation: The Four Angles and the Moon's Nodes by Melanie Reinhart

Relationships and How to Survive Them by Liz Greene

The Art of Stealing Fire: Uranus in the Horoscope by Liz Greene

When Chimpanzees Dream Astrology: An Introduction to the Quadrants of the Horoscope by Alexander Graf von Schlieffen

The CPA Master Class Series

Due to the numerous requests from students for live recordings of CPA seminars, selected seminars given by CPA tutors are now available as Studyshops – classic audio workshops supported with articles, images, charts and background information, all included on one CD. Each Studyshop contains around four and a half hours of lectures via MP3 files which play in a computer's CD or DVD drive, and are designed to play on Windows (Windows 98 or later) and any Mac or Unix platform. The CPA Master Class Studyshops are published by Astro Logos Ltd. in conjunction with the CPA Press. The following Studyshops are currently available:

The Soul in Mundane Astrology by Charles Harvey

Karmic Astrology by Howard Sasportas

Astrology, Myths and Fairy Tales by Liz Greene

Also available from Astro Logos is the Astro Logos Master Class Series. The following Studyshops are currently available in this series:

Delineation: Unfolding the Story Within a Chart by Darrelyn Gunzburg

Build Your Own Astrolabe by Bernadette Brady

Information on the purchase of CPA Master Class Series Studyshops, and Astro Logos Studyshops available from Astro Logos, can be obtained on line at www.astrologos.co.uk or by mail order from Astro Logos Ltd., PO Box 168, Fishponds, Bristol BS16 5ZX, United Kingdom.